BUSINESS COMMUNICATION PRACTICES

MODERN TRENDS

BUSINESS COMMUNICATION PRACTICES

MODERN TRENDS

Uma Narula

ATLANTIC

PUBLISHERS & DISTRIBUTORS (P) LTD

Published by
ATLANTIC
PUBLISHERS & DISTRIBUTORS (P) LTD
7/22, Ansari Road, Darya Ganj,
New Delhi-110002
Phones : +91-11-40775252, 23273880, 23275880, 23280451
Fax : +91-11-23285873
Web : www.atlanticbooks.com
E-mail : orders@atlanticbooks.com

Branch Office
5, Nallathambi Street, Wallajah Road,
Chennai-600002
Phones : +91-44-64611085, 32413319
E-mail : chennai@atlanticbooks.com

Printed in India at Nice Printing Press, A-33/3A, Site-IV,
Industrial Area, Sahibabad, Ghaziabad, U.P.

For My Family

To

Paradigm Shifts in Business Communication Practices Integrated Scenario of Globalization

Acknowledgements

The deliberations of the intellectual and business community in seminars, conferences and group discussions, that I participated in, and participants in my training programs gave me insights and updates about how the business practices were changing due to globalization, economic liberalization and technology. These were changing the communication practices. These deliberations inspired me to highlight such changing modern trends in my book.

My sincere acknowledgements are due to them.

UMA NARULA

Preface

There is a paradigm shift from the past in the business practices of today, and the same can be expected for the future. It is equally true of emerging economies of India and China or the developed world. The trends in how people do business around the world are changing; there is globalization of business practices as the businesses themselves are getting globalized. Developed countries are outsourcing manufacturing, IT & IT enabled services from companies in developing countries like China and India. However, business practices are still unique to a particular country within the globalization framework, because of its cultural ways and values.

We define business practice as not just producing, marketing and delivering products and services for economic gains (capital development) but they also include the practices of human development, social responsibility (in business contexts), and business etiquettes. Therefore, leaders planning to do business in alien country must understand and relate well to the business practices, business cultures of the particular business and in general, and to the bureaucratic and government practices of dealing with businesses.

Historically, robust communication channels and timely flow of critical content have been the key enablers for successful business enterprises. Globalization, technology and economic liberalization are changing the business practices and how they are communicated. There is a paradigm shift both in business contexts, models, practices and business communication models and practices. We cannot deny the importance and significance of how MICE (media, information, communication and entertainment) technologies are contributing as well changing the business practices. Many of the business models today and in the future are possible because of the new channels and modes of communication.

Business practices and communications both human and non-human (technological) are intertwined. Business transactions occur in every human activity — be it big or small. There is little difficulty in identifying a particular instance of social action as *Communication.* The problem arises in specifying what human actions are *not communications.* From these perspectives, many social actions that otherwise would not be defined as instances of communication, are shown to be powerful means of creating and managing business reality.

The complexity in interaction results from human and non-human communications. Communication is interaction with our ownselves, with others and with our external and internal environments. The conventional concept of communication is that we use communication to express our inner purposes, attitudes, and feelings; to describe events and objects of the external world and to produce sharing between the speaker and the audience addressed.

Messages in a shared environments relating to personal or business could not only be oral, written, non-verbal, visual or olfactory but these could also be laws, customs, practices, ways of dressing, gestures, buildings, flags, gardens, exhibits, etc. Language and body synthesizers that are culture specific are essential components of messages.

Human systems are not connected and coordinated by mechanical means or force of matter and energy but rather by exchange of information. The most important for information sharing is the communication network circuits, by which individuals within the system are interconnected. A circuit is a circular loop with two-way exchange of information that is a prerequisite for feedback. Feedback produces action in response to input of information and through its reactions modify its subsequent behavior. Research overtime suggested the necessity of both positive and negative feedback loops for communication effects.

In the era of communication revolutions, communication is far more important and central to human condition than ever before realized. Connectivity refers to the means by which people are connected to or are able to access communications channels such as the media channels, people networks, Internet, email, and computer. There are community initiatives that use the Internet and other digital communication networks, media channels and people networks to access markets, skills and opportunities to derive real economic benefits.

Business relates to markets for any product and services. Products essentially relate to tangible goods, and the services are either the by-product of these tangible goods and allied to them, and are essential for delivery of products. It is a wide term being used for all categories of businesses such as consumer goods and services of durable and non-durables, banking, insurances, hospitals, schools, real estate, travel, stock markets etc. Further, these are classified into segmented markets for different classes of people who do consume but differently, and have the capacity to pay differently such as poor, middle class, elite class etc. There are different geographic areas such as urban and rural that determine the patterns of consumptions and the market demands. There are different cultural groups globally who also determine the market segments. These differentiations create different business dealings.

There are business theories and concepts, paradigms and guidelines that give a general framework for businesses to operate in any market. We do need specific approaches, models and guidelines to deal with differentiated markets.

These specifics change with the times, business and technology moves, as well with the changing characteristics of the customers and consumers.

In the text of the book, the term *Products* is used interchangibly both for tangible and non-tangible products and services. The term *Customer* is used for customer in the supply chain of goods and services and term *Consumer* is used for consumers of durable and non-durable products and other services.

In any business transaction — small or big, the relationship between the consumer and business is established. This relationship with your day-to-day vendor or retailer is personal and warm and business tries to give you the best of services and products according to your preferences and would even suggest to you a product in the same category. For non-durable goods and services whether it is a refrigerator or car you also patronize a retailer who has credibility in the market or recommended by word of mouth. Market Credibility is important in this context. Other products and services like hospitals and schools, you also go by credibility factor about the capability of the personnel such as doctors and teachers and the quality of services they provide.

Businesses communication deal with the core competencies of people, processes and technology. Interpersonal communication is essential and is used significantly in business. Technologies of computer, telecommunication, satellites, and other information communication technologies and other auto-ID business technologies such as evolutionary technologies of Bar Code and RFID are predominant on the communication scenario. These provide technological solutions for business processes.

The readers are familiarized with certain business concepts, contexts and business practices but we have not gone in too much depth discussing these topics. We discuss in depth and highlight the communication framework in which business is practiced and that is the main objective focus of the book.

Organization of the book gives the readers insights about communication realities in the business world. Business communication framework defines the scope, concepts and essential components of business communications and its tools. It presents the salient models of Business Communications. It introduces the readers to business communication typology, contexts and patterns. Chapter 1 presents this.

Chapters 2 and 3 highlight the inflow and outflow of information and sharing with the external and internal links of the business organization. This is important for successful business development, viz. marketing of the products, services and ideas and people. The dynamics of business communications are discussed in the context of performance, productivity and human relations of external and internal links.

Marketing and Innovations are two main business communication tools. In Chapter 4, Marketing from its various approaches, and Innovations of products and services are discussed.

Advertising is an effective tool for both marketing and innovations. This is also an effective tool for creating image and credibility as well as awareness and motivation for buying products and services. Advertising through its various channels, directly or indirectly, creates and enhances the image of the corporate and particular businesses. We have highlighted this in Chapter 5. The *Image* of the corporate and particular businesses, its leaders and management, and its products and services are further projected and enhanced through Public relations tactics with public, media, government and other businesses. Chapter 6 discusses about corporate Public Relations.

Communication technologies as well as other technologies related to business are pulsating very fast and they create waves. Applications of these technologies are creating waves in the business communications. Chapter 7 is focused on these applications. We need communication skills to deal with ever changing dynamics of communications in business whether they are internal links or external links in business, marketing, advertising, public relations and communication technologies. We have discussed a few salient techniques for development of people, processes and products in Chapter 8. Cultural sensitivity and communication skills are as important and significant as other professional skills for successful dealings in business.

Our concluding observations in Chapter 9 present the paradigm shift about rapidly changing business practices. Globalization, technology and economic liberalization have tremendously changed the business practices worldwide. Business practices have to keep pace with the rapid technological change to be successful. Best practices of yesterday may not serve the consumers of today; therefore the practices are on a continuum of change. Three models of Globalism, Globalization and Outsourcing in the context of Globalization may profile business practices differently. Globalism is the awareness that local events have global consequences and understanding of global impact. Globalization is merging local and global trends. This model operates in two ways: one is adapting and fitting global trends to local ways such as fitting global business practices to local business cultures. Second, local trends are changed into global trends. Such as business practices are changed to global practices of doing business.

The emerging economies are booming because of these three factors — globalization, technology and economic liberalization. Further models of *Globalism* and *Globalization* shape the focus of their business, products and services. In addition, they are competitive and achieve more when they follow a *Collaborative model* of Business Communication practices. Catering to *Low-end Mass Market* is new upcoming business practice in the emerging markets.

It is an observation that different emerging markets have their business strengths and weaknesses according to their specific models of business communication practices. Some of these are emerging as booming markets as interplay of above-mentioned three factors and other additional models but their markets develop according to models of their predominant business strengths. As such emerging markets of China and India are taking different paths to economic prosperity as per their business strengths.

A wide variety of business transactions cover entire gamut of human life both from general and specific focuses. To cover the entire gamut cannot be within the scope of my book. I have titled my book, *Business Communication Practices: Modern Trends*. I endeavor to discuss about those aspects of business communications that we encounter daily in dealing with business people, processes, products and services; and the communication skills and technologies we need to deal with them efficiently and effectively. We do encounter a paradigm shift in business communications due to fast changing business practices. I endeavor to highlight the changing business practices and modern trends.

UMA NARULA

Contents

7. Concluding Observations: Chinese [illegible]

[illegible]

List of Figures

1

Introduction

BUSINESS DEFINED

What is the purpose of a business? One may say making money, helping economy. The valid definition may be, that the purpose of business is *creating customer*. Businessmen create markets. The customer may have felt the want a business satisfies before he/she is offered the means of satisfying it. It remained a potential want until the action of businessmen converted it into an *effective demand*. At times there may not have been a want unless business action created it by innovation. Such as want for computer or cell phones was created. Or want may be created by advertising (when people become aware of it such as a vision magnifier) or by salesmanship through persuasion appeals for a specific product. *It is business action that creates the customer. It is the customer who creates the business. It is the customer who creates the wealth, economic resources by his/her willingness to pay for goods and service.* What a customer is buying and values determines what business is, what it produces and whether it is going to prosper. Business enterprise has three basic functions — marketing, communication and product development through innovations. These produce results.

The simplest representation of any business organization is in terms of customer and supplier. An organization develops/provides a product or service for which it receives payment, of some kind, from a customer. In this case the organization is the supplier to the customer. There is supply chain to the organization for the product. Here the organization is customer to the suppliers. This simplistic dynamic is a very simple way to think about all the relationships in a business setting. It is this dynamic that determines the power balance in the relationship and defines the frame work in which relationship will proceed. It is therefore this dynamic and the factors described above that provide the framework for all business communications.

Expanding further, one can look at any business organization having several external customers and several external suppliers. Within the business organization there will be several functions some of which will be customers and suppliers to each other. Therefore, in a realistic business organization one will have a multitude of customer – supplier relationships of which many will be internal and many external. *It is the dynamic between all the individual elements that will influence how communication channels are developed and proceed in this complex system.*

The earlier models of management by objective, diversification theory, zero-based budgeting, value chain analysis, decentralization, quality circle excellence, portfolio management, matrix management is outdated now. Early models of decentralization and management system are not effective now.

What is important in the present business context are three factors: Customer, Competition, and Change. Customers' demand for products and services unique to them has changed. It has changed customer-buyer relationship. Technology has changed the nature of the competition. Change as such is pervasive and persistent and the pace of change is accelerated.

BUSINESS COMMUNICATION: A FRAMEWORK

Connectivity refers to the means by which people are connected to or are able to access communications channels such as the Internet, email, computer and people networks. There are community initiatives that use the Internet and other digital communication networks and people networks to access markets, skills and opportunities to derive real economic benefits. Business communication framework focuses on perspectives, types of communication, contexts and patterns. It

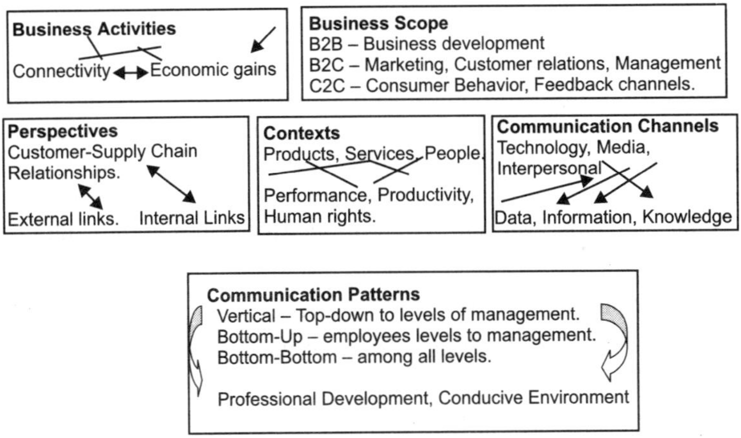

Fig 1.1. Business Communication Framework

defines the scope, concepts and essential components of business communications and its tools. It presents the salient models of Business Communications.

Communication in any business operates from three perspectives: One, customer — supply chain relationships including both external and internal links; two, employee-management relationship including internal links only and customer-consumer-product relationships.

The dynamics of business communications are customer — supplier relationships in the context of product, services and people. Communications occurs in different forms in these relationships. It may be a set of data, information or knowledge about product, services and about people. These may be conveyed through technology, media, and oral interpersonal or through written word. The employee-management relationship is in the context of performance, productivity and human relations. These may be assessed and conveyed through technology, media, and oral interpersonal or through written word. But in addition, the human relations approach — of developing reciprocal good attitude and behavior to create good and healthy work environments and professional development is important to assess and boost the performance and productivity in any business organization.

We have defined customer as a supply chain link of the organization and it becomes both as external and internal link. We define Consumer as of durable and non-durable products and services. Products do include both tangible products and intangible services. Usually we mention 'products and services' as inclusive, wherever omitted, it implicitly implies both products and services.

Types of Communication

There are three typologies that define communication. One typology defines *communication as a process*. It could be linear, non-linear and circular. Second typology defines *communication as hierarchical*: vertical or top to bottom, horizontal i.e. among one another in the same hierarchy and bottom-up i.e. communicating from lower level hierarchy to top level. Third typology defines communication vis-à-vis different *communication environments*. Different communication environments call for various types of communications. Communication always occurs in a context and not in a vacuum. Sender sends the message in *his/her* context; the receiver receives the message in *his/her own* context. The message is understood and is effective when the contexts of both of them match. Business communication is meaningful when it is in context of perception, expectation and demand.

Communication environment creates context. In a business, the internal links i.e. management and the employees, and the external links with the businesses such as supply chain for product components, distributors, whole-sellers, retailers, competitors, consumers, community, government and media act and react in communication environments (situations). There are five basic dimensions of communication environment in a business: the physical dimension refers to the work place, social dimension refers to the type of functions we are attending — whether working alone, in team, with the manager, or in a professional meeting etc. The social dimension also shows whether the environment is friendly, hostile, indifferent, formal or informal etc. The third cultural dimension suggests the prevailing value systems, the unwritten codes of acceptable and unacceptable behavior of the employee and employers i.e. the business culture of the organization. Fourth dimension is time. The senders and receivers function in relation to the time. They operate in the present but with some reference to the past experience and future envisions. Fifth is technological dimension that essentially creates channels for transmitting messages to and fro. All the five dimensions are important; they are not exclusive but overlapping and interdependent.

Contexts of perception, expectation, demand, communication and information are important for business from the point of internal links of employees and management, and from the point of external links of customer and consumers, government and media.

Contexts: internal links

Context of perception in business: Perception is experience. We always perceive in configuration. The silent gesture, tone of the voice, environment, culture and social referents cannot be disassociated from the spoken language. Without them the spoken word has no meaning and cannot communicate. Percept and concept are not separate. We cannot perceive without conceiving. To communicate a concept to a person is not possible unless it is within his/her perception. In communicating it is important to know whether whatever is being discussed is within the range of a person's perception (we loosely may term it as within the person's understanding). The range of perception is set by physical, cultural and emotional limits. The last two dimensions are more important. For example, some people cannot be convinced by rational arguments, they do not have the ability to perceive a communication that goes beyond their range of emotions. If they have to be convinced, if they have to learn then their perceived emotions have to change on the basis of experience. Perception is conditioned by what we are capable of perceiving. The disagreement and conflicts are likely to be the result of incongruity in perception.

Business is multidimensional but each person is likely to see different dimensions of it according to their range of perception. How do we expand the range? One has to talk to people in terms of their own experiences and language. They have to be exposed to other dimensions of business, which is likely to give them *different perception.* Only then they are able to receive the message otherwise it exceeds their *perception capacity.* If they are able to understand the message, they are ready for dialogue, training and coaching.

Context of expectation in business communication: As a rule we perceive what we expect. One generally thinks what is unexpected is resented (in business). But more than that what is important is that unexpected is not received at all. It is not seen or heard but ignored or misunderstood.

The human mind tends to fit its impressions and stimuli into a 'frame of expectations' and it resists any attempt to 'change its mind' or to perceive the unexpected and not to perceive the expected. In this context therefore, before communicating it is necessary to understand what the recipient expects to see and hear. Only then we know whether communications can utilize his/her expectations, and what they are. Whether there is need for 'shock of alienation', or 'for an awakening', that breaks through the recipients' expectations and forces him/her to realize that unexpected is happening. Gradual small incremental steps in change do not work since it will only reinforce his/her expectations.

Business management is equally concerned with making business profits as well as creating and providing good and healthy work environments to its employees. They have certain expectations from its employees for performance and productivity to enhance profits; and good attitude and behavior to create good and healthy work environments.

The employees expect from the management not only good and healthy work environments through understanding and good employee-management relationships but ample interest in developing them professionally to add on to business productivity and their performances.

Communication makes demands. It is believed that communication is always persuasive in which communicator wants to get something across and to change the attitude and behavior of the receivers. This may be or may not be heard at all. It is powerful when communication fits with the aspirations, values, and purposes of the recipient. If it is against his/her aspirations, values, motivations, either it is resented, resisted or not heard at all. Communication is not effective unless it keys in with the receiver's attitudes, or behavior.

The management makes demands on the employees for productivity and performance according to the main objectives of their business — make profits through Capital. It makes demands on their human capital in relation to achieve their first objective. These demands can be met if management on one hand has regular programs of information, education, communication and motivation (IECM) about the corporate business policies and products itself. And on the other hand they spend time, effort and resources to professionally develop them more and more to fit efficiently with the tasks of the corporate. This is what employees demand from the management. The reciprocity of these demands does lead to better relations and effective communication.

Communication and information as contexts are interdependent and necessary condition for each other. Communication is perception, and information is logic. The problem is how to isolate information content from perception? Information can be processed as communication when the receiver decode according to his/her perceptual set.

In business communication, the contexts of perception, expectation and communication demands are significant for dialogue, training and coaching. It is necessary to change the employees perceptual sets for exposing them to different dimensions of business (information) so they are receptive to learn more than what they know and learn novel ways of doing. Their receptivity (expectations) also has to be changed by creating awareness, knowledge, and motivation about better practices. Their barriers to change and receptivity to unexpected can be done through persuasion where their self-esteem, confidence is not threatened. In such communication environment, the employees become open to dialogue. They are open to training to know better practices of doing business and building organizational capacity. They are open to coaching (one-on-one or by mentoring) by acknowledging their weak points and to build their strengths.

Information is important and necessary condition in various business contexts. The processing of information is more efficient when the employees' perceptual sets are changed and widened, and when they are persuaded to change their attitudes and behavior to fit the business culture of the organization. Efficient processing of information leads to knowledge sharing and better communication environment.

Contexts: Internal and External links

The Communication Patterns in business can be top-down, bottom to top, bottom-bottom, and circular. Top-down communication is from top-level management/employees to various bottom hierarchical levels. The bottom-bottom communication among management and employees of the same levels is normal pattern. But when top-level management and employees are ready to listen and talk to lower levels, dialogue occurs between the two. Communication is circular when top-down, bottom to top, bottom-bottom communication occurs. It leads to robust and candid dialogues among various levels of management and employees. This happens in efficiently organized businesses.

The communication patterns with customers in the supply chain can be two-ways with many feedback loops. The objective of communication is to understand the needs and demands of the organization vide its products and services, and the inter-dependency among the various supply chain links. Customers deal with different levels of employees and management in the organization, with those who deal with specific supply component that they supply. The communication is horizontal, *bottom-bottom*, and *top-top* from customer to the top senior leaders. It has to be circular since bottom, top and customer must interact for efficient delivery. Feedback loops are necessary condition to get the right supply without delay. Since the supply chain links are inter-dependent, they must communicate with each other, among themselves (whatever the case may be) effectively and efficiently to keep the supply chain moving. Thus Communication among the supply chain links is two-ways, circular and with feedback loops.

Communication mode is interpersonal — both formal and informal, both in groups and one-on-one and supported by technologies. Use of different information tiers, databases, computers, telephones both landline and cell, various audio and video devices and Internet support interpersonal mode of communication.

The communication patterns with consumers of goods and services are both formal and informal interpersonal communication modes and various media channels. The main objective is to understand the consumer behavior. Market researchers and analysts interact with consumers interpersonally one-on-one, with groups — organized unorganized and focused groups and exposure of company and product related messages through media channels for product development and product launching. The patterns are direct communications.

Sales teams interact with consumers through loops of distributors, wholesellers and retailers to know the consumer behavior about the acceptance and rejection of the products and services and brand loyalty, their allied demands for products and services, and consumer driven innovative ideas. In conjunction with distributors, wholesalers and retailers, sales team plan strategies to push the sale of product and services to the consumers. Sales people thus have indirect communication patterns with the consumers. They use interpersonal modes supported by technology to communicate directly with distributors, wholesalers and retailers to keep the supply chain moving. They use technology to collate databases and information for them about the products.

Communication about various products and services to the consumers is done by the corporate through Advertising on various mass media channels of print, broadcasting and telecommunication, Internet, through outdoor publicity modes and by word-of-mouth publicity. Corporate also use both personal and media public relation channels to create good and optimum visibility and Image for itself, and for its products and services.

The latest trend is co-creation in business. This entails different communication patterns with the poor consumers having low level purchasing capability. The rural markets need development and co-creation of business. The communication patterns with consumers in rural market are different from urban consumers.

Feedback to business communication lies in three domains: First, B2B is communication between business to business. This deals communication with product manufacturers, developers, and product researchers on one hand and on the other hand with product and services distributors, wholesalers and retailers. The focus is on planning of products and services, communicating marketing and sales strategies and delivery of goods and services. In short, focus is on business development. Second, B2C communication is aimed at from businesses to consumers through marketing and advertising strategies such as product launches, campaigns about product and services, and co-creation of businesses. Third, C2C, i.e. consumer-to-consumer communication is through advertising, feedback to business (for business products and services) as well among themselves for acceptance and rejection of the product and services. This is responded by consumer behavior.

The three business communication approaches deal with specific relationships associated with these. In B2B approach, the communication relationship is for research and development, resource management, product life cycle management. In B2C, communication focus is on strategies for marketing, advertisement, product demonstrations and campaigns, customer relationship and media management. C2C communication focus is on feedback channels both media and interpersonal and customer relationships, viz. product as the priority, and consumer behavior.

Business Concepts

The most important and basic concepts in the business world are: First, *know the market forces and recognize the changing market dynamics*. Second, business leaders must *do the right things right*. Doing things right is not enough in today's market place. First, know what is right and then handle them in the right way. They argue that facing facts may be a leader's most important asset but they may fail the test of intellectual honesty. In an era of globalization and commoditization unrealistic corporate behavior can be fatal. The most widespread unrealistic behavior when the game changes drastically is to violate the first Law of Holes (when you are in one, stop digging) is when people redouble their efforts to do what they know best. They often achieve heroic results but often they are pointless, because they fail to confront the new realities.

Third, *confront the reality*. Bossidy and Charan (2004) propose a new set of tools for confronting reality. In their business model, goals and actions are forged not in a vacuum but in alignment with the often harsh realities of the changing business environment. If a company's market position is eroding, when its competitors are using new technologies, these factors must be incorporated into the business plan and day-to-day operations. Often, the harsh realities are ignored because of filtered information, selective listening, wishful thinking, emotional investment, fear and a bias towards hearing good news.

Fourth focus is on *accepted sets of values*. Many successful management theories rely on such concepts as: great teams make you better, knowing your customer is good, make more money by bringing in what you spend, and that there is an element of good business practice quite close to common sense. Industriousness, team spirit and self-control still reflect a value system based on cooperation and personal responsibility. The core values will resonate: never lie, never steal, and never cheat. Don't indulge in corrupt practices. Don't whine, don't make complaints, and don't make excuses, just move on with the times. Respect and create healthy human relationships by interacting. These sets of values have the power to transform almost every workplace. But in reality, in the business world, we find more pragmatism, practical wisdom and even corruption to an extent. These four business concepts present the business communication perspective that can impede or facilitate company leaders to recognize the changing market dynamics.

Business communication tools are: Marketing of product and services focusing on Marketing strategies, Market research, Market analysis, Product development and Sales. Product development also takes place through innovation of products and services. These are also diffused through various marketing channels for business. Goals of marketing are achieved through advertising in its various facets.

Public relations through various media channels and interpersonal communication channels are significant business tool in projecting the image of the corporate, its products and its business leaders. The trust thus built facilitates confidence in customers and consumers to create market for its products. Communication is necessary and important tool that encompasses marketing and Sales, product development, and communication with external and internal links of the corporate.

Business communication components are business intelligence and its social components, changing dimensions and areas of businesses, and the new and wider applications of information communication technologies (ICTs). These three components create a specific business culture for a particular business. Communications through conventional and new media technologies, and interpersonal channels play significant role in managing these three business communication components.

We are stepping into knowledge economies such as e-commerce through newer technologies of Internet etc. These various modes of mobile communications have facilitated global business and globalization in business.

Communication through various mass media channels and interpersonal channels facilitate management of various dimensions of businesses. Some salient conceptual moves such as business culture, business intelligence and its social intelligence model, and communication plans highlight the importance of communication management for businesses. We discuss these in this context.

Business Culture: Every business has its distinctive focus and culture like societies. These are the norms, beliefs, values and work ethics that regulate the behavior of individuals and groups within any corporate. Many may not be aware of their distinct cultural characteristics. Culture of a business is influenced by the culture of the country of its origin that sets the values, norms and general style of business dealings and rules and regulations of governmental bodies. The culture of specific business is created by personalities, ideas and business approaches taken by its founders and its top business leaders. The coordination of these two distinct cultures calls for effective communication strategies as well management of those strategies.

A business culture that is constantly changing and evolving is vibrant and thriving. Progress occurs when it changes. It is not the success but the threat of failure that compels businesses to reinvent themselves. Changes in a business occur when its leader provides ideas that challenge traditions. Successful businesses have leaders who revived, changed the culture and the course of business. In most cases, such changes are based on retaining and developing what is good in the existing culture and adding to it new elements that would stimulate the progress. Total rejection of existing culture is devastation. Therefore, the skill in reinventing the culture is to identify and retain what is good and what is to be rejected and modified. The exercise starts with review of existing culture, with its strength and weaknesses by its senior managers and outside consultants in organized and formal discussions.

To effect receptivity to change, the top management team and the levels below them must be stimulated to examine issues and implementing changes, and accepting challenges associated with it. How fast an organization should attempt to modify its culture? The wise thing is to change as fast as practicable but not that slow that organization becomes stagnant and people lose motivation and incentive for achievement.

Communications is the core of managing business culture from various perspectives and dimensions whether initiating the change, reinventing the culture, leadership roles and receptivity to these. The success depends how effective is the communications in various contexts. Both interpersonal and media channels can be used for effective communications.

Business intelligence model and its social model: Business intelligence model is in tune with changing dimensions and areas of businesses and the new and wider applications of ICTs. These create technological challenges such as technology management for cost effectiveness, competition and reaching new markets. The new market environments could be local, monopolistic to global. Technology and market environment together pose challenges for product and service quality, upgraded technology, cost competition, cost effectiveness, and motivated customers and personnel. Its social model helps in creating satisfied customers and consumers through update quality products, developing healthy national economy and striving for sharing global economy. Further, businesses contribute in the development of the local communities in which they function by setting schools, hospitals and parks etc. this is their social responsibility and social opportunity cost. This helps in the development of society in the broader sense.

The businesses need *Communication Plan,* which could be both short-term and long-term. The communication plan encompasses communication strategies to create awareness and knowledge, acceptability, marketability, and adaptability (AAMA) about the corporate product, services and technology among its local, national and worldwide customers. It encompasses communication strategies to create, develop, and whenever necessary to reinvent a healthy business culture.

Communication strategies focus on the employee-management relationships and professional development. It is essential to relate both short-term and long-term communication plans with both short term and long-term business plans. Coordinating both the plans is effective business management.

Business communication Models

We may understand the business concepts well but in practice it is important to manage the business reality well. Communication strategies are one of the components to manage business reality. The focus of business communication is on diverse dimensions of businesses. The various Business Communication Models take seven approaches. First is general approach to business communications. Second is special approach that handles business communications from various perspectives in specific aspects of different business sectors. Some of these may include negotiations in business dealings, marketing and management of products and services, product-cycle, advertisement and public relations, globalization and information technology. Third approach is communications for employee-management relationships in the context of development of business and professional development of people. It may be achieved through dialogue strategies among all levels in the organization, through training, coaching, mentoring and candid and frequent appraisals.

The fourth approach focuses on communications for human relations in businesses. These include employee relation management (ERM), customer relation management (CRM), product relation management (PRM) and resource management. Fifth approach focuses on business and economic intelligence and analysis, and economics of business communications. Sixth approach is the segmented market focus on the poor and those having low level purchasing capability. This presents co-creation Business Model. This is the recent new business model. So far the marketers have ignored this segment though in many developing countries they are almost 70% of the market. Seventh approach is the business communication to rural markets. This segment forms almost 70-80% of the market. Sixth and seventh approaches are unique to most of the developing countries. These seven approaches document seven business communication models. These models need different communication strategies to tap this market. These models will be discussed in detail in the subsequent chapters.

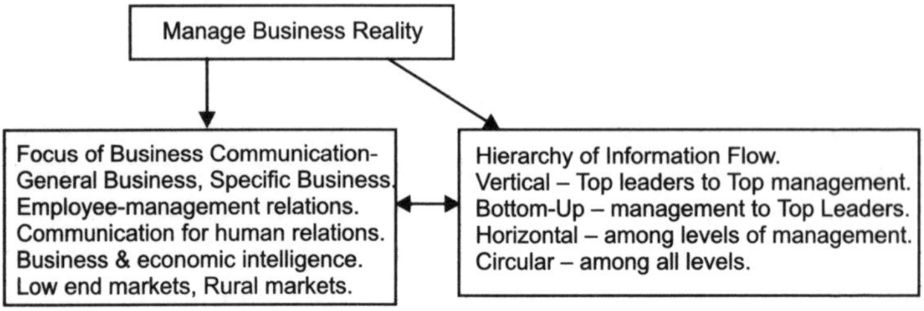

Fig 1.2. Business Communication Model

Business Model

A business model (also called a business design) is the mechanism by which a business intends to generate revenue and profits. It is a summary of how a company plans to serve its customers. It involves both strategy and implementation. It is the totality of, to define and differentiates its product offerings; marketing (marketing, promotion, distribution and Sales strategies); creation, acquisition and retention of customers/ consumers, defining strategies for the performance of various business tasks and how to configure its resources and capture profits. Every business organization will have business models according to its business objectives, products and services offered, business culture, and style of functioning of its top leaders. It may have one or multiple business models. Generally, the business models of service companies are more complex than those of manufacturers and resellers. As we have highlighted earlier, communication is the basic and essential component in all business models since all functions must be communicated in the right perspective for implementation of the business.

There are conventional and new business models. The conventional models have either already outdated or lost its utility and value because of changing business perspectives and market forces such as expansions of markets, emerging markets, and e-commerce, and knowledge economy etc. The advancement of technology both ICTs and business technologies have further created different businesses and therefore the need for varied business models and communication perspectives.

Over the years, business models have become much more sophisticated. Each of these business model innovations can give the company a sustainable competitive advantage. Companies must continuously rethink of their business designs and change their business models because of changing business environments and product values, consumers' profiles, and advancement in technologies. Ultimately the success or failure of a company depends first on how well its business design and models match their customers' priorities and relationships with it external and internal links.

Bossidy and Charan (2004) propose a business model where goals and actions are forged not in a vacuum but in alignment with the harsh realities of the changing business environment. If a company's market position is eroding, when its competitors are using new technologies, these factors must be incorporated into the business plan and day-to-day operations. Often, the harsh realities are ignored because of filtered information, selective listening, wishful thinking, emotional investment, fear and a bias towards hearing good news.

Types of business models

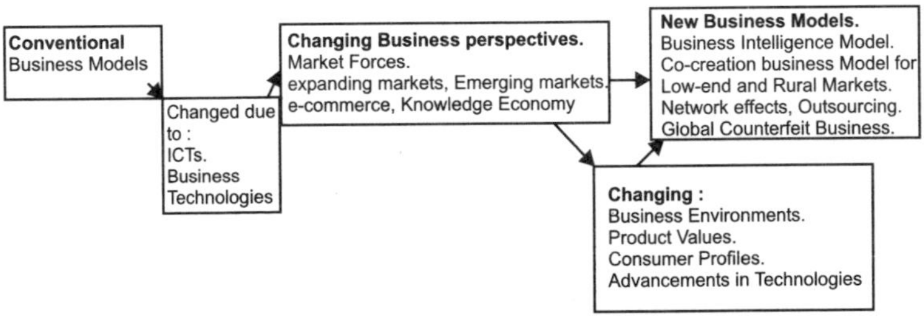

Fig 1.3. Business Models

Conventional business model: the oldest and most basic business model is the shop-keeper model. This involves setting up a store in a location where potential customers are likely to be and displaying a product or service. Now the super store, chain stores and franchises are expanded versions of store model.

The bait and hook business model is another interesting model (also referred to as the razor and blades business model or the tied products model) introduced in the early 20th century. This involves offering a basic product at a very low cost, often at a loss (the "bait"), then charging excessive amounts for refills or associated products or services (the "hook"). Examples include: razor (bait) and blades (hook); cell phones (bait) and airtime (hook); computer printers (bait) and ink cartridge refills (hook); and cameras (bait) and prints (hook). An interesting variant of this model is a software developer that gives away its word processor reader for free but charges several hundred dollars for its word processor writer.

The other conventional models may include negotiations in business dealings, marketing and management of products and services, product-cycle, Brand Equity model advertisement and public relations, globalization, information technology, employee–management relationships, human resource development. These models focus on employee relation management (ERM), customer relation management (CRM), product relation management (PRM) and resource management. All these models are specific focused.

New Business Models

There are six salient new Business Models that have substantial impact on business, economy and marketing techniques. There is a paradigm shift with the advent of new models. These are, Business Intelligence Model, Co-Creation Business Model, Business Model for Rural markets, Network effect Business Model, Outsourcing and Offshore Business Model, and Counterfeiting Business model.

Business Intelligence Model is in tune with changing dimensions and areas of businesses and the new and wider applications of ICTs. These create technological challenges such as technology management for cost effectiveness, competition and reaching new markets. The new market environments could be local, monopolistic to global.

The Co-Creation Business Model is doing business with poor consumers with low purchasing capabilities. They are the masses but they do need the basics and necessities of life and can buy according to, 'as and when and as much' they can spend for their needs. It is a mass market. As such the poor consumers' major demand is 'sachet economy'. The main strategies of this business model are: tap this mass market, and do marketing of products according to their lifestyles without encouraging materialistic consumerism, produce according to their low purchasing power, mobility and accessibility. Thus there are three essential dimensions of Co-Creation Business Model:

(i) produce products and services for the poor, low income masses matching their purchasing power and capabilities,

(ii) enhance their purchasing power by providing micro-credit,

(iii) through micro-credit, businesses also capture some share of market for regular products and services in course of time. Thus increasing their total market share (this model is discussed in detail in Chapter 3).

Business Model for Rural Markets. In developing countries, 70-80% of their population lives in rural areas. They have low connectivity with inadequate physical infrastructures such as roads, public transport etc. They have low density of telephones and only some of them are exposed to electricity and TV etc. It is only recently that businesses are understanding the importance of rural markets, these have been ignored so far. Now Rural Business Models are being developed.

This model focuses on five characteristics of rural markets and consumers: (i) purchasing capability, (ii) durable and non-durable consumer needs according to rural life styles. For example, they would need a different kind of food, different kind of soaps and detergents. Quite likely, there may not be any market for toilet tissue and paper napkins, (iii) sachet economy will be the priority for durable consumer goods,

(iv) businesses need to tap the market for farm implements, accessories and farm goods and provide doorstep delivery system, (v) delivery system is the most crucial part of the marketing strategies since villagers have low mobility, less knowledge and familiarity with the urban markets for purchasing negotiations.

In the second phase of their marketing strategies the focus should be to: (i) enhance their purchasing power by providing micro-credit, (ii) through micro-credit, businesses also capture some share of market for regular products and services in course of time. Thus increasing their total market share.

Another peculiarity of the rural market will be the fast changing consumer scenarios due to their exposure to media channels of TV where they are exposed to life styles of various Indian regions and additionally to the global life styles and consumer goods. Therefore, the businesses need to consider this factor. Businesses teams need to live with them for a while to understand their consumer dynamics for their consumer and business goods (this model is discussed in detail in Chapter 3).

Network effect Business Model

Network effects were used as justification for some of the business models for dot-coms in the late 1990s. These firms operated under the belief that when a new market comes into being which contains strong network effects, companies should care more about growing their market share than about becoming profitable. This was believed because market share will determine which company can set technical and marketing standards and thus determine the basis of future competition. A good example of this strategy was that deployed by Mirabilis, the Israeli start-up which pioneered instant messaging ("IM") and was bought-out by America Online. By giving away their ICQ product for free and preventing interoperability between their client software and other products, they were able to corner the market for instant messaging. Because of the network effect, new IM users gained much more value by choosing to use the Mirabilis system (and join its large network of users) than they would by using a competing system. As was typical for that era, the company never made any attempt to generate profits from their dominant position before selling out.

Network effects become significant after a certain subscription percentage has been achieved, called *critical mass*. At the critical mass point, the value obtained from the goods or services is greater than or equal to the price paid for the goods or services. As the user base determines the value of the goods, this implies that after a certain number of people have subscribed to the service or purchased the goods, additional people will subscribe to the service or purchase the goods due to the positive utility — price ratio. Until this point has been achieved, however, only early adopters will subscribe.

One consequence of a network effect is that the purchase of goods by one individual indirectly benefits others who own the goods — for example by purchasing a telephone a person makes other telephones more useful. This type of side effect in a transaction is known as an externality in economics, and externalities arising from network effects are known as network externalities.

The increasing number of subscribers cannot continue indefinitely. After a certain point, most networks become either congested or saturated, stopping future uptake. Congestion occurs due to overuse. The applicable analogy is that of a telephone network. While the number of users is below the congestion point, each additional user adds additional value to every other customer. However, at some point the addition of an extra user exceeds the capacity of the existing system. After this point, each additional user decreases the value obtained by every other user. In practical terms, each additional user increases the total system load, leading to busy signals, the inability to get a dial tone, and poor customer support. The next critical point is where the value obtained equals the price paid again. *The network will cease to grow at this point, and the system must be enlarged.* The congestion point may be larger than the market size. New Peer-to-Peer technological models may always defy congestion. Peer-to-Peer systems, or "P2P," are networks designed to distribute load among their user pool. This theoretically allows true P2P networks to scale indefinitely. But market saturation will still occur.

Network effects are commonly mistaken for economies of scale, which result from business size rather than interoperability. To help clarify the distinction people speak of demand side *vs.* supply side economies of scale. Classical economies of scale are on the production side, while network effects arise on the demand side. Network effects are also mistaken for economies of scope.

Examples, ***Software:*** There are very strong network effects operating in the market for widely-used computer software. Take for example, Microsoft Office, for many people choosing an office suite; prime considerations include how valuable having learned that office suite will prove to potential employers, and how well the software interoperates with other users. That is, since learning to use an office suite takes many hours, they want to invest that time, learning the office suite, which will make them most attractive to potential employers (or consulting clients, etc), and they also want to be able to share documents with potential co-workers. Similarly, finding already-trained employees is a big concern for employers when deciding which office suite to purchase or standardize on. The lack of cross-platform standards results in a situation in which one company is in control of almost 100% of the market.

However, network effects need not lead to market dominance by one company, when there are standards that allow multiple companies to interoperate, thus allowing the network externalities to benefit the entire market. This is true for the case of x86-based personal computer hardware, in which there are extremely strong market pressures to interoperate with pre-existing standards, but in which no one company dominates in the market. The same holds true for the market for long-distance telephone service within the United States. In fact, the existence of these types of networks discourages dominance of the market by one company, as it creates pressures that work against one company attempting to establish a proprietary protocol or to even distinguish itself by means of product differentiation.

In cases in which the relevant communication protocols are under the control of a single company, however, the network effect can give the company monopoly power. The Microsoft Corporation is widely seen by computer professionals as maintaining its monopoly through these means. One observed method Microsoft uses to put the network effect to its advantage is called embrace and extend (derisively called embrace, extend, and extinguish).

A limited handful of *websites* also feature a network effect. Generally, web marketplaces and exchanges feature a network effect, in that the value of the marketplace to a new user is proportional to the number of other users in the market. For example, eBay would not be a particularly useful site if auctions were not competitive. However, as the numbers of users grew on eBay, auctions grew more competitive, pushing up the prices of bids on items. This made it more worthwhile to sell on eBay and brought more sellers onto eBay, which drove prices down again as this increased supply and also brought more people onto eBay because there were things being sold that people wanted. Essentially, as the number of users of eBay grew, the prices reflected better supply-and-demand and more and more people found the site to be useful.

The collaborative Encyclopedia Wikipedia also benefits from a network effect. As the number of editors grows, the quality of information on the website improves, encouraging more users to turn to it as a source of information; many of the new users in turn became editors, continuing the process.

Social networking websites are also good examples. The more people registered onto a social networking website, the more useful the website is to its registrants.

By contrast, the value of a news site is primarily proportional to the quality of the articles, not to the number of other people using the site. Similarly, the first generation of search sites experienced little network effect, as the value of the site was based on the value of the search results. This allowed Google to win users away from Yahoo! Without much trouble, once users believed that Google's search results were superior. Some commentators mistook the value of the Yahoo brand (which does increase as more people know of it) for a network effect protecting its advertising business.

Interestingly, Alexa Internet uses a technology that tracks users' surfing patterns; thus Alexa's related sites results improve as more users use the technology. As theory would predict, no competing technology has emerged to compete successfully with Alexa, but this may be because of other factors. Alexa's network relies heavily on a small number of browser software relationships, which makes the network more vulnerable to competition.

Google has also attempted to create a network effect in its advertising business with its Google AdSense service. It places ads along the relevant news or other matter. Google AdSense places ads on many small sites, such as blogs, using Google technology to determine which ads are relevant to which blogs. Thus, the service appears to aim to serve as an exchange (or ad network) for matching many advertisers with many small sites (such as blogs). In general, the more blogs Google AdSense can reach, the more advertisers it will attract, making it the most attractive option for more blogs, and so on, making the network more valuable for all participants.

Network effects and technology lifecycle: If some existing technology or company whose benefits are largely based on network effects starts to lose market share against a challenger such as a disruptive technology or open standards based competition, the benefits of network effects will reduce for the incumbent, and increase for the challenger. In this model, a tipping point is eventually reached at which the network effects of the challenger dominate those of the former incumbent, and the incumbent is forced into an accelerating decline, whilst the challenger takes over the incumbent's former position.

Outsourcing and offshore Business models are now open to new combinations of outsourcing, service providers, and off-shoring. The outcomes of such business models are: globalization, global delivery models, multi-country supplier and delivery models, hub-and-spoke model in globalization of services, captive centers model, small and medium enterprises using off-shoring. There are product development and design facilities off-shoring model, the 'Second wave' model for expertise-driven jobs and iGen consumerism model in outsourced countries and the reverse outsourcing model.

There are Intercultural learning and training models including language facility, mannerisms, and ways of handling situations both in business and social set ups, business culture learning and training models of both outsourced and outsourcing companies in different countries. They are offshoots of outsourcing and creating business and business models of different kind.

The developed countries are outsourcing their various business processes to developing countries because of cheaper costs and thus more profitability. The capabilities, which are outsourced offshore, have moved from IT-centric functions into business processes. The complexity of these capabilities continues to climb with functions such as patent research, drug research and development, legal services and equity research beginning to emerge as the high-end of offshore outsourcing. There are services such as data entry, technical support and financial analytics, which require vastly different skill sets, end up being lumped together and evaluated as "offshore business" process services.

Educated English speaking younger age manpower, IT centric trained personnel, low labor costs, growing infrastructure, suitability of time zones and willingness of business and the government to regulate, facilitate outsourcing to developing countries. Broad categories like people skills and availability; business environment, and financial structure facilitate it further. Apart from cyber security, other issues that are critical to growth of IT are infrastructure and human resources. For example, India has depth and breadth of technologically skilled labor, available at a low cost; English language skills that facilitate communications with the developed English-speaking countries; an improving telecommunications infrastructure and extensive IT experience.

Different developing countries have different outsourcing strengths such as India has more IT centric, software development strengths. China has manufacturing strength both garments and hardware mechanical devices. Stiff competition is growing up among countries with high or low strengths as outsourcing product and services scope is widening.

However, while complexity is increasing, respective cost expectations are not shifting accordingly. But selling BPO services is becoming tougher and tougher as clients get more knowledgeable about outsourcing and competition increases with an ever-growing number of players.

Increasing acceptance for off-shoring is a foregone conclusion for multinational corporations that must keep pace with global competition, global supply and global delivery models. The role of offshore outsourcing will continue to grow in importance as off-shoring moves to a corporate "must have" and as companies develop more sophisticated global delivery models across IT and multiple business processes. General Electric's recent spin-off of its India BPO unit. We also predict the emergence of multi-country supplier and delivery models that span the globe from India to China to Central Europe. In the client market, US companies will no longer be the dominant buyers as Western European firms create strong demand for offshore services. A longer list of contenders will only reflect the rapidly spreading interest around the world in getting a piece of the BPO action. Off-shoring will grow in size and complexity as clients leverage on early lessons.

While the amount of back-office work that is currently sent outside their national borders by Western European and Japanese companies is still a tiny fraction of the total amount of such work that these companies outsource. Still it constitute a substantial source of revenue and employment for recipient countries, as India has demonstrated.

Despite Gecis' spin-off, the increasing complexity of processes being off-shored will lead to more wholly owned offshore subsidiaries for BPO, often referred to as captive centers. Existing captive shared services centers will become targets for further efficiency and expansion. It predicts that over 40% of offshore initiatives will not yield anticipated savings, scale or risk diversification. The key reason for these disappointments will not be due to supplier capability but buyer preparation and management.

In 2006 the expectation is that small and medium enterprises will finally be clients for off-shoring as they weigh the benefits of off-shoring due to budget pressures and a more accepting political environment for off-shoring.

The next big emerging phenomenon is a hub-and-spoke model in globalization of services. Singapore already has become a BPO off-shoring hub whose spokes extend to India, China and the Philippines, and some day could reach out to Sri Lanka and Vietnam. Dubai has the potential to be a Singapore-like hub in the Middle East. It is stable, forward looking and technological advanced. While the role of BPO hub by definition will be reserved to a chosen few locations, the spokes are likely to proliferate. It is as much about labor availability as it is about cost.

A 'second wave' seems to be coming in off-shoring of business processes in which English language fluency will not be a decisive factor. These will be expertise-driven jobs, requiring mainly the ability to analyze and solve complex problems.

For example, these workers may be involved in bioinformatics, or risk analytics for insurance, or scenario management in sell-side equity research, and then, someone in the US can wrap the English language around their work.

Some businesses are off-shoring product development and design facilities. The problem with it is that technology will leak out to local competitors. For companies that rely on cutting-edge innovation, protecting intellectual property is critical especially as local competitors are also going up the technology ladder.

There is outgrowing trend of reverse outsourcing also. Bharti telecommunication, India's premier telecom has outsource maintenance of its telecom infrastructure to IBM and Siemens who have set up business facilities in India (Gurgaon) to service it (2004-05). This trend is likely to grow worldwide.

China comes second owing to its cheap and plentiful labor supply and fast-improving infrastructure, but lags behind India because of its relative lack of English skills, cultural barriers and a weak legal system. Overall, Asian companies dominate the rankings, occupying six of the top ten locations.

The Economist Intelligence Unit's ranking model measures the attractiveness of 60 countries as destinations for off-shoring, scoring each country on nine criteria commonly used by companies when deciding where to offshore. Countries were scored on labor costs, labor skills, labor regulation, proximity to major sources of investment, political and security risk, macroeconomic stability, regulatory environment, tax regime and infrastructure. "With outsourcing and off-shoring becoming critical forces for business, it is important that businesses look internally both at their motivation for off shoring and their ability to manage such a function," said Andrew Briggs, Dimension Data's head of contact centers business. "Off-shoring cannot fix broken processes but in fact may only serve to exacerbate the problems, irrespective of the location chosen," he added.

Outsourcing Model for high end: To be precise, global consumer electronic majors are now launching many of their latest innovations in India, much ahead of even the US, Europe and Japan. For example, Hitachi recently launched a range of 32 to 42-inch plasma TV models in India, the second country in Asia after Singapore. Samsung introduced their 'Pleomax' range of IT products here just after their South Korea launch, 'Electrolux' global launch of 'talking' washing machine included India. The trend is now really picking-up. A few like LG, Philips and Electrolux are even significantly investing on developing features and technologies largely suited for India. They have realized that the domestic consumer is no more price-conscious and is ready to pay for superior technology. Quite naturally, there is a mad rush by the companies to enjoy the first-mover advantage.

"The market is showing a swift shift from low-end and mid-end segments to high-end, and the first one to invest will ultimately drive the volumes," Electrolux India's vice-president (sales and marketing), told Economic Times. Currently, about 60% of product innovations at Electrolux are targeted at the Indian markets. "There is a growing demand for premium audio and visual products in the Indian market. Hitachi wants to carve a distinct niche for itself and has, as a policy, identified India as a priority market," said Tadashi Nishiuchi, managing director, Hitachi Home Electronics Asia.

Interestingly, the companies are also relying on premium products to drive their brand values. "With extremely high pressure on bottom line, every company is now striving to derive higher brand values with latest technologies. It ultimately boosts the sales of low and medium product segments as well". Efforts are on to develop the market for premium products.

Some of the challenges of outsourcing: Companies make the decision to outsource after careful strategic planning and review of the pros and cons of each scenario. They chose either a third party outsource company or set up their own facility in host country — say India. Companies invest time, resources (including people) and have a few key executives to manage the operation, on the ground. These people are now responsible for managing the operational challenges in India in context of its business cultures and social cultures. Creating challenges of culture learning.

There are political and economic ramifications from outsourcing/offshoring countries, for example in US when people are losing jobs to other countries. But there were 100 sectors where there were no job losses associated with service outsourcing. This, according to them, implies that a worker could lose his/her job due to outsourcing, but may later find a job in another firm within the broader industry classification.

Hence, they conclude that there are no net job losses when there is sufficient job creation in another sector, which indeed seems to be the case. They contend that even if outsourcing leads to some shedding of labor, increased efficiency could lead to higher production and an expansion of employment in other lines of work. Share of imports of "private services" — educational, financial, insurance, telecommunications, business, professional, technical and others — from developing countries to the US, though increasing, is still quite low at 32%. The remaining 68% originates in other industrial countries.

The other social challenges for outsourced countries are to handle the consumerism among younger generations who are able to earn more at a fairly young age. Though such consumerism is creating markets and boosting economy of the host countries.

Global Counterfeit Business Model is another new Business Model in operation. It is a complex and ingenious model. The counterfeit business is targeting everything from computer chips to life saving medicines, consumer electronics and luxury goods, DVDs, watches, auto parts, motorcycles, memory chips, computer accessories, cigarettes, shoes, bags and many more. It is estimated 7% of world merchandise trade in 2004 was bogus.

What is the business strategy? Counterfeits can make products more cheaply than legitimate manufacturers. Their profits are huge with no marketing, R&D and advertising costs to defray. They have skilled labor, smart distribution and product savvy without getting bogged down with research and brand building. The marketing techniques are: for distributorship, authorized licensee who decides to counterfeit can tap legitimate channels to enter retail outfits, some mix counterfeit one with the real ones. Containers loaded with fakes are shipped from many ports not to let their origin be determined.

Counterfeit business model deals in multiple ways: It may be genuine product when it is manufactured by ex-employees who know the know-how but without the license and is therefore encroaching on the business profitability of the genuine manufacturers of products and providers of services.

Another times the duplicate is made by cheap product mix, giving it the outward product appearance and packaging of the genuine product to mislead the wholesaler and consumer. Many times there is name mix with the established brands to confuse the buyer. Such as in India made in USA (Ulhasnagar Sindhi Association) played on people's craze for foreign good to get it at any price. So this group good overpriced the consumer durables Indian goods as imported goods. Sometimes the counterfeiters may be fly-by-night operators but other times it may be the licensed producers of brand goods who run extra-unauthorized shifts and sell out through back door. So the products, 2 times out of 3 times may be genuine but produced and distributed clandestinely. There is the instance of piracy of Software that is ubiquitous in many developing countries because of the high cost of the genuine product involved. There is pirated movie DVDs and videos.

The tricks of the trade are getting sophisticated. The key steps to faking are: seed money comes from various sources including criminal sources. The expertise comes from current and former employees of licensed manufacturers of branded goods. They disassemble the products and reengineer them or they actually know the know-how. Sophisticated packing equipment is acquired to give them authenticity and digital technology helps them. For example, in case of memory chips, discards from real chip plants are smuggled. Counterfeiters etched the brand names Intel etc.

Outsourcing and counterfeiting has interesting connection also. For example, when product development and designs are outsourced such as in China computer chip designs, manufacturing of Reebok and Nike shoes or Nokia mobile phones. They learn the intricacies of products, reengineer it, market it under the same brand or putting in the market as their own brands and they are in competition with the genuine brands whose products they have copied. Chinese have the skill to duplicate to the closest details.

The scale of threat is prompting new efforts by multinationals to stop and curb the spread of counterfeits. They are even hiring detectives around the globe and pressuring governments to crack down countries that are doing it. They lose market for their products to some extent as fake products capture some markets and some markets are lost by the bad image created by bad products that may not wear well.

Counterfeiting has gone from a local nuisance to global threat. It is thriving on the whole process of globalization. Globalization is the spread of capital and new knowledge and know-how to the new markets that in turn contribute to low costs to create the ideal export machine, manufacturing first the cheap stuff then moving up the value chain. Even fakes have different shades of quality depending upon who is faking it and at what level.

It is the story of South Asia and China. Counterfeiting pack all the punch of skilled labor, smart distribution and product savvy without getting bogged down with research and brand building. The result is a global industry that is matching the multinationals in speed, reach and sophistication. For example, Chinese are ingenious, inventive and scientifically oriented and they are becoming the world manufacturers of counterfeit products.

Even the counterfeiters are skilled at duplicating the holograms and smart chips and other security devices to differentiate the genuine from fake. Many fakes are getting so good that even it would take a forensic expert to distinguish it from the real. Armed with digital technology, the counterfeiters can churn out perfect packaging – a key to duping distributors, retailers and consumers.

Once they sneak out, they get mixed into genuine supply chain, and phony components get used in authentic components. Unscrupulous wholesalers, small office supply stores, independent pharmacies would say they are offering goods at bargain price and get fakes accepted by consumers. If they can push them off as high quality products they have good profit margin.

While the counterfeiters are piling up profits, the multinationals are spending more money in stopping them. They are hiring sleuths, investigators, lawyers and informants within the factories making fakes. Even Pfizer will soon use RFID tags to its medicines in USA that will enable to track drugs from lab to the consumer medicine cabinet. Biggest challenge is in getting cooperation from China who is faking the most but now if its products are faked then what?

SUMMARY

The purpose of business is creating customer, markets, and effective demand for the products. It is business action that creates the customer. It is the customer who creates the business. It is the customer who creates the wealth and economic resources by his/her willingness to pay for goods and service. It is the dynamics between all the individual elements that will influence how communication channels are developed and proceed in this complex system.

Business communication framework suggests that communication in any business operates from three perspectives: customer – supply chain relationships including both external and internal links; employee – management relationship including internal links only; customer-consumer-product focus. Business communication framework comprises of types of communication, contexts and patterns. It defines the scope, concepts and essential components of business communications and its tools. It presents the salient models of Business Communications.

It focuses on different types of communication typologies. One typology defines *communication as a process*. It could be linear, non-linear and circular. Second typology defines *communication as hierarchical*: vertical or top to bottom, horizontal i.e. between each other in the same hierarchy and bottom-up i.e. communicating from lower level hierarchy to top level. Third typology defines communication vis-à-vis different *communication environments*. Business communication is meaningful in the contexts of perception, expectation and demand in both internal and external links.

The Communication Patterns in business can be top-down, bottom to top, bottom-bottom, and circular. The communication patterns with customers in the supply chain can be two-ways, circular and with many feedback loops. Communication mode is interpersonal — both formal and informal, both in groups and one-on-one and supported by technologies. The communication patterns with consumers of goods and services are both formal and informal interpersonal communication modes and various media channels.

Scope of business communication lies in three domains: B2B — business to business, B2C business to customer, and C2C customer to customer. These three have different business as well communication focuses. The three business communication approaches deal with specific relationships associated with these.

The four business concepts: Know the market forces and recognize the changing market dynamics, business leaders must do the right things right, confront the reality, and accepted set of values present the business communication perspective that can impede or facilitate company leaders to recognize the changing market dynamics and the business communication tools.

The three main business components are: business intelligence and its social components, changing dimensions and areas of businesses, and the new and wider applications of information communication technologies (ICTs). These three components also create a specific business culture with distinctive focus for a particular business. We present Business Communication Models, and conventional and new business models. The various Business Communication Models take seven approaches: general and specific business approach, communications for employee–management relationships, for human relations in businesses, business communication to rural markets and to the poor having low level purchasing capability, communicating through economic intelligence analysis, and economics of business communications.

There are six salient new Business Models that have substantial impact on business, economy and marketing techniques. These are, Business Intelligence Model, Co-Creation Business Model, Business Model for Rural markets, Network effect Business Model, Outsourcing and Offshore Business model, and Counterfeiting Business Model apart from conventional business models of super store, chain stores and franchises expanded versions of store model and specific models for business related functions.

2

Corporate Communications

CORPORATE COMMUNICATIONS

'The simplest representation of any business organization is in terms of the customer and supplier. An organization develops and provides a product or service for which it receives payment, of some kind, from a customer. In this case the organization is the supplier to the customer. This simplistic dynamic is a very simple way to think about all the relationships in a business setting. It is this dynamic that determines the power balance in the relationship and defines the frame work in which relationship will proceed. It is therefore this dynamic and the factors described above that provide the framework for all communication.

Expanding further, one can look at any business organization having several external customers and several external suppliers. Within the business organization there will be several functions some of which will be customers and suppliers to each other. Therefore, in a realistic business organization one will have a multitude of customer-supplier relationships of which many will be internal and many external. It is the dynamic between all the individual elements that will influence how communication channels are developed and proceed in this complex system'.

A business organization is a system. There are two ways of operating and communicating in this system. One is operation of internal links of people, processes and core competencies in the organization. Communication is necessary condition of operating these three at optimal success level. Second is operation of external links of customers, supply chain vendors and other external vendors of community, media, civic organizations and government.

The customers pay money for acquiring your (business) product. This money compensates all other stakeholders viz. shareholders, financiers, suppliers, society and last but not the least, employees for investments they have made in the organization. If your customers desert you or if you fail to attract them, your business will close down. The customer has a special stake in your organization. If the product he/she purchases does not provide him/her the desired performance, the hard-earned money is wasted. Thus, the customer has great interest in efficient functioning of your organization. He is, therefore, a stakeholder of your business.

The employees buy your organization's business concept and concretize it by providing their knowledge, skill, effort and time. They interact with all other stakeholders and satisfy the interest of each of the stakeholders. Your organization, in turn, fulfils the needs of the employees like physiological, security, social needs, etc. There is similarity in the interests of both customers and employees vis-à-vis the business organization. If you look at the definition of Customers, you will find that Employees have many of the attributes of the former. And, therefore, the Employees can also be described as 'Internal Customers'. If the Customer is the purpose of the business, then the employee as the Internal Customer is the means. Organizations having *satisfied employees* create satisfied customers. An enlightened management should try to bring synergy of all the different stakeholders so that business is able to flourish; and satisfy to a great extent the needs of the shareholders, financiers, suppliers and also the society.

From the discussion so far, we can say that customer relationship management cannot be successful without employee relationship management. It is not enough to be a customer centric organization! A truly smart company is one that is centered on both customers and employees. Customers are the primary (core) focus and employees are the secondary focus of such an organization. The management of such companies focuses on building relationships with their customers and employees. That makes the relationships enduring and lifelong.

Business Communications in a corporate can be focused from two perspectives: One, customer-supply chain relationships including both external and internal links; and two, employee-management relationship including internal links only. The dynamics of business communications are customer-supplier relationships in the context of product, services and people. The dynamics of business communications in employee-management relationship are in the context of performance, productivity and human relations. The focus is on vision and leadership qualities of the top leaders in the organization, performance of employees at all levels, development and upgrading of capabilities of the employees and dialogue strategies to communicate, coordinate the business reality through candid appraisals.

The core processes in any business are people, strategies and operations and the end result is 'product' which must be achieved through Action. The effectiveness of these processes depends on both internal and external communication in the corporate organization. Internal communication focuses on employees and management interactions for the three core processes and the Action; whereas, the external corporate communication is associated with business development. This could be facilitated through communicating with external links to the corporate business such as supply chain for the product components, distributors, wholesalers and retailers, consumers, product marketing and sales through its positioning in the market and product campaigns, its business competitors, media, public relations, business focused conferences and government.

CORPORATE COMMUNICATIONS: INTERNAL LINKS

Employee and Management Interaction: Internal communication is mostly interpersonal. This channel is used both for formal and informal interactions. It is both vertical and horizontal interpersonal communications encompassing employees' interaction and management interaction within the different business divisions and facilities of a corporate. Feedback is important component in the interpersonal interaction process. There is technology support to interpersonal communication also. People at all levels communicate with each other by telephones, emails, intranets through computers, formal presentations and after question hours to clarify their doubts and also through informal interpersonal interactions. The informal internal communication is facilitated in staff lounges, lunchroom, cafeterias, around the vending machines and water coolers, and people interact and exchange information and views informally even when they are walking through the office corridors. These social operating mechanisms help to get to know the office happenings, informally exchanging both positive and negative views about people and products, and sharing new ideas and knowledge effortlessly and inadvertently.

Social scientists advocate these 'decentralized self-organizing systems'. Collective wisdom shapes business, economies, societies and nations. Heeding to collective intelligence is greater than the smartest decisions of one man or woman. So decisions made by a group are always better. Sometimes tapping into the crowd can pay-off, other times the group can go wrong as in stock market decisions.

The strength of internal business communication lies in coordinating the three core processes of people, strategies and operations and motivating for Action implementation. Implementation is in a way exposing reality and acting on it. Interpersonal communication dynamics play significant role in this context.

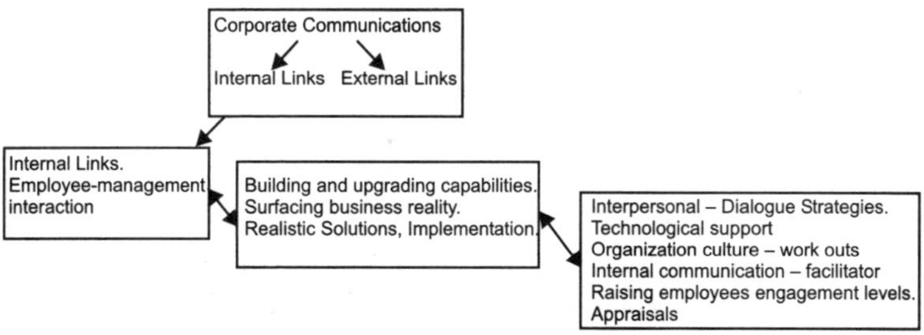

Fig. 2.1. Corporate Communications Internal Links

Employee and Management Interaction focus on building and upgrading the capabilities of the organization and its employees, surfacing the business reality and accountability, finding realistic solutions and implementing them. Some salient communication interpersonal channels including organization culture facilitate the communication process. The characteristics of the communicator are important in this process. Further, appraisals as communication tools, help in getting the right person for the right job.

BUILDING THE CAPABILITY

The interaction among employees, between staff and different heads of divisions, managers, chief executive officer and the top leader of the corporate is both essential and important for development of the business and to know the reality of the particular business they are dealing with. Through communication, management levels within the corporate know the strength and weaknesses of their employees; and also they themselves, in turn, get appraised about their own strengths and weaknesses. Through this processes even the employees get appraised of their own strengths and weaknesses and also they appraise their management levels in their own work and professional contexts. This is an efficient way of management levels knowing their employees and own self; and employees knowing themselves and their management levels. Such an appraisal is in context to organization's capabilities, business development strategies, linking strategies to operations and how these have to be executed. Since implementation is the main objective to achieve results in any business. Top leader must appraise the capabilities of different levels of management and employees by interacting with them and not through filtered information from selected sources only.

Such knowledge helps to build the capability of its employees by pulling and developing the weak and as well developing the weaknesses of others; and playing on the strengths and filling in the gaps (by hiring new) in the capabilities and talents needed for business strategies and operations. Hiring new may bring in the fresh ideas and newer perspectives to the business on hand and promotions and incentives for the old. It is only through communication, top leader assesses the need for new and fresh ideas and perspectives, and performance incentives for the old employees. He/she is able to assess the capability of the people who would implement strategies. He/she would be able to synchronize people and various disciplines within, and link performance rewards to the outcome.

The weak employees are given chance to develop their business and technical capabilities through *in-house coaching and training programs*. They are not decried for the weaknesses. While training and coaching programs are ongoing; the employees are moved around and are put in positions where their strengths can be utilized and put to optimum use. This way, the corporate is not at loss nor the employees' morale goes down. Thus for the complex role of the ultimate leadership communication is a big facilitator. Internal communication also provides a *mechanism for changing assumptions* as business environments change, and upgrading capabilities to meet the challenges of the ambitious new strategies.

SURFACING THE BUSINESS REALITY

Interactive communication — dialogue with people concerned helps to surface reality of the business, to discuss accountability of the person responsible for the results. Dialogic interaction helps in knowing the capabilities of the accountable person for the task and if need be to upgrade the capabilities beforehand to achieve results. If such step is not taken, corporate may be wasting its money, time, energy and tarnishing its business and product image.

In interactive communication dialogues, people concerned, argue about the doable initiatives, search out the reality, reach practical and specific conclusions, and everybody agrees to take the responsibility as well as commit to the responsibility. They further take accountability for the action. Thus interactions clarify the points of doubts, encourage responsibility, commitment, and accountability.

Dialogue is the core of culture and unit of work. How people talk to each other determines how well the organization will work. Is the dialogue stilted, politicized, fragmented and lowers the morale of the employees. If it is so then reality will never surface. Or is it candid and reality-based, raising the right questions and debating them and finding realistic solutions. If it is so then people will move on. The leader has to be in the playing field with his management team consistently and forcefully.

Importance of *Robust Dialogue* brings reality to the surface through openness, candor and informality and being focused. Even such a reality may make people uncomfortable. It makes an organization effective in gathering information, understanding the information and reshaping it to produce decisions. It fosters creativity, and even innovations are incubated through robust dialogue. People have to start with open mind, hear new information and choose the best alternatives. They listen to all sides of the debates and make their own contributions. The aim is to invite multiple viewpoints, see the pros and cons of each one, and try honestly and candidly to construct new viewpoints. This is the dynamic that stimulates new questions, new ideas, and new insights. Finally, robust dialogue ends with a closure where people agree what each person has to do and when. Since they have committed to it in the open forum they are accountable for the outcome. How do you get people to practice robust dialogues when they are used to classical corporate dialogues? It has to be practiced from the top leaders first. Others will take the cue.

Candid dialogue is also necessary along with robust dialogue. It is critical and needs integrity, honesty, a common approach, a common language and frequency. The people-development-and-assessment model focuses on four competencies: functional skills, business skills, management skills and leadership skills. The candid dialogue is — the dialogue of the organization, the process of observation to common criteria, and culminating in candid assessment and feedback.

Leaders should follow through the execution process. This ensures people are doing the things they are committed to do according to the agreed time-table. It exposes any lack of discipline or connection between ideas and actions and forces the specificity to synchronize the moving parts of an organization. Leaders can either follow one-on-one, or in group-settings as feedback method. In the group, everybody learns something. The variety of viewpoints raised help people see the criteria for the decisions, the judgments exercised, and the tradeoffs being made. This exposure calibrates people's judgments and aligns the team.

Organizations do not face realities when their dialogues are ineffective and it shows in their results. Dialogues alter the psychology of a group. It can expand a group's capacity or shrink it. It can energize it or drain energy. It can create unity or create bitter factions.

COMMUNICATION ABOUT BUSINESS STRATEGY

If the leaders in the corporate are clear about the building blocks of a business strategy. They can discuss and debate about it with its employees and sensitize them about it. This process helps them to find if it is good or bad strategy and needs alternatives. Discussion with employees give good feedback.

Strategy process is related to people and operation process. Strategy is to win the customers' preferences and create a competitive advantage. Debating and discussing, constant exchange of ideas and best practices among diverse business managers create intellectual capital and better business strategies. Strategic value is also added by initiatives to improve performance throughout the company such as six sigma, digitization, and people process. The initiatives can help people move to environments where they can grow and be ready to take on more responsibility in the future.

A good strategy allows people to learn about the business, external environment and not just data and facts. It helps them to analyze it, use judgment, develop insights and intuitions, and learn from mistakes. Discussing these things create alignment among the employees and build energy in the process.

An operational plan focuses at number of factors such as assessment of external business environment, assessment of the existing customers and markets, who are in the competition, and the critical issues facing the business. The major concerns are: are the short-term and long-term strategies balanced and if business is capable of executing the strategy.

After the plan is constructed, reviewed at the corporate level, it must be reviewed with the people who are the real people to implement it. The people are the real executing power. When a business decides about the new strategy, it ought to have dialogue about the quality and aptitude of the people involved.

The human resource leader in the corporate must be trained in tactile skills of how to teach people, develop them, make them interested in staying with the company, and know what is important to build morale and momentum in the organization. In addition he must have the characteristics of a business leader such as business acumen, ability to understand how company makes money, ability to think critically, passion for results and ability to link strategy to execution.

Endorsing the same type of communication approach James Welch (2002) suggests a *work-out* communication process which he used for transforming General Electric Company. He projects how workers within the business get frustrated when they feel they know more about the work, they have great ideas but no empowerment for action. They can't change things that needed to be changed. Managers have authority but no time. Work-out is the solution. Though work-out is a kind of transformation process missing in most of the large and global organizations.

Work-out is based on the premise that people who are closest to the work know the work best. Things happen when the ideas of those people are solicited and immediately turned into action — unencumbered by fleets of meetings, approvals, forms and reports. This way the unleashed energy of people is tapped and there is gain in productivity.

A small group of employees and managers, at cross-functions, or cross-levels or both, meet for a day or so and address the critical issues of the business and develop recommendations for action (GE calls it town meeting). After the open dialogue, the leader on the spot approves or disapproves a recommendation and empowers the person to take action if approved. He reviews it again whether the results are being achieved. In the meeting, the managers can suggest the issues or employees can raise the issues. The business issues addressed may be minor or mind-boggling. It may take a day or several months for implementation depending on the issues. There is an open dialogue on the issues.

The dimensions of work-out are: *Stretch,* i.e. stretching the goals high. It forces an organization to think about challenges to their performances, which should not be just a small incremental gain but high-level performance. The stretch goals challenges people to think about new ideas.

Sensitize employees about company's Brand: This is the second approach of getting employees involved with the company. How do you sensitize employees to the value of the brand? Employees at all levels should be involved, feel motivated and committed to make a product successful. The shop floor needs to be motivated too. They need to feel that they are part of what the companies do. The managers should talk about the new products that they are in the process of launching and give all employees a sense of involvement. Very often in companies, when you see a new product or a new project, a sense of belonging is created. Employees wear badges, labels on their sleeves, special caps. In these times of economic change, we need to make it our responsibility to expose employees to the company holistically. This kind of awareness can perhaps be built best by moving people into positions where they have to face different constituents.

Plant people can be sent to customer-service operations to enable them to see the different kinds of problems people face in the field. Otherwise, it is their production and somebody else's problem. Employees have to believe that they are responsible for the company. How do you create that culture, that sense of belonging? It is something that has to be created by the CEO of the company. The CEO has to be concerned with all kinds of things, not just the bottom line, production figures or the company's image. A holistic concern should be created.

Third approach, *important initiatives* can be taken such as the Tata Business Excellence Model and Tata Quality Management Services for a big corporate in India. Through this they have been assessing the quality of products and the quality of the manner in which operations are run — and having a scorecard for that. This is a process that can create a business culture where employees and CEO feel holistically involved.

Here are a few examples of Indian companies who engage its employees through newsletters, credit cards, war cries and a whole host of other activities to upgrade the engagement level between the company and its workforce. At the Goodlass Nerolac paints factory situated in Maharashtra India, the workers bring out their own newsletter. A simple hand-written single-page letter called 'Spandhan', which gives news about happenings at the factory and also about its workers. At Johnson & Johnson the field sales personnel have been given credit cards under the cashless admission scheme. The card, which can be used in select hospitals, enables the staff to pay for medication for their dependants in case of an emergency, thus saving them the trauma of arranging for finance. At the corporate office of Procter and Gamble in Mumbai, the walls are plastered with posters saying 'To the top — Non-stop.' This follows an earlier war cry 'Now or Never,' which donned the walls earlier.

Amidst all the technology, million-dollar investment and global game plans that one hears about, it is the *human capital*, which is central to any company's long-term strategy. The realization is that for a company to move ahead, its employees need to move in tandem. Everything comes to a naught if the employees don't care about where the company is going. That is why it is crucial to attain higher levels of employee engagement. Employee engagement is essentially a gamut of activities and feelings to be addressed in the lifecycle of an employee in any organization. So aspects like motivation, commitment, training and development, communication and compensation etc comprise engagement. It also reflects the attitude of employees towards the company.

A survey was conducted a few years back on the engagement levels of employees in India with companies, whether they are MNC, big or middle level. Few comments given below give negative feedback from employees: "In India, employees are constantly reminded about their accountability but they aren't given feedback on their performance. Queries on what is expected of them or how aware are they on the company's vision draw a blank". ".....there is a realization that initiatives at the organizational level usually don't reach out to employees". "We are now trying at an individual level. If we aspire to be world class, then we have to chalk out what's in it for our employees, what are their expectations and how do we meet them," "employees do not have role clarity. Instead of outside communication, we realized that internal communication is needed".

Raising engagement levels doesn't have to involve a big show of tender loving care — a small initiative can sometimes yield big results. Johnson & Johnson, for example, has a Peer Award, where an employee can recommend his or her colleague for accomplishment. "A simple initiative like this enables the company to build camaraderie among its employees," believes, head of human resources, Johnson & Johnson.

The seriousness of employee engagement can be assessed by the statistics given by regional practice leader for Gallup. He reveals that the actively disengaged employees, who form around 20-25% in any organization are very destructive, as they undo the work of committed or engaged employees, who roughly comprise of 25-30% of the work pool. The balance are the not-so-engaged employees, who work within their parameters, content with what they have but are open to flirtations by rival companies. The ratio between the committed and actively disengaged groups is 1:1, whereas the ideal situation should be around 4:1. And if ratios or percentile aren't persuasive enough, here are some hard numbers.

He further comments that a study of the Singapore workforce reveals that the cost of disengagement for companies is around $5 billion; while in the US it's around $300 billion. In the Indian corporate arena, there is good news, as there seems to be a heightened sense of engagement. The realization is there, which is good, though there's a long way to go. One of the aspects of the realization is the need to make communication two-way. Merely passing on management's viewpoint, as a diktat, is passé. Employees need to be equally passionate about the strategy. Companies also realize that this can be achieved by taking the employees' perspective into the overall vision (2005).

The creation of BAT (business analyst team), CAT (creative analyst team) and soon to debut RAT (rapid action team) at Nerolac reflects the company's attempts to garner ideas and thoughts from employees. "People management should be all the way. If companies can create quality communication at the level of team managers, then one will have an engaged organization."

At Procter & Gamble India, each group is expected to take the strategy to a functional level. For example, at the plant, the functional group chalks out an action plan to ramp up the capacity for the laundry business. A plant worker is therefore able to relate to it, as the plan would take into consideration his observations. The challenge is to get the employees to become confident in decision-making. They also need to understand competition, the direction consumers are going in, how products are faring and how trade is going to behave.

At Procter & Gamble engagement efforts are carried out keeping in mind the long-term vision of the company. Accordingly, the move from 'Now or never' to 'To the top — Non-stop' is the next phase after the success achieved in the past couple of years.

"The current younger generation employees want to be heard. They want to be given importance. A company can ignore that only at its own peril".

Similarly, Johnson & Johnson hold the Strategy Plan challenge meeting, which gives executives an opportunity to challenge the strategy plan. They get a chance to fashion and shape the strategy plan in the presence of senior management. If the feedback is feasible, then it can be incorporated. The learning curve goes through phases and each curve merits a fresh look. New skills like streamlining process speed up decision-making. The leadership also has to be dynamic to incorporate changes in the strategy.

Hero Honda (India) wants to bring in the same dynamism — of employees and leadership, even as the company is enjoying its peak position in the industry. Success brings in complacency. Management feels the need to communicate to the employees that the market is changing and one has to be prepared to meet the demands of change. No words are minced when it comes to telling the employees about the competition that lies ahead.

The issue is how employee engagement is rewarded. Employee engagement enables a company to find out whether the best employees are being adequately rewarded or not and whether a system is in place to track that. But if remuneration is sub-standard, then a company definitely has to look at ways to get it on par with industry. Moreover, if a company works on aspects like work environment, workplace innovation and cares not only for its employees but also for their families, then it makes an employee think twice before taking a leap with more money as the only consideration.

Motivation is both effort and commitment

Peter Cappelli, professor of management and director, centre for human resources, Wharton School Interview to Economic Times 14 Jan 05, comments on employees engagement in companies.

Indian companies, like their western counterparts, will have to look more seriously towards keeping employees engaged. Cappelli spoke on the various issues concerning engagement, the consequence of ignoring employees' needs and where India stands in the engagement stratosphere.

If you look across regions, then companies in the US have more of a financial orientation. They're always looking at ways to drive costs down and aren't paying much attention to employees. In comparison, companies in Europe take a long view on motivation and commitment. They focus on developing individual employees' careers in the organization, investing in them through initiatives like training and development.

In India, as the economy heats up, companies are more willing and able to hire talent away from each other. That is creating a market, where the potential to lose talent is higher and it's making them pay more attention to the human capital issue.

Indian companies are reaching the engagement issue faster compared to other countries. The Indian business scene has moved away from limited mobility across companies, and that's a challenge in a highly dynamic labor market. How can companies attain higher levels of engagement? A company wants employees to stay on the job. That's the primary objective, globally. However, as companies delve deeper, the facet that comes out is motivation.

Motivation is both effort and commitment. Employees can be judged on the basis of the work and the effort they put in when no one is watching. There are some who stay with you, work hard when monitored, but do nothing when the senior management or the immediate supervisor isn't watching. Commitment is more to do with psychology rather than economic incentives. People are committed when they feel a sense of ownership for the work executed by them. There are simple questions that can be asked to judge whether employees are engaged or not.

Do they feel some control over their responsibilities? Do they believe they have some personal stake in what they do? Do they believe they will be identified and recognized for their performance? Getting committed employees means that a company has to involve them in decision-making. For that, the managers have to give clearly defined tasks, which can be judged. Managers have to see that there is feedback. And the feedback should also have some kind of recognition, which isn't necessarily monetary.

How critical is remuneration to engagement? Most companies believe that compensation is the most important management tool and is particularly important in retaining people. Some employees work very hard and are committed, mainly because it's their personality. But they still quit because they aren't paid enough money. So adequate remuneration is critical in maintaining people's attachment. But a company has to do a balancing act between pay and performance, because that's crucial in keeping employees motivated. Employees want to see themselves paid more if they work hard and also realize that they don't get rewarded for non-performance.

The biggest problem with motivation, particularly in white-collared jobs, is that people are often not rewarded for doing a good job. Rewards are often pointed in different directions for example; higher pay comes with seniority, where you are rewarding people for just staying around. That's the biggest problem in motivation as the actual rewards are for something different. Employees across the board want to see rewards coming on the basis of the performance and not the longevity of tenure.

If remuneration isn't the solution, how do companies motivate employees? Most companies in the US have been grappling with employee motivation issues for a very long time. Companies need to realize that the employees are in a market, where they can leave if someone else offers them better terms. That's a reality that companies have to accept. The other aspect is that employees tend to stay back, not tempted by more money, because they are attached to a group of people. Social relationships hold people back even though the money is better elsewhere.

Cappelli and Hamori's (2004) researched about the changes in the attributes of Corporate Executives 1980 to 2001, suggests that "corporate executives tended to be model organization men who stuck faithfully with the companies that first hired them, and they climbed methodically up the corporate ladder until, at last, they retired. The dominant notion during this time was that a business career ran its course inside a corporation."

Second, the new model clearly underscores that "different skills are being rewarded, and that a new type of executive will benefit from this trend. People who can promote themselves clearly win. It's tempting to say that people with more merit get ahead now, although I'm not exactly sure that this is true because it's hard to judge real merit. But the people who appear to have merit clearly have the advantage in this model."

Corporate hierarchies are flattening. "We measured a considerable change in the distribution of executives by job responsibility between 1980 and 2001. Not all companies have exactly the same hierarchy of titles, but most have three tiers — CEO and chair level, EVP level and VP level ... We found that the percentages in the top and middle tiers declined (27.8% to 22.8%, and 65.1% to 59.3% respectively), while the percentage in the lower tier expanded substantially (from 7.1% to 17.8%), again supporting the perception that corporate hierarchies have become flatter."

Different types of companies offer different prospects for advancement. "It's clear, for instance, that there are huge advantages to working in a growing firm. Executives are much more likely to be promoted in companies with healthy growth rates than in stagnating companies ... Other things being equal, younger companies offer faster advancement, perhaps because of their tendency to have flatter hierarchies." Also, "the youngest firms — presumably the fastest growing — do the most recruiting of outside talent."

Changes have also taken place along the "inside track" to the executive suite. Through the 1970s, "marketing was the preferred track into the executive suite, but the results here suggest that finance now offers by far the best path (it offered the best path in 1980, too, but consulting and human resources were close behind). The finance track will remain the dominant path to the top job as long as the investor community wields a powerful influence on corporations."

Employees want to feel they have some attachment towards their immediate supervisor that he cares as a person and is interested in helping them. Companies can foster and develop this sense of belonging. One way of strengthening the social fabric in an organization is to encourage employees to interact more through group discussions, strategy meetings and social gatherings.

How the issue of communication in the organizations can be handled? The biggest area of friction is that companies keep employees in the dark. When nobody tells them what's going on, it's difficult for employees to feel a part of an organization. They need to know what's happening in the company. Is it expanding or shrinking? Lack of internal communication leads to discontent among employees. And the management has an even greater problem when employees start making up stories without knowing the real picture. For example, if there is a rumor that a plant will be shut down and the management says nothing, then people start talking. The management's reasoning could be that it doesn't want to scare the employees, but by not communicating, it clearly ends up scaring them even more.

Most companies in the US have still not paid enough attention to communicating openly. They fear competitors and investors will come to know and so they hide it from their employees as well. Often decisions taken at the top aren't communicated even to the senior management team.

The traditional employee-employer relationship has undergone change in Indian businesses. With changing times, the Indian corporate culture has also undergone a great change. As globalization has brought the world closer and the Indian professional has gone places, courtesy his global career; work standards, ethics and practices have been changing in the Indian corporate culture. The traditional employee-employer relationship, too, has undergone a metamorphosis because of this change. The image of formality and formidability that over the years has been associated with that of the employer has changed. Instead, in its place, an informal, accessible and easily approachable employer is visible and not a distant and authoritative superior. For many, he has also become a philosopher, guide and mentor, rolled into one.

Employees think it is essential to have a good working rapport with your superior since he/she is the connecting link in the hierarchy chain, it doesn't make sense to antagonize him/her. One must manage the boss well as it affects your day-to-day work capabilities, motivation, commitment to work and appraisals. It affects your career progress both in the short-term and long-term.

As competition peaks, the corporate world has become the survival of the fittest. With high-stress jobs becoming the order of the day, most professionals are realizing that it takes more than simple good work to be able to climb up. Networking, building the right image and trying to portray an image of self-assuredness and confidence have also become important criterion. You might be a great at work. But if you have a bad PR with employees or a bad superior, then the overall impression suffers. Even in the best of companies, it is important to project a good image.

INTERNAL COMMUNICATION FACILITATORS

What count is the substance of the communication though various facilitators? The salient channels are board meetings, mentors, specific meeting forums of top leaders of all divisions, team meetings, workshops, training and coaching programs, and both formal and informal one-on-one talk of the boss with the employees. The organization culture also facilitates the internal communication.

Board Meetings. The board directors meet at around quarterly frequency. They discuss about the operations of the businesses, profits and loss and growth and image building of the company. The heads of various divisions — finance, operations, business strategies and marketing of the company along with the CEO will be meeting the directors and communicating about their divisions plans, strategies, operations, and shortfalls. The board of directors in their meetings discusses and approves the matters about the company for public disclosure and action.

In specific meeting *forums of top executives* of all divisions, the CEO may review all aspects of their businesses and external environments, identify the company's greatest opportunities and problems and share best practices. He also uses this forum to observe how the top executives think, how they work together and execute the particular strategies, how they lead their divisions, mentor the group and coach them. The interface communication in this forum gives opportunity to the division heads to be appraised frequently about the company policies and plans, changing short-term strategies and the CEO's contribution to share with them their handling of problematic issues, other issues, feedback about handling opportunities and best practices.

Mentors in any organization are important to develop a person befitting the needs of the business. *Teams* are necessary. Team can focus on different functions, and some may focus on cross-functions of the company. They should be put together to work on well-proven and provocative management ideas to work with energy and passion. Why? Business at its best is critical to individual and social wellbeing-material and psychological. The focus should be on leader-managers at the middle level of a business because they are the men and women charged with turning ideas into reality, turning abstract thoughts into human value. Without their drive, innovation, change, and leadership, an idea is simply an idea, a wish, a dream, and unfulfilled promise.

There is power of people working together to do what no individual can do working alone. Little of any significance in the world is achieved without a team willing and able to wield individual talents, knowledge, and expertise to a shared purpose. The power of teams resides in the full expression of talents available to the individual men and women who come together with their diverse experiences, cultures, and personal styles. Diversity is the engine of life, the force that propels us forward into imagining new possibilities. Without differences, life and business degenerates. In short, the beneficial power of business at its best, is the power to innovate, improve, fulfil, transform, and empower.

In team meetings, the members of the team interact, plan about the strategies and operations to handle a particular piece of assignment and members commit to responsibilities according to their capabilities. Through the interactions, they iron out the wrinkles among themselves, doubts are clarified and even new ideas are suggested and incorporated. Team communication focuses on dialogue, collaboration and coordination among the team members. The circular communication among the members helps in reaching consensus about handling the assignments. Feedback loops are important component in these situations.

The team interaction with the higher levels of management and top leader is the next essential step. Employees-team members assess themselves objectively and also communicate their own ideas and suggestions about the assignment itself wherever there is disagreement. Such talks appraise higher levels of management and leadership about the reality of particular employee team's capability — strength and weaknesses in handling particular piece of the work assignment and the Action motivation. They are also able to appraise the team members of any shortcomings and the need for coaching and training etc. This kind of knowledge sharing and involvement improve the quality of the work.

As discussed in earlier sections, companies must sensitize even employees at the lowest rung through proper in-house channels about their business strategies, policies and plans and actions for better involvement, motivation and commitment to work. Even one-on-one informal talks between the employee and supervisor facilitate this.

Two types of *in-house workshops* are organized. Their duration is mostly 1-2 days. One, when a group of people from particular business division/s attends the workshop. The objectives can be to appraise them about the recent developments in their work areas including innovations in techniques and technologies both in their own corporate and also in related businesses. The higher levels of management may appraise them of the developments. In the second type of *in-house workshop*, outside experts are invited to appraise the participants about the recent developments in their work areas including innovations in techniques and technologies in related businesses.

In both types of workshops, participants are also encouraged to present their experiences by presenting discussion papers and participate in the open discussions at the end of the workshop day. It further facilitates information and knowledge sharing. Learning is an important part of developing people in the company. The in-house education through identifying issues of the company itself provides good learning.

Training programs focus on either upgrading employee/s particular capabilities to fit in a specific assignment. Or they may aim at general professional development of the capabilities. *Coaching* is intense training of a person for developing his/her minus points to fit in the assigned work. It aims at upgrading specific capabilities in particular and professional development of the person in general. Here the training is one-on-one. Most effective way to coach a person is to observe him and then give the feedback. Generally, the supervisors do the coaching but some corporate may have group of persons specially assigned to coaching employees.

Organizations culture is its shared values, beliefs and norms of behavior. These beliefs are conditioned by training, experience and what people hear inside and outside about the company's prospectus and what its leaders are doing and saying. Behaviors are beliefs turned into actions. Behaviors deliver the results. The norms are the expected and accepted ways of groups of people how they behave in the organization setting and work together. These are rules of engagement.

These are called 'social software' of an organization. A key communication component of software is social operating mechanisms. These are formal or informal meetings, presentations, even memos or email exchanges — anywhere that dialogue takes place. Two things make these operating mechanisms work. First, they are integrative, cutting across the organization and breaking barriers among units, functions, disciplines, work processes, hierarchies, and between the organization and external environment as well. Second, these create new information flows and new working relationships. These let people, who normally do not have much contact with one another exchange views, share information and ideas, and learn to understand their company as a whole. They achieve transparency and simultaneous action.

CHARACTERISTICS OF THE CORPORATE COMMUNICATOR

The main characteristic of the communicator is that he/she is willing to talk as well listen. They are receptive to others. Therefore, the qualities of a communicator/s are equally important. Communicator at whatever level of line in the corporate must have: *self-awareness* – that is they must know themselves well. So that they are comfortable with their strengths and weaknesses and have no emotional blockages to admit their mistakes and have the capability to learn from their mistakes as well their successes. They should be *authentic*. That is they are the same as what they do and what they say. It builds trust. *Self-mastery* is the self-confidence with which they can communicate, adapt to change and can encourage debate to bring up the opposite views and set up the social ambience for learning from others. *Humility* keeps the ego under control and they listen to people and admit they do not know answer for all and are receptive to others' ideas. A person who is not categorized as high performer needs to be valued rather than more attention being given to star performers.

On the negative side, sending micro-inequities characteristics of the communicator can sap the motivation of the employee and they may feel devalued. Micro-inequities are the subtle putdown snubs, dismissive gestures and sarcastic tones with which your boss or other colleagues may treat you and exclude you from the task or team. When your boss or someone else takes credit for your work. When a senior manager cut shot a timid worker conferring with him by taking a casual call without even saying excuse me, and continues on the phone for a long time. The worker feels ignored and insulted. Such offensive attitude and behavior can sap worker's motivation. How to stop the snubs that demoralize you and your colleagues?

This is a subconscious phenomenon that hurts everyone's career and productivity. Sending too many negative messages can lag team's performance. These cumulative little acts of exclusion can make an organization unsuccessful. And people leave organizations since they do not feel valued there. Anytime we feel hurt about not being recognized we take it personally. But taking things personally is a way to get stuck. On the other hand, ignoring subtle slights is bad and so is explosive retaliation. With personal attack you start feeling you are no good. The way to handle it is to firmly ask to be included. Let the person be aware of his/her offensive behavior and that it will not be tolerated. Make the person aware what affect it is having on the productivity of the organization. Let this message be not from one person, but from all other persons and from team members to have cumulative effect. If you have been sending micro-inequities, you will realize, in paying closer attention to people you overlook consistently, you will discover ways to turn their differences into advantages. If you have devalued a worker because he/she is slow, ask her, what other things can you do to make him/her feel more included.

Awareness of micro-inequities and how to handle it improves business relationships. Micro-inequities training can facilitate better organization communication. We have presented Micro-inequities training program module in Communication Skills Chapter 7.

APPRAISALS: TOOLS FOR TALENT PLANNING

The focus of employee appraisal is on performance, behavior, potentials, marketability, and promotion in context of their jobs in the corporate.

Why the right people are not in the right jobs? The reasons could be that the leaders lack knowledge to select the right person. They lack courage to tell people when they (people) under perform. They have the psychological comfort factor where the other person does not challenge them since he/she is loyal to him. Leaders do not acknowledge these limitations and do not make efforts to fix it. The right people can be in the right jobs when information about people, how they work together and deliver results – or fail is processed along with fixing the two above-mentioned limitations of the people. The expertise of choosing the right person can be developed by consistency of practice and appraising. There are certain tools for talent planning which can help the organization leaders to put the right persons in the right jobs in the organization and improve both performance and productivity.

The essential tools for talent planning are: periodic evaluation reports of the employees, leadership assessment summary reports, continuous improvement summary, succession depth analysis, and retention risk analysis. All these needs candid appraisal by the assessing leaders. People-process begins with one-on-one assessment, but when developed and practiced as a total process it is effective for Action implementation.

Review reports, or Evaluation reports are communication channel of interaction with the leader about employees' activities. The usefulness of the evaluation depends on how they are assessed. They should be reviewed after talking with person concern in the context of his jobs done. These points should be illustrated with specific observations made and the leader making the assessment should indicate how to remedy the person's shortcomings. Whether person needs coaching, mentoring, or shift to another assignment. The person appraised is also invited to add his ideas, opinions and suggestions. The person finally accepts about his learning needs and willingness to participate. The evaluations should be done more frequently and not just annually.

The candid appraisals through evaluation teach the leaders to focus on the quality of people's talents, develop and upgrade them. The focus is to help and overcome the person's gap in information, knowledge, experience or capability; or to move him/her to a befitting assignment. This will be a consistent and systematic process of getting the right person for the right job through appraising people and developing them through useful feedback, rather then to fire the person. Even tolerating such employee will be wasting the resources of both the person and the company.

Leadership assessment summary report is useful talent planning tool. Its overview identify which persons in the group have high potential and are promotable, those who exceed standards in terms of performance but needs improvement in behavior, as well both who are below standard in both the areas. *Continuous improvement summary* is a performance appraisal where key performances are highlighted – both accomplishments and missed targets. It includes clear, specific and useful information on development needs. This summary helps the individual to become a better performer.

Succession depth analysis determines whether the company has enough high potential people to fill the key positions. It also looks at whether there are high-potential people in the wrong jobs and whether key people will be lost if a higher job is not unblocked for them.

Retention risk analysis looks at a person's marketability, his/her potential for mobility, and the risk organization faces if he/she leaves. If she is blocked for upward movement she is susceptible to leave. Both these techniques are essence of talent planning and building a leadership pipeline of high potential people and are the foundation for discussing people's needs as well as for lateral and upward moves.

The above discussion highlights the importance of *interpersonal oral communication* through dialogue strategies for performance, achievement and productivity. In small groups and team meetings, it is important that both employees and managers, and top leaders participating on equal levels (breaking the boundaries of the hierarchies) understand the operating group dynamics where everybody is encouraged to raise an issue and discuss it. There is no blame, no complaint but constructive discussion and solutions for the problematic issues. The open interactions contribute to the productive meetings.

Open interaction strategies, operating group dynamics help the leaders to promote healthy interpersonal communication among people in the business at all levels. Through these strategies leader develops acumen to communicate with finesse and to handle difficult interpersonal situations with the employees. One situation may be where he/she has to convey bad appraisals to the employee but at the same time preparing him/her to participate in programs of coaching, training, mentoring to build his/her capability. In another situation, the person is totally unfit for the job assigned, either he may be conveyed the option to move around in another assignment or be fired. There may be third situation where the leader might have to give good reference for such persons when they are fired and are later hired by other company. In this case, rather than giving a total biased opinion, the leader must pull up the employee's strengths first (as experienced in the company job), mention his weak points and then his potentialities for improvements, and suggest other potential capabilities. The other employer gets wide options and discretion in employing the person according to his company's needs by such handling of the situation. He also gets good image of the communication processes and group dynamics in the first company. All these three situations call for *communication competence* of the leader so the employee's self-dignity and self-confidence is not damaged.

We cannot undermine the importance of *intrapersonal communication* where people at all levels of business organization from top-leaders, managers, and employees aim to improve their capabilities through self-assessment of their strengths, weaknesses, opportunities available and grabbed, training needed (SWOT). SWOT analysis is needed at personal level first then at organizational level. These are the basics of people process.

Self-assessed people are ready to make use of their strengths through opportunities available, and through demand. They demand training programs to develop their weaknesses into strengths. This is excellent for human talent development programs. Organizational SWOT can be done in the framework of self-appraisal SWOT.

In the above sections, we have discussed about the corporate internal and external communications that could facilitate business development, performance and productivity if practiced well. Probably our discussion suggests this as an ideal situation for a corporate. But one size does not fit all. Different corporate would be practicing the communication styles differently and achieving differently. But a total ignorance of the effective communication elements and rules in an organization can result not in low achievement but even as a dead organization.

Let us talk about a research and training organization. It started with high objectives but within 10 years not only it was a failure but totally dead organization.

When it started, it was provided ample funds and offered high-level information communication technology devices. There was high vision that it would grow up to the national stature. The first Head of the organization had low vision, rather then utilizing technology devices for training and research, he ordered these to be stored away. According to him, they were only gimmicks and not really useful. This was failure No. 1.

He had no leadership qualities of a high visionary, had no self-confidence to lead a new organization with high stakes. The working of the organization over a period of ten years showed that the coordination of the people-process, strategy-process and execution was not well and efficient. This was failure No. 2.

The performance in applied research deteriorated since it never got linked to the needs and demands of society, industry etc. Secondly, even if client sponsored research was done efficiently, its results were never communicated efficiently, in time for implementation, to the clients. Organizations' own research was never done efficiently and training programs for clients also suffered the same fate.

Why this was happening? The faculty was highly educated and trained. Then why low performance?

The internal communication links were ineffective in the organization. The leadership was poor at all levels. There was low interaction among the employees and management, head of divisions and the lower level faculty and staff. In fact, there was no dialogue about how research projects and training programs should be planned, executed and what Information communication technologies should be utilized rather than dunking in the storeroom. There was never consistent communication about the research and training strategies for training and research programs, operation plans and implementation of the strategies, between faculty and staff, and head of the organization. In fact, there were no robust and candid dialogues to surface the reality even when it was deteriorating. In short, people-process lacked consideration.

Workshops, in-house training programs, coaching and one-on-one talk were not used at all to upgrade the capabilities of the people. The supervisors did even the annual evaluation reports routinely and casually. These were not the candid appraisals for few reasons. One, they were not based on actual observations made by the supervisor. Two, they were never discussed with the employee (who is being evaluated). Three, no suggestions were given about how his/her weaknesses can be upgraded. Fourth, since there is no discussion with him/her about the evaluation, and it is not in his/her knowledge, no suggestions, ideas for self-improvement are discussed. Will this type of evaluation help in improving the performance? Further, if he/she has done well he/she is not recommended for reward. Even though he/she may be having high-potentials but is not recommended for promotion. No proper fit would have been tried in the organization to move him/her around even though he/she had not been doing his job well. Since either the evaluation report was being treated a mystery, or too routine and casual not to be relied upon. Therefore, nothing would be disclosed or acted upon. This evaluation report for lack of proper communication has neither served to improve the performance of the person nor the performance of the organization.

There is big turn over of people from the organization when there are lack of opportunities to upgrade oneself, be rewarded for good work and potentialities for promotions. When proper appraisals are not done efficiently, frequently and continuously for performance, behavior, potentials, marketability, and promotion in context of their jobs in the organizations.

Its external communication suffered because of inconsistencies in internal communications. The organization was not getting research projects from the high-profile clients. It lost its credibility both with the clients and for research quality. Its training programs did not attract trainees. So the organization suffered heavy losses in revenue, functionality and credibility with related professional organizations and media. The ten years past, and the organization exists but only as 'dead organization'.

The Business week's list of best managers of (2004) reflects a variety of skills and strategies that enabled some companies to prosper in 2004 while other sank. Good management is never one size fits all. Winning in some cases was simply a matter of execution, or investing in new technology to increase profit margins. Others have focused on holding down costs to expect profit rise. Few managers did well in turning around struggling companies. Other CEOs did well by listening to customers (Joseph M. Tucci of EMC Corporation) he revamped the data storage product line to reflect desires for less expensive options. Other CEO helped boost quality and customer satisfaction and GE a customer-driven company focused on innovation.

One key skill a CEO can supply is the ability to size up and nurture next generation of executives. Such nurturing of leadership enables to stand out and tap new markets. Sometimes the best Managers are not found in blue-chip boardrooms. No doubt there will be new challenges in 2005 but the lessons offered by these top managers in 2004 are suited even to tomorrow's business conditions.

Our above discussion has highlighted the process and importance of communication with internal links in the corporate through various channels and in various contexts. The internal links are people — as employee and management in business. There is pointer that people as customers and consumers are equally important for business development. This will be the focus of our discussions in corporate communications and external links (Chapter 3). The communication dynamics of people with people develops business realities.

SUMMARY

Business Communications in a corporate can be focused from two perspectives: One, customer-supply chain relationships including both external and internal links; and two, employee-management relationship including internal links only. The dynamics of business communications are customer-supplier relationships in the context of product, services and people. The dynamics of business communications in employee-management relationship are in the context of performance, productivity, and human relations.

The strength of internal business communication lies in coordinating the three core processes of people, strategies and operations and motivating for Action implementation. Implementation is in a way exposing reality and acting on it. Interpersonal communication dynamics play significant role in this context. Feedback is important component in the interpersonal interaction process. There is technology support to interpersonal communication also.

Employee and Management Interaction focus on building and upgrading the capabilities of the organization and its employees, surfacing the business reality, and communication about business strategy. This calls for robust and candid dialogue strategies.

Debating and discussing, constant exchange of ideas and best practices among diverse business managers create intellectual capital and better business strategies. Strategic value is also added by initiatives to improve performance throughout the company. After the operation plan is constructed, reviewed at the corporate level, it must be reviewed with the people who are the real people to implement it. The people are the real executing power. They can discuss and debate about it with its employees and sensitize them about it.

Work-out communication process is based on two premises, one, that people who are closest to the work know the work best. Secondly, workers within the business get frustrated when they feel they know more about the work, they have great ideas but no empowerment for action. Things happen when the ideas of those people are solicited through open dialogues on the issues and immediately turned into action — unencumbered by fleets of meetings, approvals, forms and reports. This way the unleashed energy of people is tapped and there is gain in productivity.

Development of human capital is central to any company's long-term strategy. The realization is that for a company to move ahead, its employees need to move in tandem. That is why it is crucial to attain higher levels of employee engagement. A holistic concern should be created among the employees for the corporate. They should be involved and sensitize to business strategies and brands of the company and not just robot producing the products. The biggest area of friction is that companies do not communicate openly to employees. When nobody tells them what's going on, it's difficult for employees to feel a part of an organization. Lack of internal communication leads to discontent among employees.

What count is the substance of the communication though various channels of Internal Communication facilitators? Characteristics of the corporate communicator are important mainly if he/she is willing to talk as well listen and are receptive to others ideas.

The employee appraisals are tools for talent planning. The focus is on performance, behavior, potentials, marketability, and promotion in context of their jobs in the corporate. Such tools are review reports, evaluation reports, leadership assessment summary reports, continuous improvement summary report, succession depth analysis, and retention risk analysis report.

Open interaction strategies, operating group dynamics help the leaders to promote healthy interpersonal communication among people in the business at all levels. The intrapersonal communication is important, the people at all levels of business organization from top-leaders, managers, and employees aim to improve their capabilities through self-assessment of their strengths, weaknesses, opportunities available and grabbed, training needed (SWOT). Organizational SWOT can be done in the framework of self-appraisal SWOT. There are skills and strategies that enable some companies to prosper while other sank. Good management is never one size fits all.

3

Corporate Communications: External Communication Links

CORPORATE COMMUNICATIONS

External corporate communication is associated with business development through the visibility of the corporate and its products and services. This could be facilitated through communicating with external links to the corporate business such as supply chain, distributors, wholesalers and retailers, consumers, business competitors, Community, Media, Government and Civic bodies.

Market Information System (MIS) is organized flow of information among external links. The concept is that the flow of the information is continuing, interactive with people and procedures to take market decisions.

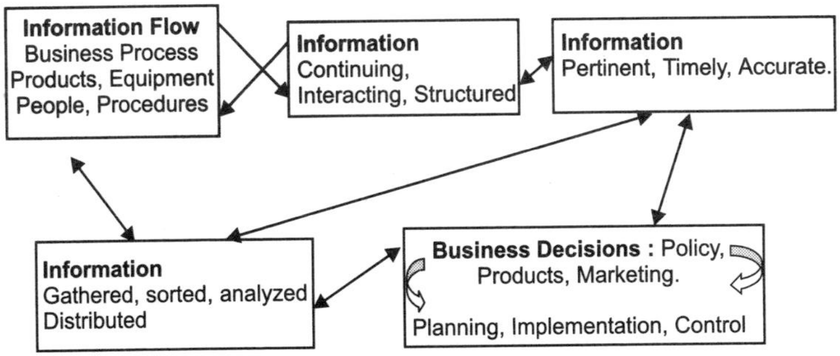

Fig 3.1. Market Information Flow

EXTERNAL COMMUNICATION LINKS: INFORMATION FLOW

Inflow and outflow of information and its sharing is important for successful business development viz marketing of the products, services and ideas. Outflow and inflow of information occur with ten major external links with the corporate within the framework of national and international economies. Six external links: supply chain, distributors, wholesalers and retailers, consumers, business competitors facilitate business development and market decisions about product and services. The two-way communications from other four external links of community, media, government and civic bodies regulate the business development with checks and balances and social responsibility.

Communication, strategic interactions and coordination, coherence (precision), persuasion, reinforcement are functions of external corporate communication links. These occur through different hierarchy of information needs of several business vendors. The mapping of information inflow and outflow between the business and external links, and its various focuses highlights the communication in business practices.

- There is outflow of information from corporate to supply chain and in-flow of information from supply chain for product and services.
- There is inflow and outflow of information from consumers to corporate about their needs, demands and preferences for products, services and new ideas. There is inflow of information from business to consumers about innovative ideas, products and services. There is inflow and outflow of information between both corporate and consumer about customer services and promoting good customer relations.
- There is inflow and outflow of information between corporate and distributors. Corporate outflow information to distributors about products, services, consumer segments, market segments and supply chain links.

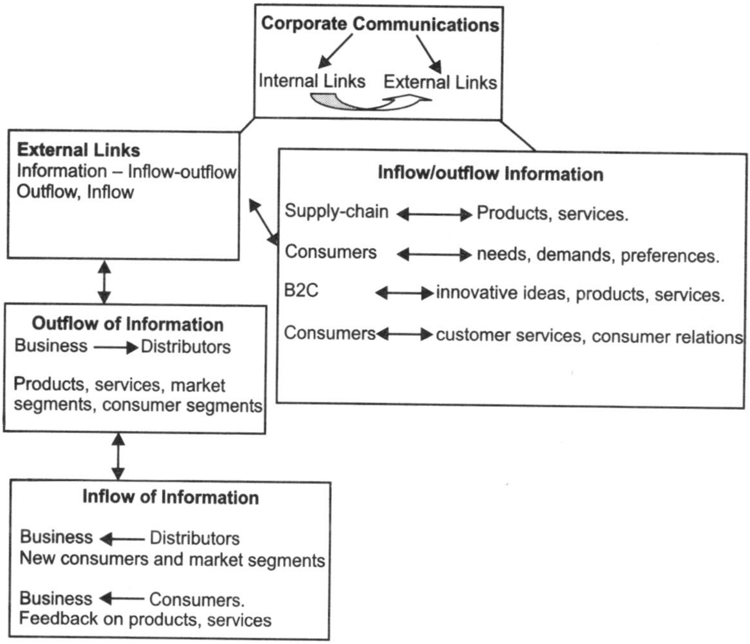

Fig 3.2. Corporate Communication External Links

Distributor to corporate inflow information is feedback on receptivity of existing products and services, consumer segments and markets.

Feedback on new consumer segments, new demands for products and services, and new markets.

- Distributors and wholesalers share both outflow and inflow information about consumer and market segments about products and services.
- Outflow and inflow of information from wholesaler to retailer is about consumer segments, market segments of product and services.
- Retailer to wholesaler the inflow is demand for new products and services, and new consumer segments. There is also feedback about changing demand for old products and services.

Thus corporate gets inflow information on old products and services, its salability, consumer segments and markets for it and also when consumer preferences for those products and services are changing and creating demand for new products and services, and new consumer segments. Corporate gives outflow information on old products and services, consumer segments and markets and supply chain. It shares information for an innovative idea. It also provides information identifying needs for new product and services, consumer segments and markets for them. Thus outflow and inflow of information bond the corporate and its external links for better execution and productivity.

- There is inflow of information from *community* about the social acceptability of the products and services within the cultural and social value matrix and healthy physical environments.

  The outflow of information from corporate addresses the issues of harmless products and services, environment pollution, its business practices being accountable and transparent to social and cultural values – avoiding scams, frauds and violation of societal norms for clean ethical life.

- Information flow from businesses through various *media channels*, create consumers, markets, brands for its products, services and ideas and overall development of the business. Media create and projects Public Image of the Company. Public credibility to media information outflows can promote or mar the image of the company, its leaders, business procedures, ethics, and its products and services.

- Information flow from national and international governments is about the taxes, treaties and laws, rules and regulations about businesses, market growth and economic policies, and particular checks and balances from time to time to keep control and being transparent about these.

The outflow of information from businesses is being accountable in following rules and regulations, demand in new rules and regulations, economic policies to facilitate business development and progress, if these are inhibiting. Further, such information must communicate about transparency of their business activities.

- The information flow from Civic bodies, both government and NGO demand creating clean and healthy environment by waste disposal, recycling, zoning, property taxes and contributing to the social welfare of the community through schools, medical facilities, setting parks, gardens and playgrounds etc.

  The outflow of information from business confirms their social responsibility and contribution by their products and services.

EXTERNAL BUSINESS COMMUNICATIONS LINKS

The simplest representation of any business organization is in terms of the customer and supplier. An organization develops and provides a product or service for which it receives payment, of some kind, from a customer. In this case the organization is the supplier to the customer. This simplistic dynamic is a very simple way to think about all the relationships in a business setting. It is this dynamic that determines the power balance in the relationship and defines the frame work in which relationship will proceed. It is therefore this dynamic and the factors described above that provide the framework for all communication.

Expanding further one can look at any business organization having several external customers and several external suppliers. Within the business organization there will be several functions some of which will be customers and suppliers to each other. Therefore, in a realistic business organization one will have a multitude of customer-supplier relationships of which many will be internal and many external. It is the dynamic between all the individual elements that will influence how communication channels are developed and proceed in this complex system.

Bossidy and Charan (2004) offer a model for facing facts in three areas – external realities, internal realties and financial targets; suggesting how these are linked and how to reassess them.

Communication: Customer-Supply chain relationships

Products are developed for the customer and supply chain vendors who provide materials for the product. Both customers and supply chain are external links with the business organization. Customers create revenue for the organization whereas the organization pays to the supply chain. These two are important to create and develop business. Therefore, right kind of communication with them is important.

Our discussion highlights that communication with multiple processes of production of end product, such as of supply chain, customers and internal specialized communication teams focus on coordination, coherence (precision), reinforcement and persuasion through different hierarchy of information needs of these vendors. Some of these vendors may need set of data, or specific information on the product market, customer demographics etc, others may need advance technical information and knowledge about product specifications to facilitate manufacturing processes. Finance may need more update information and knowledge on economy of both market and the country. Administration may need update information on taxation, revenues and budget co-ordinations both at internal and external levels.

For every process and its information hierarchical needs, there is an objective in the context of a customer and customer's needs. The customer can be external or internal to the organization depending on the particular process at hand. For example, the internal customer of the organization may be marketing division. They have assessed the need for a particular product. They may approach product development team or engineering division to develop product prototype on the basis of their market analysis. Further, supply chain develops, as engineering division is in touch with the product development division, manufacturing division and bringing product into the market through marketing and sales divisions. Thus communication, coordination, coherence (precision), reinforcement and persuasion through different hierarchy of information needs occur. Different types of information will have different values to the organization primarily because of the needs of the customer. For example, some companies may spend a lot of money on solutions about products and supply chain management rather than on knowledge management.

An organization may have three primary business divisions. If three deal in the same product line, there may be inter-communication at the level of the top leaders for business strategies. But they may be using the different marketing, sales, finance, administrative resources in all the three divisions. There may not be direct day-to-day inter-communication but there may be strategic interactions and coordination for the sake of creating efficiency of resources. All divisions may share the resources of the data and information bank, research and development division and manufacturing and production. All actions and interactions will be based on and driven by the purpose of the business. Within a company that has several businesses, the need of the common resources and targeting of the common customers will determine coordination between businesses.

Communication with supply chain is multiways and circular since there will be many vendors in this chain who will be ultimately supplying material to the manufacturing division for the product. Within this supply chain there will be other chain links that would be supplying to one another in the process. So there is process of demand and supply between supply chain (links) and organization, and communication process between them to identify demand for right type of material, resources and issues relating to it. Communication is multiways and circular as many employees at different levels are involved in the organization and in supply chain. Loops of feedback are imperative for understanding and finding solutions for the issues to create smooth line for the end product to be delivered to the customer.

Communication with the customer is important and the interaction with the customer takes place in three phases. First phase is the pre-product phase when the product is being planned. The two-way interaction with the targeted audience takes place through organization's multilevel employees to identify customers' needs (felt and created), preferences, demographic and geographic market segments and purchasing power of the customers. This type of communication is significant at this point for the future success of the product.

In phase 2, communication with the customer is equally significant when the product is launched in the market. Acceptance and rejection of the product, its high and low sales, and its market positioning — all depend on how characteristics of the product are communicated to the customer in the framework of phase 1 assessments. In follow-on period of phase 3, communication with targeted customers is necessary for two reasons, (i) the reasons for acceptance and high sales and reasons for acceptance but low sales; (ii) the reasons for rejection and low sales or no sales. Modified or new business strategies and products would be based on phase 3 assessment data. In fact, in follow-on period of phase 3, communication with targeted customers has to be repeated frequently and consistently by the organization for gaining new insights and for the success of the product. It will be *cyclic communication* process.

Interpersonal communication is the main communication channel in organization-customer relationship. It is multiways, circular with feedback loops. Media channels and other outdoor channels reinforce communication assessment data of all three phases and follow-ons and thus support interpersonal communication channels. The reinforcement component is product advertisements through media channels of print, TV, radio, film, Internet and outdoor channels of billboards and even by word of mouth — an interpersonal channel. Interpersonal communication channels are both personal and impersonal. Friends, relatives and other consumers, and even your retail store may recommend new products or dissuade you to buy certain brands. It is strong and persuasive word of mouth publicity for the products. These are unorganized and at random but these people can be organized in focus groups where the marketing people may focus on certain products and brands with organized briefs.

The communication channels for communication and reinforcement with supply chain vendors is organization's internal links of *specialized communication teams* such as marketing team, product development team, engineering team, manufacturing team, sales team, finance and administration teams.

Marketing team of market researchers and analysts will identify or develop market requirements initiated through an innovative idea or customer driven idea. Product development team will develop market requirements and product specifications. Engineering divisions work on the product specifications and develop prototypes. Again product development team and marketing team will communicate for marketing strategies and with sales team. Sales teams in turn will interact with supply chain of distributors, wholesalers and retailers and reinforce and persuade the product sale deals. These special communication teams have communication links with finance and administrative teams in the organization. Both finance and administrative teams create balance for the end product to be positioned in the market and earn revenue through productivity. Coordination and coherence with all communication teams and with supply chain vendors is essential for effective communication for the end product.

Communication: Supply Chain

There are two categorizations of supply chains: the different businesses are supplying various components for the product and services to the primary business. Secondly, even the bigger component suppliers may be supplied smaller components by suppliers specializing in those. For example, the suppliers, supplying doors of the automobiles may be depending on bolts and hinges from other suppliers. Thus supply chain is multiple of suppliers specializing in different processes of the product and services.

Communication between interdependent suppliers, other ancillary suppliers and main organization is necessary. Not only communication but also coordination with different suppliers in the chain is important for effective delivery system. Interaction within and among the supply components is of utmost importance for understanding the needs, resources available and needed, supply time, other related issues and problems. Coordination by the organization with different suppliers for various components of product is necessary and important for effective delivery. The organization will always be confronted with the issue, will their suppliers be able to deliver in time, just enough, and at the right prices?

Second category is where the Sales team of the organization deals with a supply chain of distributors, wholesalers, and retailers. The distributors supply chain create market segment for the product and services through wholesalers. The wholesalers in turn, position the product in the market through retailers. Retailers sell product directly to the consumer.

In this communication and interaction process all four (sales team, distributors, wholesalers, and retailers) are interdependent to sell the product but not in circular fashion rather communication is vertical at first stage: Sales team to distributor, distributor to wholesaler, wholesaler to retailer and retailer to consumer. In the first stage the feedback is also between the two (of the chain) only. In the second stage, the communication may be horizontal such as among many wholesalers in the chain or many retailers in the chain. In third stage, for aggressive sales, the communication is circular and with several feedback loops and among all the five links including consumers. In the fourth stage, the Sales team may be communicating and coordinating with the internal specialized teams of the organizations and top leaders for effective sales of the product and services.

The interesting feature is, all the first four are customers as well suppliers to each other at different points of rotation for actual sale of the product. They are also in the communication and feedback loops with one another in the complex supply chain. But the smooth functioning of the chain depends on timely coordination and coherence of communication. Interpersonal communication channels with support from media channels facilitate it.

Communication: Business Competitors

The forces of globalization, technology and economic liberalization combined are increasing the pace and alerting the shape of competition across the world. The competitors with sharper value propositions and low cost have emerged. They have challenged unleash innovation and productivity. Every corporation requires in varying degrees, labor, raw materials, a communication infrastructure, production facilities and capital. Globalization has integrated the low-cost economies into supply-and-demand base; technologies have exploited the networking and communication infrastructure. The efficient and computing power in emerging countries have made possible a large number of people available for physical and knowledge work.

Plentiful, cheap and global labor, capital, capacity infrastructure and information have three broad consequences: (i) aggregation of formerly distinct markets; now competitors in one geography compete with others; (ii) enhanced market clearing and efficiency suggesting buyers can make more efficient purchasing decisions; and (iii) there is increased specialization in the supply-chain. As transportation, communication and coordination costs fall, suppliers can easily spread production across facilities and geographies. Companies also learn to take advantage of scale, proximity to end consumers, differing costs of labor and raw materials.

The zones of extreme competition are emerging markets. They are getting more open and greater competition is evident in many sectors. India and China are fast developing emerging markets. In fact there is extreme competition among the emerging markets because of outsourcing from the western countries. This will pose new communication challenges.

In extreme competition four factors need monitoring by businesses: the value proposition risk — will a cheaper product knock the company out? The cost curve risk — will a low-cost competitor take the company's market share? The bad-conduct risk – will a price war destroy the company's profitability? The bad-bet risk — will the company's assumptions prove too optimistic? Companies should assess the source, extent, and timings of all these risks. They should communicate them appropriately to the investors and define activities that will mitigate them. Such assessment should help the businesses to adopt a forward-looking perspective and implement radical solutions rapidly otherwise the traditional players will be toppled if they do not.

One source of competitive advantage is to diffuse throughout the company a unique, proprietary knowledge about customers, competitors, products, and techniques that resides in the minds of its employees. But many efforts at knowledge management have failed to deliver that advantage, because they haven't focused on the creation and broad exchange of knowledge within a company. Establishing an internal knowledge market with its own unique approaches to pricing, exchange, market facilitation, and competition can solve that problem and boost productivity.

Communication with Consumer

What if cornucopia of choice becomes overwhelming for us? There are growing number of alternatives available to people. The selecting from these confuses them. Social scientists research into how people make these judgments. Friends or store recommendation may guide the pre choice. Or why consumers cannot make choices and buy nothing from the store they are visiting. These are some of the forces shaping consumer behavior. The focus on consumer behavior is through three perspectives: consumer creation, acquisition, and retention — building consumer trust and loyalty and consumer service and relationship.

Consumer creation, acquisition, and retention: Businesses create consumers for their products and services through their own innovative ideas and consumer driven demands and ideas. The focus is on consumer preferences for products and services, consumer market reach and consumer satisfaction. Companies identify their consumers and segmented markets through market analysis and research. This data they use for product development. Further, they use marketing strategies to sell the products and services to the consumers. Communication strategies and plans are important for market analysis and research which are key for creating the consumer and markets for them.

Consumer satisfaction with the products and services rendered is of prime importance. Customer satisfaction is assessed by post-market research and feedbacks from the customers. The company must consider both the post-market research and feedbacks to improve on their products and services. Customer acquisition and retention is the by-product of good customer services and relations. Systematic programs of customers benefiting and customer retention are planned by corporate. What might be done to attract and hold the customer for potential product? By acting on the suggested technical changes, marketing research findings regarding customers' attitude for their products, problems they encounter in market reach and delivery.

Customer service and customer relationship are important for businesses. In today's world, what customers are looking for, are products that suit their purpose best — in terms of price, features, quality, and appearance. They expect to receive sales and service support for products like vehicles and air-conditioners. They expect to receive timely and competent attention, along with a definite solution to their problems from the service people, dealers or channel partners. The concern of business ought to be the interface with the customers. They must ensure excellent service. This would involve training of their channel partners and improving the interface between them and us so that they can give the customer the service he or she wants. To illustrate, if Tata Engineering Company (in India) is not backing its dealers, for instance, in the changing of parts of car during warranty, then obviously the dealer is going to haggle with the customer. The customer pays the cost of that in terms of inconvenience. This in turn reflects on the image of the product. Eventually, Tata Engineering pays the cost of customer dissatisfaction.

We need to create *trust* for the customer. Customer does not have to prove his *bona fides*. Where we have direct dealings with our customers, it is important that, at the middle-management levels, they are shown courtesy, dealt with fairly, and made to feel that they are receiving the attention they deserve. The interface with the customer should be a seamless one. It is difficult to understand why all our managers and officers cannot be courteous at all times to all people. It is part of the Indian psyche to say, "I will treat important people with great courtesy, and I will treat everyone else, not with scorn, but as second-class citizens. I will show my superiority as an individual." This is really not in business interest. The multinationals coming to India are showing that their customer interface is dramatically different from what we find in major Indian companies.

Building consumer trust and loyalty: Companies should enjoy customer trust and loyalty. This may not be happening only at senior management levels, but certainly happening at interface levels. We should be treating the customer in the same way that we would want ourselves to be treated as customers. In India we have to address this issue proactively and a lot to learn on this front — and a lot to change. Formal training within the companies at the sales and dealer levels are needed to make their interface with customers truly seamless.

Does the customer value a brand just for the brand's sake, or for a particular business, for example, Tata group in India has a brand advantage? This group has a tremendous brand advantage through its diverse products. It has long-term goal of being the biggest household name in the country. How can Tata group customer loyalty be built when others are also vying for this position? What should the group do to ensure that the difference remains in the eyes of the customers for years to come?

Being a household name is very much a function of the products you sell. It can become a highly respected brand with consistently high quality, and a constant attempt to refresh and improve their products so that they are at the leading edge, rather than followers of other products. They have to ensure that their products are genuinely appealing to customers and that they service their customers well. What are some of the challenges companies face with respect to customer acquisition and retention? A fundamental change of outlook is necessary in terms of their products or business lines, companies need to create products and strategies that are based on what the market wants. Often businesses deliver products or work on strategies that are based on what they want. People sometimes hide behind market surveys.

If Tata introduces a new vehicle, for example, and the management cannot adequately determine what the market wants, the company is in trouble. Theoretically, the top managers of a company should take up the role of that ideal customer: they should be driving their competitors' vehicles, they should be driving the best-of-breed vehicles, and they should be making cost comparisons. They must have an idea of what they, as customers, expect from a Tata vehicle. And they should try to ensure that the product is within the price parameters a customer would pay for. While a top manager should be the ideal customer, he should also be the greatest critic of his company's products. If the CEO compromises, or is only looking at the margins, then even if he is successful, the company's success will be short lived. That is because the market will determine whose product works and whose product is successful. That, in turn, will bring everything else into play. How important is market feedback vis-à-vis internal quality or service parameters? Market feedback is very important, but it has to be stripped of its bias. It should be viewed objectively, not defensively.

Customer relationship management is important from the point of customer satisfaction and from the importance of human interaction in managing customer relationships. Businesses have to ensure that their products are genuinely appealing to customers and that they service their customers well.

Customer services: Increasing number of consumers are upset at how their complaints are addressed by the customer services departments of retail stores. Over the past three decades companies have tried new approaches to keep consumers happy. They have established call centers, expanded budgets that give irate customers monetary relief such as coupons or reimbursement, and installed automated telephone response system. In 2003 North American companies spent $1.75 billion in software that helps manage every aspect of their relationship with the customer. But the report found that half of the respondents never want to do business with company again or threatened to talk to management or yelled or uses profanity. Still the report revealed it was easier to gain customer confidence by getting their products or services fixed, giving them an explanation, an apology or a chance to vent their frustrations and assurance that the problem won't occur again. 115 wanted revenge and 3% legal remedies. Many were raged because of the lost time in efforts ('Customer Rage' research report, Customer Care Alliance 2003).

Customer development is also facilitated when consumers seek satisfaction through actions and consumer forums. The companies must aim to improve customer care and enhance customer relationships. In outsourcing, IP (Internet) telephony makes customer care innovation possible. IP telephony and IP contact centers an alternative to traditional siloed systems. It can help companies enhance customer care relationships while reducing costs.

Using the standard IP standard customer interactions speak the same language, offering customers the choice to use self-service, agent-assisted service, face-to-face service, web phone or chat to conduct transactions or to receive information. With IP voice and data flow seamlessly across these channels without costly translation technologies. IPT makes it affordable to integrate telephone, web, and direct customer care for the first time. Customers reach the right person in your business regardless of the expert's location. Specialists can support multiple branches. Flexible work place options become reality.

A distributed business can act as one unified entry enhancing service and reducing overheads. Customized features and support options become affordable on IP. Call authorization, project tracking, call accounting and web-based reporting can be integrated into existing systems to reduce overhead costs.

In terms of customer acquisition, with so many competing brands and products available today, what is, or should be, the Tata differentiator? Very often it is said about several companies that they take a lot of pains to make a sale. However, once they get the order, customers cannot even get anyone to answer their calls. Tata would like the customer to say that the next product he buys will also be a Tata product because of everything that he has experienced. That is really what customer retention is about. You cannot afford to have a customer say, "I made a mistake. I'll never buy another product from this company." You cannot even afford to have him say he is merely happy with your product. It needs to go further than that. He has to say, "The next product I buy will be a Tata product." Any consumer product that I buy will be a Tata product, because there are so many things about the company's products that I admire or respect. That's customer retention. (Illustrations are based on profile; Tata Sons)

The company's special teams of marketing and sales communicate with the consumers to identify their needs and the market segments and demographics. The advertising team creates awareness and information and motivation to buy the products and services and create brand images and building brand loyalty. The retailers ensure timely delivery to the customer by communicating with the other supply chains of whole sellers and distributors by assessing the consumer need and choices. This they assess by directly interacting with the consumers personally, through store surveys and through certain technology used in the store to assess their preferences and product choices and satisfaction. The service support teams interact with the consumers to solve their problems with the products and services and give efficient after-sales. The efficient service also depends on how the consumer is serviced by the service center staff. Do they understand their problem? Do they direct them to the appropriate personnel to handle the problem? Are they courteous in their dealings? Do they service in time?

The Public relation team interacts with the consumers/ customers both directly and indirectly, through interpersonal communications with the clients, press, seminars and conferences. Various media channels of print, television and even Internet are used to facilitate it. Certain media technologies are used to further it. The major objective is to create positive visibility for the company in general, its top-leaders and management in particular and for its products and services.

Thus the interaction with the company's employees special teams is multi-ways and circular to understand the consumer behavior viz product and services. At times it is direct interpersonal interaction and other times it is indirect. There is indirect communication with the consumer through technologies used. Feedback loops from the customers are important component of communication process. To understand communication process of consumer behavior, one must understand the communication process between the special teams of the company and consumers in *consumer creation, acquisition,* and *retention.*

Consumer Behavior: Have you wondered why so many iconic brands of yesteryears are falling by the wayside even as relatively newer brands are capturing the imagination of the consumers and share of the market? This is happening because the old and established brands are moving away from old and established marketing basics. Changing consumer behavior and its implications on marketing communications supports this. Customer relationship management is important from the point of customer satisfaction and the importance of human interaction in managing customer relationships. The retailers have changed the rules of engagement of consumer in buying. Retailers have altered consumer behavior by offering discounts, gift cards, sales and other incentives. The role of customer is important in developing marketing strategies for tomorrow and this has changed over the past few years. The customer of today is well informed and exposed to a barrage of advertising visuals and imagery on number of communication channels.

A few years ago, in India, one had to hunt for Life Insurance (LIC) agent to pay premium or buy a new insurance policy. Today, one can do it on the Internet or at the nearest post office or even better, one can simply leave a standing instruction with one's bank. LIC has recognized that the consumer of today has no time to go to the vendor. The vendor has to come out of his ivory tower to where the consumer is located. The reasons could be many and increased competition being the major one. The point is that LIC cannot ignore the changing consumer attitudes and behavior.

Another development in the consumer space is the growing diversity and individuality of each consumer. Take the example of credit cards. While most banks have a generic Gold and Silver card concept, even within the Gold card segment, there are various customizations — fee-waivers, free add-on cards, extra credit limits, balance transfer facilities, embedded insurance, etc. This makes credit card marketing extremely complex as every consumer would have his or her own requirements and each credit card account would have to be structured accordingly. The same can be applied to many other verticals like telecom, insurance, retail, travel, healthcare, etc. With the increasing service element in verticals like automobiles, IT and even manufacturing, many other traditional product verticals will soon face the problem of individuality.

Today's dynamic business environment calls for flexible strategies and decisions for organizations. The same is true for individuals and consumers. The changing personal, societal and economic landscape influences consumer requirements. A newly promoted executive would move up the lifestyle strata and this would be reflected in his/her need to upgrade various aspects of his/her life — car, banking accounts, savings and investment portfolio, etc. Thus consumers would need access to products and services anytime. With the development of new interactive media like email, web, SMS, ATM kiosks and now even Interactive television, it is possible for consumers to react to marketing communication immediately and short cut their way through the actual transaction process.

Consumer behavior Models: Dynamics of Consumer behavior models highlight the three different dimensions of consumer behavior: sequential analysis of consumer decision-making process; development of consumer confidence in brands through decision-making process; and selective perception of the consumer that predominates and guide consumer behavior.

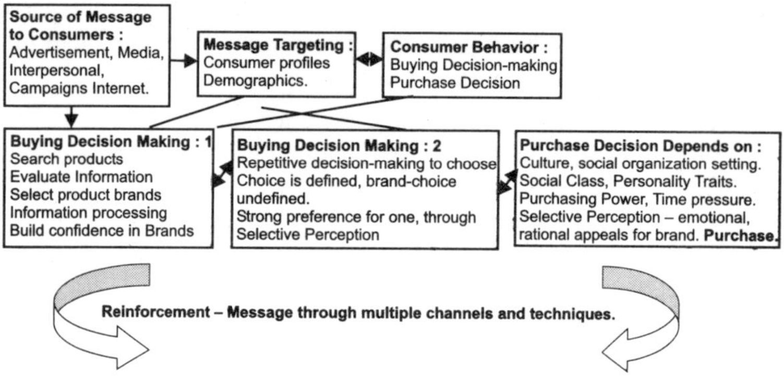

Fig. 3.3. Dynamics of Consumer Behavior Model

This focuses on advertisers (source) of the message to the consumer's attitudes and feedback. It is about consumer decision-making in a sequence:

Sequence 1: advertisers (source) of the message exposes message to the consumers.

Sequence 2: advertisers appeal and frame the message according to the attributes of consumers such as predispositions, experience, consumption and purchasing behavior.

Sequence 3: the consumer attitudes towards the products stimulate him/her to search and evaluate the products before making any decision to buy.

Sequence 4: the marketers motivate the consumer further through reinforced advertising and marketing on the basis of feedback from consumers.

Another consumer model focus on development of consumer confidence in brands. This model has two aspects: four important variables and consumer decision-making stages. The four important variables are input, output, hypothetical constructs and exogenous variables. Hypothetical constructs reflect perceptual and learning constructs of the consumer. Perceptual construct reflects the internal state of the consumer that facilitates information processing. Learning constructs functions for concept formation of how he/she develops confidence in the brand. Exogenous variables that describe the contexts in which consumer behavior occurs are purchase, culture, social class, personality traits, social organizational setting, time pressure and financial status.

The model emphasizes the development of components of each construct, their interaction with input, output and exogenous variables to let the consumer develop confidence in the brand. Decision-making takes place once brand-confidence develops.

The consumer decision-making is three-stage process. First, extensive problem solving stage suggesting repetitive decision-making as the consumer has not yet well-defined and structured choice criteria. Second is limited problem-solving stage where the choice criteria are well defined but consumer is undecided about the choice of brands. He/she has high predispositions but no strong preferences. Third is routine response, where the choice criteria are well defined and structured, the dispositions are high for one or alternate brand. There is strong preference to buy one.

The dynamics of consumer behavior or motivation is the relationship between the driving force and the object or condition towards which that driving force is directed. Motives are not stable. They are only consistent in a general sense. Motivation can be both primary and secondary. Consumer motivation is the key concept in advertising.

The presentation of the product through advertising or in physical form as done in product demonstrations, displayed in stores etc. exposes the consumer to the product. The product catches the attention of the consumer. The consumer will selectively perceive the positive or negative characteristics of the product. He/she will comprehend the product characteristics through self or an outside agent, the advertiser, friends, and the retail store. They will convince him/her about the product. Once convinced, the consumer will yield to buy. *But the consumer will retain selective perception and behave accordingly.*

The dynamics of consumer behavior further suggests that consumers' attitudes to products, brand confidence and selective perception for the products motivate him/her to take decision-action for buying. It also suggests that marketers would frame and expose the message according to the predispositions, experience, consumption and purchasing habits of the consumers. The marketer would further motivate the consumers according to their feedback on the marketing of the products and services. At the third tier the marketer would focus on consumers' attitudes (for the products and services) developed after their reinforced marketing.

Marketing tactics does affect consumers' behavior to the extent that these create awareness, information, emotional appeal and motivation for the consumer. But consumer's choice is not always rational dictated by needs and purchasing power. It is many times swayed by emotional appeals by the marketers and lure of novelty of the products.

Low income Segment Markets: The Mass Markets

The two recent business approaches, which could be advantageously operative in developing countries, focus on segmented markets of the poor and having low level purchasing capability. So far the marketers have ignored this segment though in many developing countries they are almost 70% of the market. The other approach is the rural market and this segment forms almost 70-80% of the market. These two approaches are unique to most of the developing countries. The first focus is (i) *to create market for the poor through consumers' experiences*; (ii) *to create rural market through consumers' experiences*. Second focus is to *create new business models* in these contexts. Dealing with these two market segments suggests Co-Creation Business Model.

Prahalad C.K. *et al.* (2004a) advocate the theory of Co-Creation for creating product market through consumers' experiences. The future of competition is in co-creating unique value with customers by letting individual corporate customers and consumers' fashion products and services. They suggest how to change organizational behavior to co-create naturally. Alterations must be made to every corporate function from product development to sales and marketing in this context.

The authors advocating co-creation theory of business is asking businesses to move from demand manipulation to co-creation of value along with the consumer. Given the information explosion that has made consumers most discerning and selling more difficult, they are asking companies to do business in a different way. For riding the next wave of competition, they have to change their business models, starting not with the raw materials and logistics but with the consumer experiences. They have to begin with the heterogeneity of demand and build a supply chain — a network of sales, marketing, NGOs, self-help groups, and individual entrepreneurs around the consumer's experience.

He suggests (in an interview with *Hindustan Times*, Aug 18, 2004c) that Indian companies can co-create since they have a history of breaking away from convention. A handful of IT firms are MNC today. India has been a more experimental playground for both companies and consumers. Here consumers always co-create their value. India's biggest strength is its heterogeneity.

In co-creation, the two major consumer segments are low-income and poor (both in urban and rural sectors), and rural population. The dynamics of co-creation would differ in both these segments. In the low-income and poor, the dynamics are a definite demand, but low purchasing power. These two dynamics drive home to the businesses the fact to shape and market their products according to experiences and value demands of this set of consumers and offer services to augment their purchasing power. The rural population's unconventional demands for new consumer durables and non-durables are driven more by exposures to products through media channels.

They need value products for their conventional demands also. They have sufficient purchasing power but would like higher value for their products as compared to urban population. In rural population the demand market can be tapped by three-way efforts: reliable and consistent delivery system, real time product promotions and demonstrations, and media advertising through media channels, outdoor and word of mouth especially targeting the characteristics and understanding of the rural consumers, and relevant to their needs. Even the low-income and poor in the rural segment would need the same kind of efforts in additions to the market dynamics of the low-income and poor *per se*.

Prahalad & Hart (2004 b) developed the concept of 'Fortune at the Bottom of the Pyramid'. The premise is that low-income markets present a prodigious opportunity for the world's wealthiest companies — to seek their fortunes and bring prosperity to the aspiring poor. Pursuing the bottom forces us to rethink our conventional wisdom about: technology and business models, Scale and profitability, Price-performance relationships, Productivity and capital efficiency and sustainable development. Over and above the communication infrastructure and channels to reach this segments.

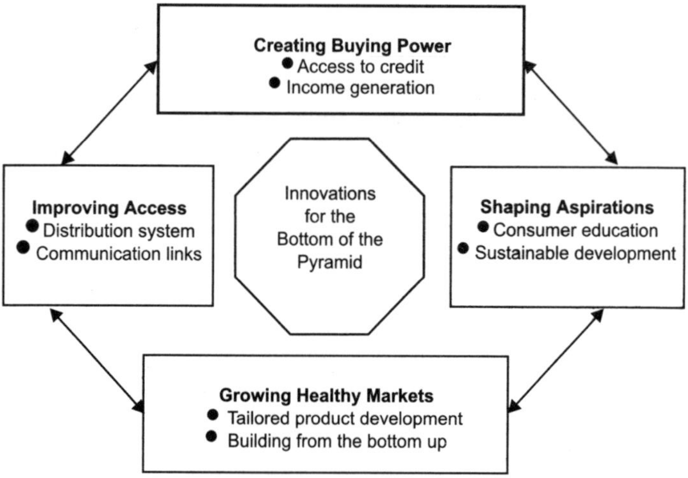

Source: C.K. Prahalad/Stuart Hart

Fig 3.4. Commercial Infrastructure at the Bottom of the Pyramid

In the above context they suggest that MNC can do it since they can bring together a global knowledge-base that is unique and not accessible to local entrepreneurs. They have the clout to bring together the range of actors required to develop tier 4 — the bottom markets. Innovations from the bottom can be adapted for use in the resource-energy-intensive markets of the developed world. Few local entrepreneurs, NGOs, or governments have the managerial or technological resources to create this infrastructure.

The new model for the bottom that MNC will follow: price performance, robust products, capital efficiency, labor intensity, new alliances, volumes, logistics, packaging-single serve and sustainability.

Soni V. (2004) presenting the 'Three approaches to creating New-Growth Businesses' argues that integrating the two concepts of, (i) focusing on the bottom of the Pyramid (concept of Prahalad & Hart), and (ii) sustained and disruptive technologies suggest that: new products, applications required for sustained innovation will not be drivers for big growth. Disruptive products that can target non-consumption with appropriate business model, such as bottom of the Pyramid, can create significant growth opportunities. Key to success with disruptive approaches, even those spawned in BOP markets, is proper management of the whole value chain. Emerging countries can be test bed for innovations worldwide.

Many of the Indian technologies in the Indian Strategic sectors in developing and applying technologies are at low cost due to budget constraints and earlier the major constraint was access to 'dual use' technology. Indian businesses in recent years do not have these constraints and products are developed fast and at much lower cost than in the developed countries.

Going forward we have to be creative and innovative to develop business models for growth based on new models. The key is to coordinate among various business parts on such initiatives. Best practices for developing the capabilities and organizational structure is needed for 'disciplined innovation'. New products and Applications development activities are business led and market driven. Technology or (platform) development activities are business led and R&D.

The Pyramid

Annual per capita income based on purchasing power parity in Rs. | Population in Milions

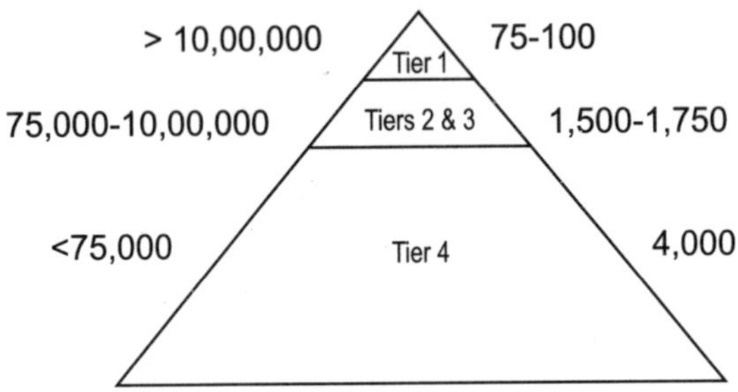

Example: Hindustan Lever

- Traditional focus: top of the pyramid
- Nirma challenged HLL in its detergent business, with a new formulation, process, packaging, distribution and pricing focused on the poor.
- As Nirma grew rapidly, HLL realized its vulnerably.
- HLL responded with its own offering targeted at the bottom of the pyramid.

	Nirma	**HLL (Wheel)**	**HLL (High End)**
Sales ($M)	**150**	**100**	**180**
Gross Margin %	**18**	**18**	**25**
ROCE %	**121**	**93**	**22**

Fig. 3.5. The Pyramid

Source: Soni V 2004

He cites the example, Hindustan lever in India (HLL), producer of FMCG has its traditional focus on top of the Pyramid. Nirma (another Indian producer of FMCG) challenged HLL in its detergent business with new formulation, process, packaging, distribution and pricing focused on the poor. As Nirma grew rapidly, HLL realized its vulnerability. HLL responded with its own offerings targeted at the bottom of the Pyramid.

The bottom of the pyramid poses challenges and questions: How do we marry low cost, good quality, sustainability and profitability at the same time? Must visualize an active market when all that currently exist is abject poverty. The primary task is to create a consumer market out of the poor, one that is conceived and structured very differently from the elite market (tier 1).

Three approaches to creating New-Growth Businesses is discussed more in Chapter 4 from the point of dilemmas of technologies — sustained and disrupted technologies.

Seely, Brown and Hagel (2003 & 2005) discusses that western countries have to innovate products and processes to serve the low-end consumers in emerging markets. They need to do it to gain cost advantage and build up capabilities to compete back home. These innovations and the forces that give rise to them is essential component of global competition. The emerging countries are the seedbed for these innovations is unsettling for the leaders in the developed countries. The best response from the companies and countries alike is to accept this shift, with flexibility, speed and openness to new ideas that gives global perspective.

The western countries have invested their skills and R&D in the emerging markets for decades to harvest the fruits. But there is shift now, the emerging markets are not getting exploited by them, rather they are generating a wave of disruptive products and processes and a new generation of entrepreneurs establishing a market on the price performance levels for a range of globally traded goods and services.

There is less of brand loyalty because of the two factors, consumers having low income and open markets providing multitude of brands. These create challenges for brand building.

A greater number of Mobile phone subscribers from both India and China suggest market opportunities for cell phones both in India and China. A greater number of subscribers in both these countries are at the low end of market. They are using more for occupational connectivity. The mobile companies of Nokia, Sony and Erickson have to decide whether they want to give the same product they are developing for developed countries markets or will adopt a radical approach to product and processes to fit both the low-end and middle level consumers in these countries. The second approach is likely to bring them larger share of the market.

The developed countries face the challenges of serving the developing markets — harder to reach and cost conscious consumers. They need to change products and processes to offer at low prices. Most of the developed countries have to reposition themselves to accept this offshore challenge.

Rural Markets: Rural consumption

Many Indian businesses are going rural. In a bid to expand their market base, companies are now exploring the rural hinterland. Hindustan Lever (HLL) for one has been continuously strengthening its marketing network in the villages and is producing goods to suit the needs and budgets of rural consumers. Others are Pepsi Foods, Tata Kisan Sansar, EID Parry — the list is expanding everyday — are all taking the rural route to expand their market base, as well as to procure raw materials for their agro ventures.

A larger number of Indians live in villages but what is significant is that villages have undergone drastic changes in the post-reform era. While the trickling-down effect of higher GDP growth and a low inflation rate have improved the economic conditions of the villagers, the exposure to new products through media especially broadcasting channels has changed their consumption patterns also. The delivery of those goods through the efforts of the businesses in various areas, in different ways further facilitates those consumption patterns.

Indian villages have become more health conscious and are now spending more on medicines — share of medical expenses in monthly consumption expenditure has increased from 5.7% in 1997 to 6.8% in 2002. Despite the fact, Government highly subsidize or provide free delivery of health and medicines to the rural consumers. They are spending higher amount on clothing also. Their conventional food consumption patterns have also changed from home-made lassi to Pepsi and other soft drinks. Higher expenditure on healthcare will keep them fit, but Indian households are no longer prepared to ignore the worldly comforts either. The most dramatic change has been witnessed in the non-durable consumer goods sector. They would like to buy TV, VCR, DVD, washing machines and refrigerators. They would like to buy tractors and other agriculture machinery.

It may be the demonstration effect caused by the opening up of the economy to the global market. But the fact remains that their expenditure on consumer goods, services and consumer durables and non-durables has increased sharply during the period. The business model of co-creation and marketing strategies targeted to this segment vice the above mentioned three tier efforts would increase markets for the businesses.

Low-income Segment

The percentage of people living below the poverty line in India has been falling steadily — down from 44.5% in 1983 to 36% in 1993-94 and further to 26.1% in 2000 according to the 55th Round of the Household Consumer Expenditure Survey of the National Sample Survey India. How to create markets for the poor who are at the bottom-of-the-Pyramid and who may be earning even less than few rupees a day? *We need different business model.*

There are billions of poor earning less than Rs. 2 or $ 2 a day. They have demand for *a* product. This is market. They are the consumers and there is opportunity for growth. This is the rationale and approach for dealing with people at the bottom.

Prahalad (2004d) talks about the 'Invisible Market'. We need a new world economic order in which there is an invisible market constituency of these 5 billion poor people. In developing countries like India, China, Brazil, Mexico, Indonesia, Turkey, Russia, South Africa — they represent 70-75% of the world population of poor.

If the poor, due to its limited purchasing power can buy small sachet of shampoo or small packets of food for a couple of servings such as quarter size or half-size bread loaves — then businesses should produce them, market them to this mass market. The demand is there and it will continue in the same proportion but in different time scale since the poor can spend limited amount on a specific consumer product at a point of time. If a business can sell cheaper the same product without packaging frills, then produce and market the same to this segment of market. In short, this segment of market has demand for the product but it has to be marketed differently. The poor want value for their money and businesses can deliver that by marketing differently and in turn they have the business of the 70-80% consumers segments to make profits.

How do we sell to the poor? Create capacity to buy through easy loan, hire-purchase system. Earlier, the poor could take loans from the moneylenders but in the process, they suffered the exploitation from the moneylenders paying exorbitant rates of 500% interest. But now the banks can give them micro-loans at 10% and develop their capacity to buy, saving and consuming simultaneously. The corporate can let them buy their products on hire-purchase system. They are paying in easy installments and consuming simultaneously.

Narula (2005), businesses are built on developing the capacity of the poor: there are 300 million cell phones in China or 40 million cell phones in India and they are adding 1.5 million subscribers per month. They are not all in the hands of the rich. In fact, in developing countries, the poor skilled or unskilled in business of plumber, electrician, carpenter or vegetable vendor are utilizing it for connectivity for their business. Diffusion of cell phones is creating business connectivity beside social change. The cell phone businesses are (being) built around the consumer demand and experience of the poor people. In these countries they have the growth opportunity.

Prahalad (2004b) argues that in the bottom-of-the-pyramid market, the problem and the solutions are known but the fundamental innovation to develop the solution to affordable product and a distribution system to make it widely available is lacking.

For example, products like iodized salt necessary to prevent mental retardation and other disabilities related to iodine lack. But only 20% of the salt is iodized in India and even iodized salt loses its potency through storage, cooking and other means. Hindustan Lever Company in India, using an advance technology developed by India's atomic-energy agency, developed a way to microencapsulate the salt, to make sure that iodine is retained. The company has to convince the consumers on two counts: that its salt was better than non-iodized salt and that it is better than iodized salt that has not been encapsulated. To educate bottom-of-the-pyramid consumers in the village they use direct education. Women are the main focus since they do most of the cooking. The communication channel of empowered local village women are used to inform, educate and motivate women to use encapsulated iodized salt — the HLL salt. In urban areas they may exposed the poor through TV ads and other outdoor publicity.

Secondly, poor are brand conscious also and given the capacity to buy, they would aspire to buy expensive Sony TV rather no name. The Brands can develop its market by providing loans through banks, or selling through hire-purchase system. Without this option people may buy anything available or nothing (Prahalad 2004b).

In India, self-help groups of companies like ICICI, the ITC e-chaupal, the adult literacy program by TCS, Shakti Initiative of HLL in India have realized the need to work their supply chain backward starting with the consumer expectations and experiences. For example, earlier, the bottom-of-the-pyramid persons have to depend on money-lenders. But ICICI and other banks saw these people as critical to its future. But how to convert them into customers in cost effective way? ICICI organized village self-help groups. These groups of 20 women are taught about saving, borrowing, investing and so on. Each woman contributes to the joint saving account with the other members of the group. Based on the self-help group's track record, the bank lends money to the group, which in turn lends money to the individual members. ICICI is working with local communities and NGOs to enlarge its reach.

Another way to sell to the poor — sell in smaller sizes, single servings that poor people can afford to buy. They can buy that much when they need and can afford it. If they do not like it, they can switch to other brand. To retain the brand, it becomes critical for the companies to continually prove itself superior, economical to other brands. For expanding the market the company has to make products affordable for the poor by reducing the serving size, price, (with no frill packaging) and sustainability etc.

We talk about best practices and pick our practices. Prahalad (2004 b,c) argues that if everyone follows every one's best practice then we converge to meet and the best practice would not give you any advantage. We should rather talk about the *Next practice*. Strategy should always be about the next practice. For example, 20 yrs back the next practice for businesses was about local responsiveness and global integration. Ten years back it was core competencies and now Bottom-of-the-Pyramid can be the next practice. There is some intellectual continuity in the three practices: a global company needs to leverage its global strength to bring technology and resources to bear. But it has to be very local; for example, McDonald selling veggie burgers in India and not beef burgers. Businesses enhanced core competencies ten years back to produce focused products. Now they are fast realizing bottom-of-the-pyramid is substantial and cannot be ignored. Only it needs different business models and marketing strategies.

Co-creation theory advocates that consumer is supreme and pivotal for product demands and the market is co-created through consumer demands and expectations whether consumer is elite or down the pyramid. There are elite and informed consumers, and then there are poor and not so informed consumers who are at the bottom-of-the-pyramid. There are urban (both elite and poor) consumers, and consumers in rural areas. All these four categories have different levels of exposure to information channels. All are important for the business to develop product and market segments for the same.

Thus consumer is the significant link; therefore effective communication with him/her is essential. The marketing team must go down to the consumers to assess their felt needs first, and then assessment of consumers' expectations about a particular kind of product synchronizing with their needs, their preferences, product price and purchasing capacity. The marketing team would further focus on the consumer demographics and market segments both long-term and short-term. During this process, in interaction with the consumers, the team *creates new needs* for the consumers for different allied products or in different categories by talking about the products and displaying them in the contexts of their (consumers') product expectations. Thus through co-creation, market team would target to identify and create markets for both felt needs and new needs.

Market team realizes that personal interpersonal communication and two-way or circular interaction with the consumers in groups, one-on-one and through opinion leaders is necessary. Unless the marketing team, the managers are in close interaction with the consumers, they do not know consumers' needs, tastes, preferences, affordability — in short their expectations and demands, and affordability.

Prahalad (2004c) talks about the invisible market of consumers (both rural and poor) and how to connect with it. As a practice in recent years, Hindustan Lever in India has made it compulsory for a person who joins the company in regular job to live in villages for three months at a stretch before starting work in the company. It does not matter who you are and at what level you join. You have to develop a project in that village, for instance, build a dam, so that you are working closely with the local people. Why? The company wants you to understand your consumers and be in close interaction with the villagers to assess their needs, tastes, preferences, and affordability. So that it can co-create product accordingly for this segment, which is a huge market.

Further, to connect with the poor consumers, every year for one day, everyone from chairman to down, have to get out of the office and visit a poor-family consumer. Then, after the visit, when they come back, they write a report about what they have learned and how it will impact upon management and product development practices.

Generally, top management and employees are disconnected with the poor and rural consumers. And there is a huge disconnect with all managers and not just senior managers, in multinational companies and five billion potential consumers in low income and poor. Because we do not interact with poor, we do not know how they live.

The companies have to connect to the consumption reality and affordability of the poor. Like how can the poor eat ice cream soft and at the right temperature on a hot day? You have to rethink about refrigeration. There are now ice cream vending machines, which do not have to be recharged for two days. The ice cream won't melt even if there is black out or brown out because of electricity failure. This method of refrigeration reduces the amount of electricity supplied, because in a country like India, 40% of the cost of ice cream is the cost of electricity in a vending machine. This looks like a simple problem. But when you break down in details, you have to change things dramatically, if you want every Indian kid to afford to buy an ice cream and every ruralite to relish ice cream. You have to create affordable prices, distribution and quality levels. If you can do that, it means very vibrant economy (Prahalad 2004c). Even market for the ice cream will expand for all tiers if producers/marketers can focus on changing the production procedures and quality or marketers think about an insulated packaging so it does not melt from shop to way back way home or it does not melt in the freezers.

Other big companies are also following the example. Most of them are even encouraging their senior managers to visit their targeted villages to have face-to-face and hand-on experience of the feasibility and marketability of their products. They work on the presumptions that sitting in air-conditioned offices in the cities, far from the villages cannot, give them reality check on the rural markets and low-end markets.

There are other examples such as affordable small car Maruti, and with bank loans, the middle class could afford it. Maruti Udhyog Ltd of India tapped the huge middle class market and boosted its sales. Another in the pipeline and planned to be cheaper than this is Tata's starter family car (2005). This is aimed at the huge lower middle class market. The person from lower middle class needs to buy two-wheeler scooter for his work commute. May be he can afford to buy it through easy loan from the bank. He wants to take his family for drive and leisure activities. He takes his wife and two children on the scooter — all four on the pinion. Rattan Tata is concerned about seeing the family safely in a small car rather all four on the pinion of the two-wheeler scooter! We have to have a starter car competing with the scooter prices but certainly with more safety. These two kinds of markets, middle class and lower middle class consumers have huge potential market for these two different categories of cars — when they are available at affordable prices and when the purchasing capacity of the consumers is augmented.

James Hookway (Dec 2004) discusses about how as hard times squeeze middle class, companies are seeking ways to cater to the low-income consumers, seeking a broader market, Philippines goes downscale. It is a challenge for Ayala Corp and other consumer-oriented companies normally associated with wealth and conspicuous consumption. As the urban middle class is being squeezed by country's economic problems. The upscale business is gone. The blue-chip Ayala Corp is casting net for the new consumers in low-end mall, mobile phone and lower-income housing.

Its newest shopping mall — 'Market Market' — a low-end mall does not operate in the company's usual state-of-the art buildings but the market roof is made of tins, shoppers browse through bargain bins instead of fancy boutiques. A wet market that sells seafood and produce is occupying the prime space where one time company might have displayed new Toyotas or Hondas. They have to keep prices low to tap the new customers — the poor, the low income.

'Market Market' reflects a broader shift in Ayala Corp upscale business perspectives from property development, telecommunications, banking, semiconductors and water supply. It is a lower-end mall. With the Philippine economy confronting persistent high unemployment, rising inflation and worsening financial problems of government, Ayala is being forced to rethink about its target market and the poor remains a huge part of the market in many Asian countries though untapped.

Ayala's phone company — Globe Telecom Inc is tapping the poor and the rural people for its mobile phones. As a business strategy to expand business in this segment, it is offering wireless remittance services, mobile banking, cheap second hand mobile phones and ever-decreasing denomination of pre-paid telephone cards to tap what Filipinos call the 'sachet economy' — a milieu in which people who can't afford to buy a bottle of shampoo buy it in small sachet instead. Globe prepaid phone card is being offered as low as 5 pesos or 9 US cents. Mobile phone-business is profitable because of the affordability of the small size transactions made easy by cheap low denomination phone cards. New services of mobile banking and remittances are tailored to small-scale transactions. These are proving popular among poorer consumers.

Ayala is applying these lessons to its property development business also. The company has moved into lower-income housing developments to such an extent that mass housing in 2003 accounted for 13% of the consolidated revenue — equal to the amount Ayala's property development units would have got from upscale property development which is no more. Ayala is not out of business, but rather by retargeting the consumer segment — that is the poor who are no longer middle class, it is regaining its business.

"Just because more of our consumers are poorer does not mean serving them is less profitable, observed Mr. Zobel, US educated, President and CEO of Ayala. In fact catering to this broader market is forcing us to think of more creative products."

London Ted (2005). When MNCs go overseas; they typically look for customers that are the most familiar. As a result, in the developing world, they tend to target the wealthy. There's been increasing interest in reaching into the second tier of the pyramid that you could call the emerging middle class, maybe 1.5 billion people. These are people that are beginning to get some wealth but are still in the middle class in these developing countries.

What they have not targeted is the 4 billion plus people in the base of the socio-economic pyramid. The focus is on what it takes for an organization to profitably, or at least in a self-sustaining way; serve this market in a manner that is environmentally sensitive and culturally appropriate. This latter component is crucial, as we really believe the models that are going to work in BOP (bottom of pyramid) markets need to not only be economically viable but also need to address for social and environmental performance. They tend to pay a premium for services that are offered to people in the same general geographic location who are wealthier. Commenting on article by C.K. Prahalad and Al Hammond in the Harvard Business Review ("Serving the World's Poor, Profitably") that highlighted the premium that the poor pay for basic services. If the poor are poorly served and there are ways to serve them better, that's going to create benefits to the poor.

This new market requires partnerships not only with other companies but also with local communities, non-profit organizations – entities that corporations just aren't used to dealing with, but when they do deal with them it creates a much more inclusive and interesting business model.

BUSINESS COMMUNICATION WITH NATIONAL AND INTERNATIONAL GOVERNMENTS

Business communication with government is two ways and is an essential component of the business activities. To communicate with businesses is essential from political and administrative perspective of government and economy, and to formulate public policy in these contexts. From government perspective, two-way communication should focus on facilitating development of businesses by open and receptive rules and regulations, consistent business and general public policies, stability of government and capable political and administrative leadership.

The market economy should be open to create healthy environment for both domestic and international businesses. The healthy and wholesome activity of any business helps grow the economy and general development of the country. Too much bureaucratic tangles and red-tape, corruption, less common understanding of laws and prejudices, strict regulations and traditions in a country may not create good communication effects and conducive environment for business and society. Only a healthy business environment and public policies induced by government can encourage international businesses to invest and do business with the domestic businesses. This is essential to compete in this era of globalization of businesses.

Corporate must adhere to the business rules and regulations and guidelines of the national governments in case of domestic businesses and in global businesses the international rules and regulations, and treaties are to be followed and also rules and regulations of the country in which business is being done. Two-way communication is essential between the corporate and national and international governments to express their concerns and protect their business interests.

Political and administrative traditions with respect to this relationship differ in different countries. They largely determined what is right, appropriate in a country. These traditions also explain why there is confusion in some of the business practices and why it is in disarray. The increasing confusion threatens government more than the businesses.

Since both management and employees are important components of business, the government communicates in and through business environment to protect interests of both. It protects the employees from exploitation by management, plus safeguards their general welfare interests such as wages, social security of pensions and provident fund. It ensures growth of the business through satisfied workers. Government through communication protects the management also by not exploiting the business interests by undue demands and striking work protests by the employees. Good communication strategies help in handling these deals.

Formal business organizations such as in India, Confederation of Indian Industries (CII) and Associated Chambers of commerce (Assochem) and respected leaders of the business industry are good communication channels to make demands on government for good business and general policies and laws to facilitate healthy business environment and economic growth.

To a large extent, relationship to a government results from what businesses do or fail to do. The business-government relationship becomes a social problem when there are business scams and there are frauds. When businesses indulge in shady businesses like smuggling, dealing in narcotics and even illegal businesses of shipping migrants. These problems are addressed and solutions aimed at through many communication channels such as media, respected business leaders, business and industry federations and police both national and international.

The two political models that set the relationship are: one, mercantilist model, according to it the economy is seen as the foundation of political sovereignty. National economy and national sovereignty are seen as co-extensive. The main function of the economy is to provide survival for the nation-state against the threats from the outside. Within the nation-state there may be friction, conflict, dispute, competition. In the mercantilist model the business is considered socially inferior to the civil servant. Mercantile model guides, directs and pay subsidies. It tries to encourage business provided it moves in the direction of interest conducive to the national interest.

Constitutionalist Model accepts that government cannot stay out of economy and business. This model uses antitrust laws, regulatory agencies and criminal indictments. It tries to keep businesses out of government and sets limits to political morality and business activity.

These two models pertain to political and administrative theory. The present reality is different. *Today's reality is Mixed economy.* Both government activities and business activities are intertwined and compete at the same time. There are public sector companies owned by government and in active business. Professional managers manage the business both in private or public sectors. Multinational corporations promote global business and globalization process. The business and their managers require autonomy and accountability in the interest of economy, for the sake of effective government, and in the interest of society. While it needs regulation, it needs self-determination also. The performance capacity of the government rests on autonomy for business and management. Society needs management autonomy as well healthy and functioning government in complex and interdependent society. Government is needed to be the political decision maker but taking over business activities jeopardizes its capacity. That is why, time and again in India, case for disinvestment of government in business activities is put forth for consideration.

RELATIONSHIP WITH INTERNATIONAL GOVERNMENTS

The Transnational Corporations (TNC) aim to diffuse the products, services, ideas and markets to world communities through multi-corporate and focus at creating international consumerism. Both separately and together they influence the world communities in many different ways.

Earlier, the role of transnational actor has been putting economic pressures with its negative effect on national behavior; dissocializing rationality of State; legitimization of the dissolution of the public; and confrontation with a civil society identified with market oriented private interests. But now the international scenario is different because of multiple actors and nations involved in such communication, and such channels as Internet that knows no national boundaries. Multiple political, cultural and market ideologies will interact in the present scenario.

The TNC processes through information communication technologies (ICTs), create new structures, and recompose collective identities. It is paradoxical logic. The new ICTs are instrumental, and have a role in making the State strong in its possibilities and tendencies to control, and on the negative side making it weak by disconnecting it from the public functions.

Globalization gets growing into *cultural convergence* manifested in hardware and software transnational media products (telecommunication, video, TV), other commodities, business, banks, and advertising agencies etc. Others think of cultural convergence as evident in things people think about, the ways in which they think, and which things are expressed through everyday social practices. The aspect of 'cultural hybridize' arises from play of global forces through immigration, in search of employment opportunities and global trade (Narula 2005a).

Business communication with international organizations and government calls for knowing the business participating cultures to facilitate effective business communication environments and contexts.

What are the real and urgent challenges faced by managers today in the world of global business? The challenges could be high levels of business complexity and rapid change - globalization, geopolitical turmoil, technological innovations, hyper-competition, mergers and acquisitions, and alliances. There are high demands for leadership attitudes and skills throughout the business to analyze issues, execute strategies, and drive for results. The companies are experiencing these challenges in global reach of their businesses. Meeting these challenges and customer expectations increases need for team collaboration, across multiple cultural borders, to leverage the talents of everyone on the team. Intercultural communication, understanding diverse cultures and their ways of doing business are necessary and important.

Jagdish Bhagwati (2004) advocates that the most profound and polarizing tremors shaking the business world involve international trade, outsourcing, and economic development in less fortunate areas. He advocates that globalization can have positive influence when guided by enlightened government policies. Trade enhances growth and growth reduces poverty grounding the argument in statistics and real world evidence. Globalization unfairly takes the blame when something bad is going on from the erosion of cultural values and indigenous cultures to mistreatment of women and children and environmental damage.

Key ingredient for globalization in business is strategic partnership with the local player and offering high level of service quality. Managing a global business is like scaling a lofty mountain — you climb step by step higher and higher. The climb is particularly tough in a fiercely competitive era of rapid technological advances in which services (Internet based services) utilizing today's innovative ideas can often become mundane by tomorrow. The four core values: solutions, security, network management and global services create client's approval and appreciation of the scope and quality of services.

Forming mutually rewarding strategic alliances with dependable local players around the world is a crucial cornerstone to successfully globalize data services operations. You need good alliances because developing your own infrastructure is simply too costly these days. Moreover, you can get expert advice from your partners and alliances that are well versed in the local markets in which you wish to operate. Partnership also gives the basis for trust in the market places in what you have to offer (Jagdish Bhagwati 2004).

Masanobu Suzuki (Ceo & President NTT Communication Corp at the 8th business week forum in Beijing Nov 9-10 2004) reveals that mutually rewarding strategic partnerships and providing consistently high level of service quality are the two factors for success of NTT Communication Corp. It may sound simple but if we provide our customers and clients with dependable, one-stop information and communication services through partnership and quality control — we succeed.

Desai, President Asia Society (Aug 2004) argues that India has to learn more about other countries in the Asia – Pacific region in order to become a true global player and not just an economic power. What is important is the way India plays a role in global operations and projects itself as a global economic and cultural power. While India wants to project itself as global power, the rest of Asia thinks about India as an economic power only. India has all the ingredients — the hard (economic), the soft (cultural and political) powers. It still has to get the strategy right for being a global player. Indians have not applied their minds to it, may be because they are inward looking, introspective people. The country needs to go out, be proactive and pursue an outward looking strategy.

Since the late nineties it has been widely accepted that global economic growth will now be triggered by transitional economies like India, China and Brazil. The potential of the developed economies were already exploited to the full and it had reached saturation. The capital and financial markets of these transitional economies are booming with global investor interest. It is this huge interest among the foreign institutional investors that has given boost to these markets and economies on transition.

The financial markets of developing countries are referred as emerging markets. Examples include India, China, Brazil, Israel, Mexico, Malaysia, Chile, Thailand and Philippines. Emerging-market securities are the most volatile in the world. They have tremendous growth potential, but also pose significant risks — political upheaval corruption and currency collapse, to name just a few.

It is imperative to understand and adjust to the complex communication contexts and channels, modes and styles in the emerging markets of developing countries viz their economic growth and global investor interest.

The communication channels and modes, communication partners and focuses have changed with the global economic order undergoing constant change and facing new challenges like outsourcing, foreign investments both in financial markets and infrastructures, and exports.

This suggests accelerating the development of managers and special teams who can execute strategies and drive for results in today's complex and dynamic global business environment. This can be achieved by integrating the best concepts, tools, and technologies into the most powerful learning solutions. China's current training programs in public administration for its bureaucrats in US and other countries since 2002 are part of the effort to integrate the best practices of different countries for economic growth and governance.

For a long time, there was feeling that business and economic growth would let China progress. In the current decade China has progressed tremendously in business and there is economic growth but the success of economic programs for people is not visible. China is racing towards a market economy and just weaving welfare net for its people. It is fast realizing that lack of good, clean and efficient government can severely affect your economic programs.

Kennedy School of Government at Harvard University has started a training program for Chinese bureaucrats since 2002. Other participating public administration US schools are Syracuse, University of Maryland, and Rutgers University in New Jersey among others. There are also such programs offered by France, Canada, Japan, Australia, Singapore, and elsewhere. Training programs are part of the effort for good, clean and efficient government through bureaucrats exposed to different ways of dealing with Public administration in west.

Chinese government objective is to enhance the capability of the government through its trained bureaucrats, "to draw lessons from the success and failures of the other ruling parties of the world and enhance our governance capabilities in a more earnest and conscientious manner." Some Chinese participants question whether western ways of governance will work for their country. Saich, (2005) faculty chairman of the China public-policy program at Harvard thinks, despite the differences in political system and histories of China and US, the problems the government officials face are very similar at the practical level, such as management performance and strategic decision-making. The Chinese officials are acutely aware of the differences between political and social systems at home and abroad and they require different solutions. China is now undergoing substantial economic democratization and has become one of the most open economies in the developing countries.

Saich, further suggests that this training program experiment will have major impact only if the program alumni eventually joins the inner circle (government) in Beijing. Prof Li at Hamilton College in Clinton NY thinks that new generation believes these programs will have substantial impact on China's transformation.

BUSINESSES PERSPECTIVE AND SOCIAL RESPONSIBILITY

Businesses have to take social responsibility along with economic performance for common good. The public demands that businesses take the social responsibility and the society does need it. Businesses must set their objectives, roles and performance goals in this context. This is one dimension of their relationship with the national government.

Social responsibility for businesses arises in two areas: what a business does to a society (such as creating employment for community and neighborhood) and what it can do for a society such as setting up schools and hospitals. The businesses create a healthy society to work in. Government encourages the businesses to take this responsibility by giving tax shelters for such activities such as contributions for philanthropy, and setting up industries in rural and backward areas (government in India encourages that).

Keefe (2002) advocates that in the new global economy, corporations are being asked to play a more active role in addressing social problems that were once thought to be the exclusive responsibility of government and civil society. The concept of corporate social responsibility (CSR) has gained currency and acceptance among the public and within the business community itself as the appropriate response to society's rising expectations for and demands upon the corporation. Corporations are no longer evaluated in terms of financial performance alone, but increasingly on the basis of a new "triple bottom line" of financial, social and environmental performance. In this new business environment, a company's reputation has become one of its most valuable assets, and CSR has become one of the key components of corporate reputation.

CSR has been defined as "open and transparent business practices that are based upon ethical values and respect for employees, communities and the environment - [and] designed to deliver sustainable value to society at large, as well as to shareholders (The Prince of Wales Business Leaders Forum).

Five trends that are defining the global economy of the early 21st Century seem to provide a framework for understanding these developments. They are: business transparency, an increased knowledge base among consumers, the sustainability imperative, the challenge of globalization and the failure of the public sector.

Transparency: We live in an information-driven economy where business practices have become increasingly transparent. Companies can no longer sweep things under the rug. Whatever they do (for good or for bad) will be known, almost immediately, around the world. The Internet, the ubiquitous 24/7 news cycle, thousands of media outlets, web sites, online newsletters and NGOs using electronic communications to mobilize constituencies; all contribute to placing corporations under a permanent microscope in this new age of transparency.

Knowledge: The transition to an information-based economy also means that consumers and investors have more information at their disposal than at any time in history. They can be more discerning, and can wield more influence. Consumers visiting a clothing store can now choose one brand over another based upon those companies' respective environmental records or involvement in sweatshop practices overseas. Likewise, investors can choose stocks or mutual funds based not only on financial factors but on social and environmental criteria as well. This is a fundamentally new phenomenon; potentially altering the balance of power between consumers/investors and corporations in ways we are only beginning to understand. (Kanter Moss 2002).

Sustainability: The earth's natural systems are in serious and accelerating decline, while global population is rising precipitously. We are fast approaching or have already crossed the sustainable yield thresholds of many natural systems (fresh water, oceanic fisheries, forests, rangelands), which cannot keep pace with projected population growth. Failure to address these developing ecological catastrophes will mean unimaginable changes to life including human life on planet earth. As a result, corporations are under increasing pressure from diverse stakeholder constituencies to demonstrate that business plans and strategies are environmentally sound and contribute to sustainable development. Many countries have enacted legislation mandating social and environmental reporting in the corporate annual reports in addition to financial reporting.

Globalization: In the new global economy, however, there is no Central government to legislate and enforce basic labor, human rights and environmental safeguards. Globalization represents a new stage of capitalist development, this time without countervailing public institutions to protect society by balancing private corporate interests against broader public interests.

The question therefore arises: if we can export property rights and contract rights and intellectual property protections overseas, should we not also export labor rights and human rights and environmental protections as well? Why should we export some of our values but not others? Global corporations are under increased pressure to answer these questions, and under increased scrutiny by the media, governments, workers, NGOs environmentalists and human rights groups to incorporate basic CSR standards and sustainability strategies into their worldwide operations and to disclose and report on those strategies. At the same time, a borderless global economy is beginning to give rise to borderless governance structures to fill the void once occupied by the jurisdiction, legitimacy and coercive power of the nation state. (The Global Reporting

Initiative, the UN Global Compact, other approaches e.g. labor conventions, financial accounting standards consisting of disclosure and reporting guidelines, independent auditing, multilateral treaties and related strategies).

The Failure of the Public Sector: Many if not most developing countries are governed by dysfunctional regimes ranging from the hapless and disorganized to the brutal and corrupt. Yet it is not developing countries alone that suffer from moribund public sectors. In the United States and other developed nations, citizens arguably expect less of government than they used to, having lost confidence in the public sector as the best or most appropriate venue for addressing a growing list of social problems.

Collectivist solutions having failed, capitalism itself is now offered as the remedy for solving many of the ills that plague society — the "rising tide lifts all boats" approach. Though corporations understandably perceive liberal interest groups and activist NGOs as the source of increased pressure on them to become more "socially responsible," it was arguably conservatives who unwittingly laid the groundwork for such rising expectations in the first place by discrediting the public sector and offering markets as the most just and efficient allocator of social goods.

As Steve Lydenberg (2003) has written: "With the collapse of the Soviet Union and other state-controlled economies, the world has placed an increasingly large bet on the marketplace to provide economic solutions to social problems". If corporations and markets are the solution, in other words, at some point they are going to have to deliver, and they will find themselves under increased pressure to do so.

What is remarkable about the above mentioned trends is that they are all fundamentally new — none of them were particularly significant twenty years ago, and in some instances even ten years ago — and they are altering, at a very rapid pace, the way corporations do business, as well as the way they communicate. This is true even for the "sustainability" trend. Certainly the environment was a concern 10, even 20 years ago, but arguably the notion that potentially calamitous ecological imbalances require fundamentally new, sustainable business models had not yet migrated from peripheral environmental groups and academic circles to mainstream business circles.

Corporate reputation is now inextricably tied to corporate responsibility. The convergence of the five trends identified above — business transparency, an increased knowledge base among consumers, the sustainability imperative, the challenge of globalization and the failure of the public sector have helped to bring this about. Today, a company's failure to attend to its reputation and incorporate CSR into its business model can result in unfavorable publicity, proxy fights, consumer boycotts and other concerted action by diverse stakeholder constituencies, NGOs and other interest groups. More is expected of today's corporations. CSR is no longer a collateral concern but central to business success.

For today's companies, a narrow focus on brand is therefore no longer enough. Consumers and investors increasingly want to know what's inside a company. Of the traditional competitive differentiators in the marketplace; reputation matters in addition to price, quality, service and brand. In fact, reputation today may be even more important because bad publicity can seriously undermine a company's brand and render price, quality and service irrelevant. Companies now need to develop good reputations in order to protect their brands. Reputation has become the guardian of brand. And CSR has become the guardian of reputation.

This is the new business environment that corporations find themselves in at the dawn of the 21st Century. Companies that focus on reputation, on CSR, and on sustainability-driven business strategies will have a competitive edge over their peers and be better positioned to prosper over the long-term. Those who do not will incur over time, significant new risks as compared to their more enlightened competitors. Society indeed expects more from today's corporations and corporations will have to deliver.

MODELS OF CORPORATE SOCIAL RESPONSIBILITY

There are five models of corporate social responsibility. *Philanthropic model* focused on intentions of community services. *Socialist Model* believes that the State has a key role in driving economic growth while ensuring social equality, for example, initiatives to set up PSUs by Indian government. *Stakeholder Model*, in this employees and community are considered stakeholders. Communities put pressures to integrate business and environmental goals such as improving working conditions in factories. *Shareholder Model* suggests that the shareholders need to act and look ethical due to public campaigns against unethical business practices. Image and brand protection is the key motive. *Business Model* suggests a belief that socially responsible practices will expand the market size, employee royalty and create wealth, as well create a healthy society in which to do business.

Business and social Impact: There is incidental, inescapable and unintended social impact of the businesses as a by-product of their business line. Such as creating noise or other environmental pollution because of their products, or traffic jams may occur when employees have to go to and from the business offices. These are unintended but have to be managed well through communication with the public around who are being affected covertly or overtly and the employees. Management may have to communicate with the environmental agencies to help them control the pollution, as well within the organization to streamline the disposal or reduction of the pollutants. There may be communication with the employees about disciplining traffic in the office areas. Quite possibly, the management may set up flexible office hours to avoid high traffic jams and inconvenience to their public.

These impacts cause frictions with people if not managed well and are also non-productive cost for the business. When these impacts become crisis or create scandals, they damage the business reputation. For example, 20 years ago in Dec '84, the gas-leakage in Union Carbide Company Plant in Bhopal in India. Many people were killed. It has taken many years to resolve about owning the responsibility and compensating the people. Whatever may be, the company had to shut down the operations in India immediately after the incident. They too lost the business and its reputation.

Sooner or later, the society will regard such impacts as attack on their integrity and will resent those businesses that do not find solutions for it. Such resentment when piling on for long time can damage the business as consumers lose credibility for its integrity.

These impacts need to be handled timely. For example, a few years back, people in Delhi, India were very concerned about the pollution through vehicle emission of diesel run public buses. There were strong public protests against government inaction in this matter. It took couple of years for government to introduce in the market CNG (compressed natural gas) fuel and they banned diesel fuel run public transport. Now people resented it, because government took so much time to set up the infrastructure for it. The gas filling in the vehicle would take hours and cabs were losing business.

Philanthropic model: Global philanthropy is hottest these days. There are practical reasons for companies to give big money in donations. People give away vast proportions of their wealth for variety of reasons and choose to do it in diverse ways. They go for education, healthcare, Information access technology, biomedical research, brain research, cancer research, social change, art and culture, HIV/aids, environment and global security, reducing nukes and social entrepreneurship etc.

Philanthropists believe that they should donate now in their lifetime, problems need to be solved now not after 20 years. They are urged on the belief that value of solving problems today is greater than bequeathing the money when they die. By accelerating their giving large sums now, they have better chance of effecting change. Keeping all this cash on the sidelines rather than giving it out now diminishes its power to address problems as much as by 50%.

Many companies think that successful philanthropy requires going beyond monetary gifts to embrace a cause and make a visible impact. People have called on multinationals to be stronger partners in the third world. Companies that attract customers and workers in the developing countries often are faced with poor healthcare and education. Improving those in-situations through philanthropy can help lay the groundwork for future business opportunities. This does pay social dividends in the process. Some companies are harnessing their core competencies to solve social problems.

Many companies reported their philanthropy helps in their profit-making mission by giving workers access to better health care, building employees loyalty, and building the company's reputation. For example, Citigroup has increased its support in micro lenders in developing countries in the past five years (since 99). In India alone, the company has provided grants for the loans to 90,00,000/ women. As Citigroup positions itself to be the banker of global choice, it is already building a name for itself in the developing world.

Pfizer's global fellows — a group of 30 skilled professionals — from business experts to scientists that Pfizer has loaned to aid groups in developing countries up to six months. This program started in 2003. The company's greatest resource, 'brain trust' is used to help public health problems. The program pays Pfizer some hefty social dividends. Global health fellows build employee morale and polish the company's reputation.

Intel Corp has computer club-houses providing Internet access and technology training to children in 32 countries including South Africa, India and the West Bank. eBay Inc founder Pierre Omidyar focuses on grants to individuals who are already creating social change through their non-profits. The critical tool of this mostly smallish group is Internet that enables people to give tiny ideas and give them global launch. By taking out the middleman and shifting decision-making power from experts to practitioners, he believes something more efficient and innovative can be accomplished and with a far bigger impact. It is revolutionary. His philanthropy takes up a bottom-up approach, allowing individuals to determine the vision and direction.

US companies have more reasons to fund charitable causes overseas. For one, that is where much of their new business and production is headed and their revenues come from abroad. They do hire local workforce but activists in those countries pressure the companies to take up social issues. (based on special report Philanthropy 2004, Business Week Nov 29 2004).

Under its Corporate Social Responsibility program, Reliance Infocomm Ltd in India has launched an easy-to-navigate application — 'Call History' — that helps visually challenged subscribers to access call registry, including missed, dialed and received calls.

'Call History' is an easy-to-navigate application that works on a number-to-speech engine to enable visually challenged caller's access call registry information (Dec 2004).

Manmohan Singh, India's Prime Minister addressing trade and industries high ups, said, corporate social responsibility is not philanthropy. It is not charity. It is an investment in our collective future. We need to pay more attention to the expansion and modernization of the social and economic infrastructure to realize our full growth potential. He called for public-private partnership to create world-class infrastructure (2004).

NATIONAL AND INTERNATIONAL MEDIA: BUSINESS PRACTICES

National Media: The multiple channels of national and international media play triple role of acting as information and knowledge broker, and facilitator for the public, businesses and government.

In its broader role, the national media, the national dailies, broadcasting channels and Internet give business news and its analysis from variety of viewpoints to the public. It provides company profiles, in-depth financials, competitors, and industry trends, Such as stock markets, business laws, taxations, new business models and trends, business opportunities and threats, business jobs, both nationally and globally.

In its narrow role, media channels create among public, awareness, information and knowledge for various business products, services, ideas and programs both for short-term and long-term. Media creates visibility and through advertisements and reinforced programs motivates and persuade public to adopt the programs, buy the products and consume the services. Thus media helps in marketing.

Media sets agenda for business through public, businesses and government. Media conveys back demands and needs and changing trends in consumption of the public to the businesses as well government and the feedback about how to build purchasing capability of the public. (a) This helps businesses to plan their products and services, markets and marketing strategies and follow the changing consumer and market trends and patterns. They plan strategies to develop, facilitate the purchasing capability by micro-credit, differentiated prices and sizes for low-end and high-end markets. (b) This helps government to formulate economic policies, business policies and controls, and rules and regulations. (c) Businesses and government converge their economic and business policies framework and create agenda for public.

Media play significant role in the whole process and further conveying this agenda to the public and again giving feedback to government and businesses about public reactions.

The businesses and government provide news releases, publications and a variety of resources designed specifically to assist the media and they meet the press and other channels representatives to convey the scenarios in proper perspectives. It projects corporate public relations and investor relations, government and organizational communication.

Media channels can be facilitators in its positive role but in negative role it can create bad publicity for the corporate and its leaders, its business strategies and markets products and services. This can shake credibility of the public and its brand loyalty, shake its share in the stock markets and create concerns for its stakeholders. Take another scenario, these days too much media hype for newer products has shorten the life cycle of the products, shaken the brand loyalty altogether among Generation and is pushing and challenging businesses to look for innovative products and new market segments more frequently than before.

International Media: International media channels such as television, telecommunication, Internet through email, broadband and VOIP etc facilitate globalization of businesses by creating global visibility of the consumers, products and services and markets.

Currently in 2004-05, International media is projecting aggressively China and India as emerging economies. They are highlighting China's role as manufacturing hub for outsourcing and India as knowledge economy hub for outsourcing. The news and analysis about business scope, opportunities, financial stability and economic policies, and business practices of these two countries in the International media exposes the businesses, governments and public around the world, who would seek to do business with them and import or export their product and services. International media channels also give information and analytical knowledge about opportunities of outsourcing of particular businesses in these countries and vice versa or create other geographies for outsourcing. It creates business edge both nationally and internationally. Nationally it creates interest of public from the point of job opportunities and the government (India) gets interested in widening the scope of outsourcing and maintaining competitive edge over China. Internationally it helps other players to seek businesses, competition, best business practices and business models and communication infrastructure.

International TV may expose consumers to different life styles around the world and create consumers and markets for those products. They expose businesses to new and different business practices, thus helping them to choose the innovative practices or best practices. Internet through its e-commerce use innovative and unique business practices to create international consumers for products and services worldwide. Internet has even broken the geographic and time boundaries for businesses. Internet also gives instant exposure, access and reach for the worldwide product. Online marketing and buying facilitates both businesses and consumers.

In the wake of globalization, International treaties such as WTO (world trade organization) are initiated and debated from the viewpoints of world trade partners who are concerned about protecting their business interests. It reports World Economic Summits to analyze and debate the economic policies and plans, programs and concerns of the international community and public at large. International media also projects the plight of workers in sweatshops in factories in China, or in Nike shoe factories in South Asia, or child labor in carpet factories in India. Social activists and politicians worldwide take up the issues in the international media, threatens to boycott the products till conditions are improved.

SUMMARY

External corporate communication for business development could be facilitated through communicating with external links to the corporate business such as supply chain, distributors, wholesalers and retailers, consumers, business competitors, Community, Media, Government and Civic bodies. Market Information System (MIS) is organized flow of information among external links. Communication, strategic interactions and coordination, coherence (precision), persuasion, reinforcement are functions of external corporate communication links.

Businesses create consumers for their products and services through their own innovative ideas and consumer driven demands and ideas. The focus on consumer behavior is through consumer creation, acquisition, and retention, building consumer trust and loyalty and consumer service and relationship. These are challenging for businesses. Business supply chain is multiple of suppliers specializing in different processes of the product and services. The communication channels for communication and reinforcement with supply chain vendors are organization's internal links of *specialized communication teams.*

Emerging markets are getting more open and greater competition is evident in many sectors. In fact, there is extreme competition among the emerging markets because of outsourcing from the western countries. It is imperative to understand and adjust to the complex communication contexts and channels, modes and styles in the emerging markets viz their economic growth and global investor interest. Low-income, poor consumers, and rural market are mass markets in these emerging countries and other developing countries. It is challenging for companies all over the world to develop new business and business communication models to capture this huge market.

Business communication with government is two ways and is an essential component of the business activities. To communicate with businesses is essential from political and administrative perspective of government and economy, and to formulate public policy in these contexts. Business communication with international organizations and government calls for knowing the business participating cultures to facilitate effective business communication environments and contexts. Intercultural communication, understanding diverse cultures and their ways of doing business are necessary and important.

The urgent challenges faced by managers today in global businesses could be high levels of business complexity and rapid change. There are high demands for leadership attitudes and skills throughout the business to analyze issues, execute strategies, and drive for results. The key ingredient for globalization in business is strategic partnership with the local player and offering high level of service quality. The communication channels and modes, communication partners and focuses have changed with the global economic order undergoing constant change and facing new challenges like outsourcing, foreign investments both in financial markets and infrastructures, and exports.

In the new global economy, corporations are being asked to play a more active role in addressing social problems that were once thought to be the exclusive responsibility of government and civil society. The concept of corporate social responsibility (CSR) has gained currency and acceptance among the public and within the business community itself as the appropriate response to society's rising expectations for and demands upon the corporation.

The multiple channels of national and international media play triple role of acting as information and knowledge broker, and facilitator for the public, businesses and government. National media sets agenda for business through public, businesses and government. International media channels facilitate globalization of businesses by creating global visibility of the consumers, products and services and markets.

4

Business Communication Practices

Business enterprise has three basic functions — Innovations, Marketing and Communications. The various business practices relate to these three functions.

These produce results. Thus in any business enterprise marketing and communications are the two major tools for innovations (products and services).

In economics, the main criteria by which one can distinguish between different market forms are: the number and size of producers and consumers on the market, the type of goods and services being traded, and the degree to which information can flow freely. The major market forms are: Perfect competition, in which the market consists of a very large amount of firms producing product in the same domain. Monopolistic competition, where there are a large amount of somewhat independent firms. It is Oligopoly when the market is dominated by a small number of sellers. Monopoly, where there is only one provider of a product or service.

The Product Life Cycle (PLC)

The conditions under which a product is sold change over time. The Product Life Cycle refers to the succession of stages a product goes through. Product Life Cycle Management is the succession of strategies used by management as a product goes through its life cycle. The Product Life Cycle (PLC) is based upon the biological life cycle. For example, a seed is planted (introduction), it begins to sprout (growth), it shoots out leaves and puts down roots as it becomes an adult (maturity), after a long period as an adult the plant begins to shrink and die out (decline).

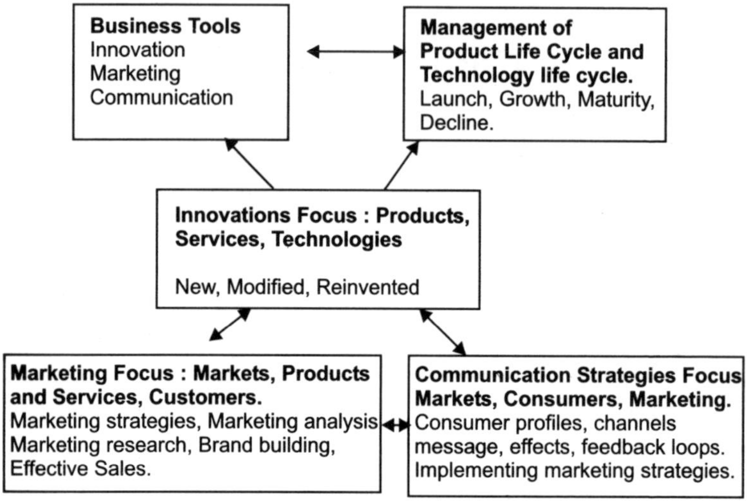

Fig. 4.1. Business Communication Tools

In theory it's the same for a product. After a period of development it is introduced or launched into the market; it gains more and more customers as it grows; eventually the market stabilizes and the product becomes mature; then after a period of time the product is overtaken by development and the introduction of superior competitors, it goes into decline and is eventually withdrawn. However, most products fail in the introduction phase. Others have very cyclical maturity phases where declines see the product promoted to regain customers.

Strategies for the Differing Stages of the PLC

Introduction: The need for immediate profit is not a pressure. The product is promoted to create awareness. If the product has no or few competitors, a skimming price strategy is employed. Limited numbers of product are available in few channels of distribution. New product development stage is very expensive, no sales, but revenue losses may occur.

Growth: Competitors are attracted into the market with very similar offerings. Products become more profitable and companies form alliances, joint ventures, and take each other over. Advertising spend is high and focuses upon building brand. Market share tends to stabilize. At growth stage costs are reduced due to economies of scale, sales volume increases significantly and so is profitability.

Maturity: Those products that survive the earlier stages tend to spend longest in this phase. Sales grow at a decreasing rate and then stabilize. Producers attempt to differentiate products and brands are key to this. Price wars and intense competition occur. At this point the market reaches saturation. Producers begin to leave the market due to poor margins. Promotion becomes more widespread and uses a greater variety of media. Mature stage costs are very low, sales volume peaks, prices tend to drop due to the proliferation of competing products, but on the whole very profitable.

Decline: At this point there is a downturn in the market. For example, more innovative products are introduced or consumer tastes have changed. There is intense price-cutting and many more products are withdrawn from the market. Profits can be improved by reducing marketing spend and cost cutting. Usually at decline stage, sales decline, prices drop and profits decline.

Market evolution is a process that parallels the product life cycle. As a product category matures, the industry goes through stages that mirror the five stages of a product life cycle. The market crystallizes as latent demand for a product category is awakened with the introduction of the new product. Market expands as additional companies enter the market and more consumers become aware of the product category. The market gets fragmented as the industry is subdivided into numerous well-populated competitive groupings as too many companies enter. Some companies tend to leave the market as there is less profit and market consolidation takes place. There is market termination when consumers no longer demand the product and companies stop producing it.

Technology lifecycle: The underlying technology subsumed within a product or product category can go though similar stages. This is typically referred to as the technology lifecycle. Most new technologies follow a similar technology lifecycle. This is similar to a product life cycle, but applies to an entire technology, or a generation of a technology. There is usually technology hype at the introduction of any new technology, but only after some time has passed can it be judged as mere hype or justified true acclaim. It is difficult to see in the early stages whether the hype is excessive because of the logistic curve nature of technology adoption.

The two errors commonly committed in the early stages of a technology's development are: fitting an exponential curve to the first part of the growth curve, and assuming eternal exponential growth, fitting a linear curve to the first part of the growth curve, and assuming that take up of the new technology is disappointing. Similarly, in the later stages, the opposite mistakes can be made relating to the possibilities of technology maturity and market saturation.

Technology adoption typically occurs in an S curve, as modeled in diffusion of innovations theory. This is because customers respond to new products in different ways. Diffusion of innovations theory, pioneered by Everett Rogers, posits that people have different levels of readiness for adopting new innovations and that the characteristics of a product affect overall adoption.

Management of the PLC

The progression of a product through these stages is not certain. In reality, very few products follow such a prescriptive cycle. The length of each stage varies enormously. The decisions of marketers can change the stage, for example, from maturity to decline by price-cutting. Not all products go through each stage. Some go from introduction to decline. It is not easy to tell which stage the product is in. Some products seem to stay in the mature stage forever (e.g., milk). Marketers have various techniques designed to prevent the process of falling into the decline stage. In most cases however, one can estimate the life expectancy of a product category.

Marketers' marketing mix strategies change as their products go through life cycle. Advertising, for example, is informative in the introduction stage, persuasive in the growth and maturity stages, and is reminder-oriented in the decline stage.

Promotional budgets tend to be highest in the early stages, and gradually taper off as the product matures and declines. Pricing, distribution, and product characteristics also tend to change.

Innovation is new product development. It may be modifications of the old. This kind of new product is in response to customer demands for better and with added utility and for some of their immediate and urgent needs. For example in 2005 Procter and Gamble Company developed Tide detergent powder for cold water machine wash to meet the need of the consumers to save in electricity bills. The innovative as well re-innovative products are driven by consumer needs and may be the result of research and development. This is discussed in detail in later section.

We need both marketing strategies and communication strategies for marketing products and services, building brands and brand values, targeting segmented markets and targeted audiences and Sales for profitability. In the later sections we discuss in detail, Innovations, Marketing and Communications in business practices.

MARKETING

Marketing in business is about products, customers and markets. In short, how business products and services reach the customers through markets and how customers in market segments access products and services of a business. Both the standpoints show that the abovementioned three basic elements of marketing are intertwined and interdependent in its reach and functioning. The basic tools of marketing are: marketing strategies, market research and market analysis, pricing policies, supply chain, customer/consumer services and customer/consumer relations.

The basic objective of any business is to get good, improved return on investment (ROI). Therefore, top-management and various other levels of business associated with marketing, plan about marketing strategies for its products and services both consumer and industrial/business products through four stages. It is four-pronged approach.

At first stage, market strategies are planned about (consumer) product development based on market analysis and market research about consumer profiles and particular market segments. If it is an industrial/business product then it is identified by need drive of the industry/business customer, and the capability of the company to supply it. The top-management and the different levels of management are involved in making decisions about prototype development of the product based on market research data.

At the second stage, marketing strategies are planned to market the prototype product. Market research is involved again at this stage to get assessment and feedback about the markets, customers and consumers' reactions — acceptance, rejection and feedback about additional features, and from supply chains involved, they get feedback about the suitability of the market segments and the consumer demand preferences. Group discussions, demonstrations and presentations are given for industrial/business product prototype to the customer group, — involved in the decision-making about the product. The customer group provides feedback about acceptance, about demand and suggestions for additional new features, total rejection or rejection of some features in the prototype product.

In fact that provides the assessment about the overall viability of the prototype product to the top-management of the product provider group in interface with the top-management of the customer group. *Interface communication* between the two management groups facilitates in deciding abort the viability of the product, pricing policies, time period, supply chain and further marketing strategies. The collective decision of many sharp and knowledgeable management helps in decision-making about the final product development. Top-management and various other levels of management decide about the viability of developing the products and services for its customers and consumers based on market research information and data, and feedback and assessments collected at the second stage, and facilitated by it, and taking into consideration other business factors.

At the third stage when product is ready to be launched, management has to think about *marketing strategies* again to position, and place the products in the market through its supply chain and pitching at the targeted consumer audience using various tools of marketing such as product promotions, product sample demonstrations and displays, different channels of advertisements, and campaigns etc. These strategic decisions are facilitated by the information and facts provided by the market research about customers' psychographic and demographic characteristics synchronizing with the launched product and the market segments and supply chain identified by the market research team. In case of industrial/business product, the market research teams of the customer group and of the provider group synchronize their information, data, feedback, supply chains about the end product and provide the same to their top-management and other levels of management to plan marketing strategies.

At the fourth stage, Market research team has to be active again when the product is in the market. They have to assess consumers' reactions — acceptance or rejection consequent to their buying and using the product. The feedback is direct from the consumers in general and consumer focus groups, and from retailers. This information helps in planning *marketing strategies* about marketing techniques, advertisements, building brand image, and handling competition in marketing techniques such as advertisements etc and consumer services and consumer relations. Market research team gets feedback direct from the industrial/business customer and from the supply chain. This information helps the management in planning marketing strategies of interface discussions, presentations, product visibility, and effectiveness of supply chain and sales viz the product and providing customer services and customer relations.

Thus marketing strategies are to be planned at four stages of marketing the product and services. The top-management and the various levels of marketing management play significant role in planning the marketing strategies at all the four stages and plan how the product and services reach markets and customers. Market research team has to be involved at all the four stages of marketing. It plays significant role in identifying the market segments, targeted audience, and important information and facts about them at all the four stages. The significance of the research lies in the fact that marketing strategies are based on them. Market analysis and customer profiles facilitate in formulating these strategies. The function of market research group of the business is to get information, and facts about these two factors at four stages.

Our above discussion highlights that marketing strategies are essential and important for marketing of products, services and ideas and to take the right kind of marketing decision-making. Marketing strategies, for product feasibility, for product development, product in the market, and post product marketing are needed.

Regardless of the marketing channels the company uses — direct sales, wholesalers, specialists, dealers, retailers and Internet. It takes skill, strategy and intuitive marketing maneuvers to handle today's increasingly complicated channels. It helps to develop, manage and execute channel strategies for channel selection and channel conflict management.

Communication Strategies: The business practices of marketing products and services and ideas focus primarily on marketing strategies. Communication strategies (CS) are planned to implement marketing strategies. The focus of communication strategies is market and consumer. Therefore, the effort is to communicate about markets and consumers. This is two-way communication — from marketers to markets and consumers and from these two components to the marketers. Communication strategies are planned from five angles:

characteristics, communication channels, message content, effects, and feedback loops.

Market characteristics such as geographic, regional, urban/ rural, high net/low mass are communicated to the marketers. Further, the characteristics of the segmented markets such as youth, old, women and children are communicated. The demographics and psychographics of the consumers in these markets are communicated. Marketers use this information and facts for market analysis in context of a particular products and services being considered. The product environment is in the market place, industries and business management offices.

Different communication channels are planned to reach different segments of markets according to reach and exposure in those segment markets. Rural market may have exposure through conventional TV and radio, outdoor publicity, billboards and interpersonal communications whereas the urban markets may have higher exposure to Internet, telephone and cinema etc. For effective communication, the channels are selected according to their high exposure for particular category of products and services, for specific segment rural or urban markets and according to the characteristics of the targeted consumers.

Message content is telling about the product verbally, through written word and through visual images. The message must project upfront what the product is, its enhanced qualities, how it satisfies the customer/consumer needs both overt and covert, price compatibility and affordability and the competitive products in the market. The message content contains persuasive appeals to buy. The message is further reinforced consistently through advertisements, product promotions, displays etc. In short, message must convey what the business wants to convey and its strength and credibility lies in the final act of sale.

Businesses and customers/consumers are both sender and receivers according to the message situations since circular communication is necessary condition for viability and reinforcement of the messages both from the marketers and consumers. This suggest the feedback loops from senders to receivers and from intervening market elements for better understanding of consumer demands and satisfaction and at the same time what marketers want to convey about the products and services.

There are channel noises. This could be customers/consumers satisfaction or dissatisfaction conveyed about the products, customer services and customer relations. There may be complaints about channels usage and credibility. It is important to take care of channel noises.

The business marketer is concerned about both short-term and long-term effects of product messages in terms of buying behavior of customers and consumers, their attitudes towards products and services, particular brands, and image of the company in general. Marketer is also concerned and it is of interest to him to assess the change in those attitudes overtime and factors responsible for it. These are some of the short-term effects. These are assessed in terms of demands for the products. The long-terms effects are assessed when there is actual purchase of the product and when services sold are used not once but again and again. Quite likely, the products and services may be rejected either initially or after initial use. These long-term effects are assessed in sales of the products and profitability of the products and markets.

The effects are assessed by feedback loops from the customers and consumers to the marketer and back. 'Effects' is essential component in all the four stages of marketing strategies. On one hand, these several feedback loops feed about the positive and negative effects of the products and markets differently at all the four stages, and on the other hand these feedback loops create better understanding about the products, its visibility, attitudes and buying behavior.

Effects are assessed by marketers through market analysis and market research. The effects are conveyed to the marketing associated management levels and top-management for action through interpersonal and interface communications supported by technological databases etc. We discuss in details about market research and market analysis in later sections.

All marketing strategies not only need support from Communication strategies but rather CS play important role in execution of market strategies at all the four stages. Market analysis and market research are the two major supporting tools of marketing strategies and communication is the essential component in market analysis and market research.

Market research team is involved at all the four stages of marketing. It plays significant role in identifying the market segments, targeted audience, and important information and facts about them at all the four stages. The information that is required to address issues, analyzing results and communicating the findings and their implications to top-management and other management levels of marketing. The systematic analysis and reporting of objective data facilitate marketing decisions.

Two broad market research activities are involved: identifying market segments i.e. market analysis; identifying customers and consumers — planning their profiles.

When the product is in the market. Market research team assess consumers' reactions — acceptance or rejection consequent to their buying and using the product. The feedback is direct from the consumers in general and consumer focus groups, and from retailers. Interpersonal communication is used and technology of video miners, shop tracking is used to get consumer reactions. Secondary data is used to prepare consumer demographics. Interpersonal communication and participatory observation helps them in preparing consumer demographics.

Feedback from supply chain is about the feasibility of the market segments and the consumer demand preferences. Group discussions, demonstrations and presentations are given for industrial/business product prototype to the customer group, — involved in the decision-making process. The targeted consumer audience using it is pitched through product promotions, product sample demonstrations and displays, different channels of advertisements, and campaigns etc.

The information and facts about markets and customers/ consumers are communicated to the top-management and at the various levels of marketing management by the marketing team through interpersonal communications. Interface communication between the two management groups (the buyer and the supplier) in the case of industry/business products facilitates in deciding about the viability of the product, pricing policies, time period, supply chain and further marketing strategies.

Products are combination of tangible and non-tangibles differentiated by design, size, color, options, status, taste, rank, achievements and aspirations. These are integral part of the uniqueness of the product. Corporate train, supervise and motivate their dealers and personnel to suggest these and uniqueness of the product by differentiating distinctions by which buyers may be influenced. Market participation, Product augmentation, and segmented markets are some of these areas.

For *market participation*, a product has to be a cluster of value satisfactions, characteristics of the expected components of the products, delivery, terms, and support efforts — purchasers may expect special applications' advice and support, and suppliers' ideas and suggestions for most efficient and cost reducing ways of using the product in various ways and in intended forms.

Product augmentation programs expand the market by advice and training programs. The corporate augments the programs by giving more information about use, patterns, handling problems, costs and other helpful aids.

Strategies for Effective Positioning, Branding, and Launch: Developing a better product is no longer enough to spur sales in a still-cautious marketplace. Reaching today's value-conscious customers requires crystal-clear product positioning, meaningful branding, and carefully timed launch strategies.

Positioning product is a strategic tool and touchstone. Check when the organization is ready to position its product. Product positioning is made simple by defining organization's space in the marketplace. Time is important for matching positioning elements to the state of the market. The product position can be extended through product line and platform positioning. It should plan for brand positioning—more than product positioning. Marketers have options for competitive positioning and choose strategies of competitive differentiation and the incremental differentiation trap. Signs of ineffective positioning reflect in perceptions, reality and the customer mind. The marketers should see the problem and their product from the customer's eyes. Can marketers position the company?

Market infrastructure communications focus on developing and managing the infrastructure-marketing plan. The market infrastructure is critical to positioning and communications. The influence-reference model for market communications facilitates in positioning the product. Building a complete message 'architecture', messaging and communicating about the position and brand is important. The Internet is changing the traditional market influence model using the 'megaphone effect' to amplify communications.

New product development and launching: The successful development and launching of the "right" product or service can be the difference between your company's continued success and growth, and its decline and failure. The path is particularly hazardous today with increased financial pressures and global market considerations. As always, you must develop the right product or service for your market, get it right the first time, and do it on time and within budget.

Typical causes of failure are: developing the wrong product or service. It is inadequate for market requirements. It is outpaced by technology and/or competition. The company has missed the right opportunity for the product. There is inadequate planning and control of the development process. The cost overruns. The product or service is overpriced. There are schedule delays. There are performance issues such as product doesn't meet requirements, the service doesn't meet expectations.

The requirements for the successful development and introduction of a new product or a new service are the same. You must decide exactly what you want to provide, how you will assure that it is what your customer wants and will buy, and how you will track it during the development and introduction process. There is no room for launch mistakes. With today's short runways, choosing the wrong early customers or premature launch timing can be expensive and often fatal. To build long-term mainstream market acceptance, post-launch strategy is as important as pre-launch market conditioning.

Launch planning: Why a product launch is so important? Launch readiness tests are the basics many companies overlook. The sequence and timing of launch are important to make the launch last. Different companies follow different launch strategies and styles. Post-launch period is as critical as pre-launch for product visibility in the market and acceptance by the consumers. There is Pre-launch preparation, Launch events, and Post-launch measurements and feedback.

The Pre-launch internal preparations starts with the launch team setting launch objectives, strategies and metrics within the context of the overall business strategy, brand image and specific project goals. For external preparation focus is about product positioning strategies, product demonstration, product training of sales persons, service persons, channel partners and employees.

During launch activities the focus is on product introduction and visibility through public relations with press and product analysts, trade shows, introduction advertisements, other events such as conferences, seminars, audio conferences, road shows, partner events, customer/user groups events etc. There are introductory market campaigns with the consumers and channel partners using direct mails, emails etc.

Post-launch stage is measurements and feedback through contacts made with the targeted press and analysts, articles placed in targeted publications, writing and speaking engagements, creating awareness about company and products through market research. The leads are obtained through trade shows and new product sales feedback and customer feedback.

Business organization functions in dynamic environment of marketing. And nothing can be more dynamic than changing consumer profiles, attitudes and behavior. Thus the core of marketing is identifying and understanding the customers. And critical to this intelligence is the ability to update the information in tune with the dynamism of the market environment. Given the individuality of each consumer, the task of gathering customer data and analyzing the same becomes even more difficult. This lack of knowledge remains a big handicap for marketers in not so sophisticated markets in many developing countries, resulting in subjective decision making and higher hit and miss initiatives. It is increasingly being recognized that cross-unit working relationships have a key role to play in the successful implementation of marketing decisions.

Market Analysis

Analysis of markets for its products and services through market research provides objective data to facilitate marketing decision. Various marketing research techniques such as Analytical marketing, Mass media advertising, Focused marketing, Measuring performance and other variations in marketing techniques provide critical insights into markets necessary for marketing decisions.

Analytical marketing: Today, the new revolution hitting marketing is analytics. The science of analytics has now entered the domain of marketing to provide that critical insight required by marketers to take better decisions. Using data mining theories based on varied sciences like statistics, artificial intelligence and psychology, and with analytic tools one can mine through terabytes of customer data and generate various business intelligence reports — customer profitability, cross sell propensity, attrition probabilities, and customer life time value and coupled with the use of alternate channels (telephone, Internet, email, SMS, direct mail).

Analytical marketing creates a platform for the marketer to precisely identify his prospect (client), understand prospect's behavior and pitch a product or service to customize his requirements, thereby increasing success rates as well as optimizing marketing budgets. Across the world, the average contribution of analytical marketing is almost 50 per cent. The role of traditional mass media advertising is restricted to creating and maintaining brand awareness as well as working on the more subjective elements of creating brand equity. Analytical marketing provides marketers the critical infrastructure that can result in significant return on marketing investment. Related to the problem of databases is the flow of information i.e. information loops. It is critical to have a centralized customer database system. This therefore requires a complete information loop where all data captured at various points get routed back into the common storage point. For example, after a particular campaign, the responses and feedback captured through various channels like a call center, website or branch offices should be routed back to the central marketing campaign management team and the database updated. In future, one does not have to reinvent the wheel by calling for reports from every station. Finally and most importantly, the entire management should be completely focused and oriented towards a successful implementation.

In India, many large consumer services companies have adopted analytical marketing or are in the process of evaluating it. There are still issues regarding awareness, learning and skill sets required to extract the full value out of this solution. But any organization which is well versed in the fundamentals of marketing both in theory and practice will find it extremely easy to take that one more step in becoming a mature and more efficient marketer. And from a consumer point of view, there is huge benefit. It means only focused marketing communication - communication that is relevant. Consumers will be spared from the ordeal of facing a deluge of spam and large-scale ad bursts.

Focused Marketing: The focus of marketing is gradually moving from customer acquisition to building lifelong relationships with customers. The old marketing adage of "existing customers being more rewarding than acquiring new customers" cannot be more apt in this age of competition. With high scale commoditization of products and services, it becomes very easy for consumers to switch across brands. In the mobile telecom sector, we have consistently experienced large-scale consumer shifts from one service provider to another, usually triggered by lower tariff plans and various freebies. Acquiring a customer is no longer the end of the marketing process. Managing and maintaining customer's relationship with the service provider is as important. This is particularly critical in verticals where revenues and profits per customer are realized over a period of time - credit cards, post-paid mobile services, after sales automobile services, etc. Thus marketing needs to focus on customer lifecycle management. The lifecycle of a customer can be broadly classified into four stages:

Pre-purchase Decision: From a marketer's perspective, this is the acquisition process where a prospect is serviced with relevant information and messages to influence a purchase decision in the favor of the service provider.

Purchase Transaction: This is the actual transaction where the prospect buys or signs up for the product or the service. This transaction would involve integration of the front office resources with back office fulfillment infrastructure.

Post purchase activation: For most products like post-paid mobile phones, credit cards, software services, etc., the first instance of usage indicates the activation of the consumer's account. This phase can be critical for marketers in cases where free offers are made e.g. a free add-on SIM card or a complementary club membership. Marketer would need to present some kind of a reminder or an incentive to the consumer to use the product.

Post purchase cross-sell: As the consumer starts using the product, his/her requirements may grow and this would trigger additional features or an upgrade to a higher product e.g. a college student who currently uses a pre-paid card may want to migrate to a post-paid plan or a pre-paid card with a higher denomination once he/she starts working. The marketer is guided with relevant strategies and tactics to execute from acquisition to cross sell.

Measuring Marketing Performance. Marketers want to know the actual ROI. They want to know it often, not annually, to plan campaign strategies on likely return. Marketing is taken as investment rather than cost or expense. They say glossy ads at TV are costing more and consumers of all ages are spending more time at videogames or surfing the Internet. Companies are shifting their ads from TV to print, Internet and direct marketing.

Companies in every segment of American businesses are obsessed with honing the science of measuring marketing performance. One way is to link statistics to different forms of marketing to sales and brand awareness. The latest is the *marketing dashboard technique* — to construct a comprehensive set of performance measures. Xerox Corp uses the measurement *techniques of Six Sigma* to analyze marketing impact on a range of measures from leads generated to cost per sale. Home Depot Inc has a proprietary computer model with sophisticated algorithms that correlate marketing investments with product sales and regional variations that have let the retailer, for example, push the ad 'paint using' the radio spot in some markets and newspaper inserts in others. Measuring marketing ROI in retailing is the most difficult thing. By *customer tracking technique*, the big carmakers have halved their ad expense while increasing sales, market share, and awareness. Still they have to be on TV to launch new models and blitz airwaves giving new rebate deal. But the budget going to TV ad spending is steadily declining. Yet the impact of image building by TV and prints ads as opposed to those pitching rebates is only educated guess.

A joint venture between the marketing and media research firm Arbitron Inc and VNU Dutch media company through 'project Apollo' next year in 2005 will track the media habits of 30000 household representing 70000 consumers. The 'panelists' will wear a pager like device that picks up all the electronically codes of TV and radio programs that they consume. That data plus online usage and grocery purchases scanned in half the households, and frequent and lifestyle choices should help marketers figure out which of their marketing tactics really pay (2004). Because advertisers work with multiple ad agencies there is push to establish benchmarks and standards for measuring ROI.

There is effort to bring science to measuring marketing performance still the art component will never go away. Figuring out how much of product appeal is due to marketing and how much stems from innovative features or quality is hard to pin down even by the individual consumers. They do not know why they like it, they just do it and that is the *human factor*.

Various Marketing Techniques: Marketing professionals, by nature, have to be innovative. Over the years, many new innovations have been introduced. When advertising became too expensive, multi-level marketing has been extended in the Internet age through variations like viral marketing; member-get-member (MGM) programs and affiliate marketing. Direct marketing, public relations, telemarketing, web marketing and now SMS marketing have taken advantage of new technology to serve the need of the marketer. Most of the bigger advertising agencies today have more business coming from non-traditional advertising services than through mass media advertising. We have discussed Web marketing in e-commerce and online advertising sections. We will discuss telemarketing since it is widely used and abused marketing techniques raising business and consumers concerns.

Direct marketing or 'Relationship Marketing' happens as a result of several factors. The consumer has come to expect continued satisfaction from the product/service. They have choices in today's competitive world and know they can exercise those choices. Hence, satisfaction is based on not just product superiority, but also on process benefits (how the transaction between buyer and seller is simpler, cheaper and more satisfying) and relationship benefits (how am I rewarding my customer for their loyalty). To be able to deliver these benefits, direct marketing today relies heavily on technology as an enabler for customer knowledge, process implementation and delivery. For direct marketing to become more robust, relevant and vital, there are several issues which need addressing.

In India, direct marketing has been growing exponentially and is a critical part of any product/or services marketing mix. But it is still not an organized industry and is plagued by the fact that there is no control over the quality of players entering this industry.

Permission-based marketing will be the single most important business tool for the new media. Interactive new media will bring one-on-one marketing opportunities based on video communications over broadband and interactive digital TV networks. It is important to realize that the users are at the centre of this concept; they are in control of the messages they want to receive.

Telemarketing is a form of direct marketing where a salesperson uses the telephone to solicit prospective customers to sell products or services. The prospective customers are identified and qualified by various means, including past purchase histories, previous requests for information, credit limit, competition entry forms or application forms.

Names are also purchased from another company's customer database, or obtained from a telephone directory or some other public list or forum. The qualification process is intended to find those prospective customers most likely to purchase the product or service being sold or advertised. Apart from commercial entities, charitable organizations, alumni associations and political parties often use telemarketing to solicit donations.

Telemarketing needs to be regulated. It is often criticized as being an unethical business practice as some companies do make unsolicited calls and often engage in high-pressure sales techniques. These practices may be subject to regulatory or legislative controls related to consumer privacy and protection. Telemarketing is restricted in the US by the Telephone Consumer Protection Act of 1991. Some jurisdictions have implemented "Do Not Call" listings, either through industry organizations or legislation, in which consumers can indicate that they do not wish to be called by telemarketers. The US Federal Trade Commission has now implemented a National 'Do Not Call'

Registry in an attempt to reduce intrusive telemarketing on a national basis.

In India marketing companies are increasingly using subscribers' data and calling people to sell their products. More than 70% of such calls made are for selling credit cards. Currently, there is no legislation that protects the privacy of telephone subscribers. Telemarketing has come under the Supreme Court (SC) scanner. The SC has directed the government to formulate laws restricting the misuse of the mobile phone networks for marketing purpose.

Telemarketing is in news in India currently. The Supreme Court issued notices to the Centre and all cellular operators and multinational banks, on a public interest litigation, seeking a law to ban "uncalled for" calls. Cellular operators are also in support of a total ban on marketing calls and want legislation on it. The PIL contended that this as an invasion of privacy and a violation of the right to live a peaceful life. The unsolicited calls for a loan, card or even a new telephone connection amounted to an "endemic invasion of privacy of the subscribers of mobile telephony at all times and hours" and seriously impaired the fundamental rights of citizens (2004-05).

Market Research

Market research is multifaceted aspect of marketing. Therefore, we define it from multi-angles. Broadly speaking, it is the process of specifying information required to address issues, designing the methods for collecting information, managing and implementing data collection, analyzing results and communicating the findings and their implications. The systematic collection and analysis, and reporting of objective data facilitate marketing decisions. Market research techniques facilitate the process of planning, collecting, and analyzing data relevant to marketing decision-making by using a combination of primary and secondary research tools to understand the situation better.

It is an effort by business to find useful information that describes the relationship between consumer, products, marketing methods, and marketers through experiments, information search, and processing. Further, to get information about the business's customers, competitors, or markets. Information may be from secondary sources (already published and publicly available) or primary sources (from customers themselves). Market research may be qualitative or quantitative in nature. Qualitative research, which sometimes precedes quantitative research, defines the themes or problem areas surrounding the subject being researched. Accurate information can be formulated for quantitative research. One of the characteristics of high-tech product marketing is the lack of historical data due to the product's short life cycle and innovative quality. Also, a quantitative analysis often involves working with product data that are going to be replaced (classic TVs with HDTV's, cassette recorders by compact disk players, and telephones by videotext computers). Therefore, quantitative analysis techniques used for high-tech products must always be dealt with carefully.

The collection of data by a business about the preferences, purchasing powers of consumers groups, segmented markets, psychographics and demographics, and business competition helps in taking decisions about projecting a market and launching a product or service on the market.

Requisite market data collected facilitates (i) various market research activities and for taking decisions about projecting a market, products, and services, (ii) launch new products and services, (iii) improve value for existing products and markets, (iv) initial surveys of the geo areas for market and product projections, (v) for improving project performance, (vi) assess capabilities within the market, (vii) for marketing strategy and business strategy, market profiling, ad testing, and brand research, and (viii) consumer research applications.

Market research do initial surveys of the geo areas in which a product or service is to be offered. These are done to determine the cost of doing business, any competition, potential sales, etc., assessment of the participants in that geo market to find out about the competition and market trends. It can give a technical analysis of factors such as volume, price trends, and market breadth that is used to predict price movement. Further, through market research information about capabilities within the market can be collected and analyzed. Secondly, business conduct market research of the changing demands or needs of consumers in relation to particular goods or services (of the business) i.e. already in the market either to boost the brand or club the brands, or phase out some of the losing brands.

Thirdly, it is a technique for improving project performance by surveying the industry. For example, by researching published data on the construction industry, it may be possible to schedule the construction of a project at a time when tenders will be more competitive. Market research may also reveal new or more economic materials, systems and methods for incorporation in the scope of work. Fourthly, it is applied consumer research designed to provide management with information on factors that affect consumers' acquisition, consumption and disposition of products, services and ideas.

Specialists in Market Research provide experienced data collection via focus groups, consumer panels, and surveys (consumer intercept, telephone, mystery customer and online Web surveys) for marketing strategy, business strategy, communication strategy, market profiling, ad testing, and brand research.

Companies identify their consumers and segmented markets through market analysis and research. This data they use for product development. Further, they use marketing strategies to sell the products and services to the consumers. Communication strategies and plans are important for market analysis and research which are key for creating the consumer and markets for them.

Marketing research department of any corporate will function on a derived demand from its marketing people when they encounter issues about the products and services of the corporate. These could be: when the company wants to identify new market segments and project new products and services there. When the company wants to launch new products and services in the market segments already being serviced by them. When there is plateau in their markets and products, and they want to research the problems and increase their brand value. When they want to build their brands. When marketers and management want information in general about market segments and products and services, consumer profiles in general, trends and competition.

The objective is that they provide meaningful inputs to the company's plans and have right bearing on the practical issues. The market research should make substantive contribution to company's profits. There are four major contributions that market research can make towards making marketing decisions: (i) systematic description and classification of marketing facts, (ii) substantive hypothesis that can be used to make predictions, (iii) logical and technological tools for classifying the variables, (iv) to solve the problematic issues and in the process find alternatives. These have to be practical issues.

Top management needs market research in order to improve ROI to the company. There are certain forces that play important role and have impact on the top-management decision-making. These are: explosion of information and information processing, increasing complexity of business, intense competition, expanding technology and advances, collapsing product life-cycle, inflationary trends, increasing R&D and capital costs, overall economic, financial, political and social uncertainties and multi-level management and high cost of making poor decisions.

In this backdrop there is need and opportunity for market research to play an expanded role in top-management decision-making through flow of information to top management. There are obstacles in the effective use of market research information for management decision-making and optimum results can be achieved by improving market researchers and top-management interface.

Top-management should be objective in making market research requests and set up responsibility and limitations, communicate regularly, support organizationally, budget it realistically and focus on research programs with high profit potential. The market research group should emphasize, pace, and style communications to top-management needs and opportunities. It should reflect top-management point-of-view otherwise it becomes ineffective and under-utilized and under-rewarded.

Marketing a Brand – Building Brand Value

Consumer creation, acquisition, and retention are important for building brands. Businesses create consumers for their products and services through their own innovative ideas and consumer driven demands and ideas. The focus is on consumer preferences for products and services, consumer market reach and consumer satisfaction. They build brand identity and value, and brand loyalty through various communication strategies to retain the consumer. These communication strategies help to understand how branding extends and leverages the product and company positioning to build brand equity. How branding extends beyond product life cycles and builds brand equity. The focus should be on moving from short-term product branding to enduring corporate brands, and to brand the experience, not just the product. Brand positioning is more important than product positioning in the market. Customer-managed brand experience through Internet may be different. Mergers and acquisitions (M&A) of business consolidation complicate branding. It does presents major repositioning and branding challenges when the merged businesses try to establish new identities, and either leverage or distance from past associations.

The value of technology branding and positioning is more critical today than ever before. Few questions are posed: why high-tech branding is important in both rapidly changing and maturing markets? How business-to-business and industrial technology marketing are different from traditional consumer mass marketing? What is the value of leadership positioning in technology markets?

Taking Technology Products to Market: Technology companies have survived the downturn and now are seeking opportunities for growth in a rebounding economy. Companies can no longer sit on the sidelines as their competitors fortify their positions and as challengers grab first-mover advantages in new markets. The rules of technology marketing are changing. The customer is becoming pragmatic. Dotcom euphoria and downturn pessimism have been replaced by a new era of pragmatism. Bad experiences with the 'next big thing' have turned many early adopting customers more conservative. The economic buyer now reigns over the technical buyer.

Marketing a brand and building brand value in Indian market is a case in example. India in 2004 is a very different country from what it was in 1994. Further, it is certain that the India of 2014 will again be very different from what it is today. Some facts stand out that can give some insight on what is happening in the Indian market today, and some learning emerges from the same. There are several changes that have been taking place in the last two decades, the impact of which is being partially felt today. The full impact of these subterranean changes will unfold in the coming years, and at that time, many marketing and branding paradigms would have had to be rewritten.

The most important change in India has been the demographic one. It is a nation with a very young population. These young consumers' mind space is currently a blank canvas, and almost every company has a chance to make an impression on this canvas. Brands and companies that have relied on the continuity factor (some of Hindustan Lever brands and strategies will certainly fall in that genre) have found, to their dismay, a surprising disconnect between the buying behavior of their older customers and the potential new consumers.

These young consumers are born in times of increasing consumerism, in an environment where each day, they are offered more choices of product and service categories on which they can spend money, and newer options within each product and service category. Whichever company or brand offers a better (perceived or real) price-benefit value proposition gets the share of customers' mind and wallet. The market surveys show that young consumers are shifting brands very quickly and there is no brand loyalty. Businesses have to rethink fast to create, recycle products and services to keep pace with shifting brands since young consumers are huge potential market.

Marketers spend huge resources on several kinds of communication strategies. There has been a great deal of proliferation of brands in almost every product category. Each category consists of brands new to the category: successful brands, which have sustained their success for a length of time and continue to be successful; and brands which have been very successful in the past and are struggling to revive their success. Certain interesting questions are raised in context to communication strategies: (a) should brand communication strategies be different for abovementioned different categories of brands? (b) what factors are to be taken into consideration before formulating the communication objectives for brands in each of the categories? (c) how should the communication be combined with promotional methods to achieve the objectives of communication?

A structured approach towards communication objectives provides a focus and it also enables marketers to take into account several changing factors in the environment relevant to the respective marketing situations. The communication objectives may change from time to time. The objective of a new brand (relatively) like Himalaya in the category of cosmetics and over the counter (OTC) drugs may be to create awareness and initiate trials before building conviction around its brand values. The objective of brands like Pond's or Fair & Lovely, which have a huge base of consumers, may be to emphasize the conviction that the consumers may have shown over the years by buying the brand. This may perhaps be achieved by ensuring that consumers try out the new herbal variant of the brand. It may be observed in this hypothetical situation considered, the brand not only has to emphasize the brand value to make the conviction stronger; it has to also ensure that at least a cross-section of consumers so convinced would try the new herbal variant in an environment which is largely shifting towards herbal formulation with regard to the product category.

In FMCG product categories of food with which consumers have been familiar for several decades, value is the criteria on which consumers perceive a branded offering. Value in a category like this is not just lower price; it is also a taste that matches with the palate of consumers in a specific geographical region. The brand may not spend heavily on advertising but it does launch *sales promotional schemes*, which MNC brands resort to frequently. This ensures that there is "an over-all' value perception associated with the brand. A new brand in any category has to provide a differentiation, which would appeal to consumers at that point of time. This varies from one category to another.

A product campaign conveys the brand benefits through *appropriate imagery*. For example, the consumers all along have perceived herbal to be good for the skin in the category of soaps, there is a need for an established brand to communicate the benefits through appropriate visuals and imagery because a number of brands have been launched in the category. This is the response of an established brand to the strategies of new brands, which have entered the market. Ayush a brand from Hindustan Lever in India uses the expert endorsement route (accreditation from a well known ayurvedic hospital) and another brand uses the "enhanced ingredients mix" route to appeal to consumers. An established brand, apart from formulating strategies to improve its market position is, also forced by new brands, to time its communication strategies and objectives.

In such context, the *frequency of advertising* also becomes important for the established brand because visibility has to be maintained to reduce the number of existing consumers trying out new brands (or to reduce the frequency of purchases concerning new brands). This is a vital objective because the loyalty of existing consumers is based on experience and a brand cannot afford to lose the trust and goodwill among the loyal consumers (in a category like soaps in which consumers tend to try different brands despite exhibiting loyalty towards a specific brand).

In FMCG categories, a strong 'product based' differentiation (in the herbal soaps sub-category, the differentiation centered around 'amplifying' or enhancing the benefits) can achieve positive results within a short span of time. Such a differentiation also backs up the communication objective of ensuring trials among a competitor's brand besides bringing in new category users who would want to try out the new brand.

There should be synergy between product-line management, changes in the needs of consumers and appropriate positioning strategies reflected through advertising imagery. The development of the product associations over a period of time and the varied offerings to diverse segments with a clear cut positioning strategy sustains the market share of the brand.

Sometimes sales promotions aspects are not very pronounced for well-established brands and are limited to ensure that consumers do not "rush" towards the brand only when a sales promotion is announced. Products may have *sales promotion contest,* which reinforces its brand values. The contest involves matching statements on why different types of consumers preferred the brand. Besides the thrill of the contest, this kind of sales promotion also is helpful in reassuring the consumers about their choice of the brand and this could prevent consumers from switching over to a competing brand. Some brands make an attempt to adapt to the changing environment by introducing appropriate product line, pricing and branding strategies, which have been instrumental in sustaining their success with the entry of other brands both in the organized and unorganized sectors.

There are brands (some of them being pioneers in the respective category), which have not been able to sustain their success or the stranglehold they may have had over the market in the yesteryears. There may be complexities, which go beyond marketing mix elements but from the viewpoint of marketing, these elements have not been timed to capture the changes in the market forces. The equity built up by brands must be sustained *through a continuous process of marketing planning, by closely monitoring consumer behavior, trends and competitive strategies.*

Have you wondered why so many iconic brands of yesteryears are falling even as relatively newer brands are capturing the imagination of the consumers and share of the market? This is happening because the old and established brands are moving away from old and established marketing basics. Changing consumer behavior and its implications on marketing communications supports this. Customer relationship management is important from the point of customer satisfaction and on the importance of human interaction in managing customer relationships.

It is increasingly being recognized that cross-unit working relationships have a key role to play in the successful implementation of marketing decisions. Brand owners or creators have to invest more time, effort and money in trying to forecast impending changes in consumer behavior and expectation.

But the brand by itself does not automatically usher in customer loyalty or strengthen customer relations. That is a human interface, and it embodies courtesy and fairness; it also embodies timely actions in terms of meeting customer needs. It strives at all times for customer loyalty, rather than mere customer satisfaction.

A certain Kinetic Honda came around with electric start and gearless driving. It looked feminine. Kinetic Honda was a huge success. An Activa rode in with nicer looks, good power, better brakes, and decent fuel efficiency. Activa became a runaway success without so much of bragging and boasting by Honda. These were mere happy coincidences on a long road littered with products born to insensitive design and brought to customers by arrogant marketing.

Targeting Segmented Markets

Building a brand for products through women: An advertisement or a hoarding showing a girl riding a scooter with her boyfriend on back seat is not enough. It is not enough to be politically correct about women. Your products should cater to what women need. Your services should take into account their pressures, sensitivities, and vulnerabilities. Your communications need to be sensitive to them. If these are short-term differentiation tactics they might increase sales temporarily but will not help in building a brand.

Your services need to reassure a woman that you will be around in a predictable way when she needs help. If she needs her washing machine repaired, assure her that the mechanic would not just be courteous, but that he would come home at her convenience with tools and cleaning cloth. Assure her that he would leave only after he clears the mess. This is a basic expectation. Women simply care more for these things than men do. If she tries your spices and the dish doesn't taste quite the way she expected, she will be relieved if she can talk to someone. If she talks to her friends negatively, that may be bad word of mouth publicity for your spices. If she gives feedback to you, she may try the product again, if only she can speak what is on her mind and be understood.

In absence of alternatives women have to use products that are not designed for them. Women crave to look good. They wish to be independent and mobile. They wish they could do without help from men. They wish to be themselves. Few manufacturers care. There are many more examples — a ketchup bottle with a crown cap which needs a man to open, a tin with tough metal seal that requires a hacksaw for cutting, a sachet of shampoo that requires a pair of scissors, a coconut oil bottle that drips with oil despite all the fancy packaging, a cell phone requiring complex menu navigating abilities and that comes with complicated telephone bills, cars with awfully low roofs requiring crawling to get inside, and movie theaters where women can not walk between two rows without feeling embarrassed.

Women no doubt can manage all the above creations by men and they do it with minimum fuss. But you would earn their gratitude and loyalty if you free them from such man-made mess. They will enthusiastically recommend your products to many other equally enthusiastic women. Women constitute about half of the market. If you consider their influence in buying decisions, you will realize that they control much more than half the market.

"Savvy" marketers know this, but only by half. They create and support women-oriented TV soaps and movies. Builders sell houses to women. IBM sells laptops to them. Some companies sell air-conditioners to them and some sell cars.

Let's see if well-known brands do all this. Lakme's Fruit Shock makeup for lips, nails, eyes or skin is said to contain do-good fruit extracts. Its recent print ad is clearly about energy and individuality. Women who look stunning in their fruity, juicy makeup convey this message. Every woman would like to get attention. Looking young is her eternal desire. The energy and individuality of Lakme women set up a desire in her to be like them. The products themselves occupy a small but inviting position in the print ad. Any woman will linger at the ad page and will imagine her wearing the Fruit Shock makeup. But she may not be familiar with all aspects of make up and beauty treatment.

That's why, since the year 2000 Lakme has been setting up Lakme Beauty Salons through franchisee route. Lakme now has about 70 salons in 26 cities across the country. Lakme Beauty Salons provide professional beauty services. The salons not only make good business sense but they nicely strengthen the brand by completing customer contact and experience. Lakme India Fashion Week provides the top tier of the brand communication structure.

We have seen examples of what are known to be women's products. But why haven't companies created and marketed products for women in other categories where there is tremendous scope? Take the case of holiday packages.

Women simply do not have enough opportunities to follow their natural behavior, because most products and services do not recognize their needs. What do women need? If your products, services, and communications combine to make a woman feel beautiful, you have a great opportunity to build enduring brand in her mind. You should enhance her self-image. Women feel beautiful in many ways. It takes earnestness and consistency throughout product cycles to nurture and enhance their self-image. It takes intensity to win their hearts.

Building Brand through iGen consumers: The Times, London conducted a survey of the attitudes of the iGeneration and concluded, "In time, the outlook of the twenty-somethings will come to dominate the social mainstream. It is well worth assessing their thinking and reckless to ignore it" (1999). Along with almost utopian concepts like the 'paper-less office', Bill Gates had talked about Generation-i in 1999, while outlining Microsoft's commitment to youth and learning, but now it has become a reality the world over.

In a nation like India, where half the population is aged below 25 years, marketers are suddenly finding that they can't find the pulse on a whole set of prospective and affluent customers, often dismissing them as 'fickle-minded'. However, those who see some method in the madness among this heterogeneous demography are discovering a gold mine.

Aged somewhere between 16 and 28, in India, this generation is a product of an incredible sociological change wrought by 15 years of liberalization. They have matured in an era where choice of brands had replaced scarcity; and technology is changing everyday life. It's a generation to which the Internet is as ubiquitous as the television was to the one that preceded it. This group — the iGen, is disproportionately important to marketers.

Not just conceptually, but also in terms of the increasing purchasing power, this group needs to be targeted. It is not just about recognizing the iGen today; rather there is a need to actively engage them. As a consumer segment, they have never been so critical ever before. With a generation that is already earning more than their parents, the concentration of purchasing power is opening product categories, which were alien to youth in the yesteryears.

Housing loans, equity investment products, digital cameras, gadgets — marketers are seeing a new category of customers lining up. Kotak Mahindra Bank finds a third of its account holders in Bangalore and half of its car-loan customers nation-wide to be below 30. Just eight years back the average age for car loan customer hovered around 38-40 years. Sony finds 80% of its portable music system buyers below 28 years, and the segment itself is growing at four digits rates annually. And almost all its camcorder buyers are of below 30 years. Reebok estimates that per capita consumption of footwear is three, up from 1.2 two years back. It's similar for almost all categories as companies churn out newer and fresh models to keep the younger generation hooked. iGen has a monstrous appetite for the new and that makes it impatient. Not only they are crazy and eager about anything new but also rather it is impossible to sustain their attention, which in turn threatens much sought after brand loyalty. Retail consultancy, KSA Technopak calls them 'Impatient Aspirers'. It's just that compared with their parents, they have had to deal with sex, drugs and debt, way too sooner.

The tipping point or the age at which a dependent consumer turns into the purchaser has come down dramatically. It is an urge to earn more and splurge further. Work hard, party harder is the mantra and there is far less aversion to credit and this age group doesn't mind consuming things today and pay tomorrow. Bankers are, however, finding a hard-working and financially savvy generation, confounding the traditional prejudices about its money management skills.

In terms of the four Ps of marketing — the stakeholders need to think of the design element in the product. Young people *prima facie* are rejecting anything that isn't contemporary. In terms of price, this age group is exceedingly value conscious. They tend to seek price bargains out of basic necessities and prefer to splurge as far as hedonistic expression is concerned. They would spend on a car straight away, rather than on a two-wheeler, but would try and be extremely careful about the price they pay for groceries and other things. In terms of place, they are moving to malls and new retail formats and rejecting the traditional provision stores. Manufacturers have to be prepared for the revolution that has already begun.

This age group also tends to switch brands and upgrade to keep abreast with their changing lifestyle. They are conscious about what their peers possess and don't want to be left behind. They have traditionally replaced outdated products but do so at a faster pace than ever before. In fact, their minds are already made up, thanks to the extensive net searches they run before they zero in on a product. Credit cards are fast catching up as the preferred mode of payment amongst this group, but hard cash still reigns supreme.

Consequently, in the emerging scenario of iGen mindset gaining ground, the structure of the market will witness a change. It will fragment further. Probably because of the exposure of Indian people to the US markets, through travels, movies, etc they identify more with the fashion sense of that market, rather than that of Europe and Japan. While in terms of fashion, Europe and Japan are considered very cutting edge markets and US is a more middle-of-road. Still young Indians are tuning in more towards American trends. Some years ago, fashion designers have to think of adapting the fashions to think in the Indian context, before bringing in any international fashion trend. But that is not needed any more.

Companies utilize other innovative ways to build brands. Many products spring from slick marketing campaigns. A few brands are however created in the lab. When analyzing the success and failure of brands in the fickle and super-competitive realm of consumer products, the experts tend to focus on tangible factors: instinct, serendipity, timing, luck, and unpredictable ability of an ad campaign to strike a major chord. Marketing gurus may tell you that success of consumer products depends a lot on changing people's tastes and little to do with actual engineering and chemistry. Whereas a leading consumer product company (Proctor & Gamble) has relied for brand building, more on research, development, and technology than on snappy ads to develop market dominating products. It has relied more on constant meaningful product innovation as a primary tool for building and sustaining brands. As a result, consumers can anticipate new and improved versions of products that they have come to know and love. Recently in 2005, it boosted its Tide detergent powder sale by re-innovating the ingredient mix. The detergent has to be utilized only with cold-water wash. It appealed to the energy saving need of the consumer in times of soaring electricity prices.

Cellular companies are constantly talking of new ways to increase their visibility. Now they have started putting up '*signages*' on restaurants too, the erstwhile preserve of the cola giants. Hutchison Max Telecom's cellular services brand Orange has been sponsoring various restaurants across the country. Chief marketing officer, Orange explains: "We have been putting up our signages on restaurants because we feel it's a good place to get brand visibility, apart from the conventional method of branding at shops and other retail stores" (2004).

Sensitizing employees to brands: When you think of marketing, chances are your mind goes right to your customers — how can you persuade more people to buy whatever it is you sell? But there's another "market" that's equally important: your employees. Colin Mitchell (2002) argues that executives by and large ignore this critical internal audience when developing and executing branding campaigns. As a result, employees end up undermining the expectations set by the company's advertising — either because they don't understand what the ads have promised or because they don't believe in the brand and feel disengaged or, worse, hostile toward the company. Mitchell offers three principles for executing internal branding campaigns. First, companies need to market to employees at times when the company is experiencing a fundamental challenge or change. Second, companies must link their internal and external marketing campaigns. And, third, internal branding campaigns should bring the brand alive for employees, creating an emotional connection to the company that transcends any one experience.

Brand Management is an important component in building brands. In 2004, in India, Procter & Gamble slashed detergent prices by 50% overnight. Within a day, competitor HLL responded by doing likewise and unleashed a mega-campaign conceived, executed and released within 48 hours. That means writing a new commercial, approving it, shooting it and buying media space to deliver the finished product. Five years ago, if you had asked any brand manager if that could be done, he/she would have said, "Impossible."

But times have changed in India. We live in a far more competitive world as evinced by a report that research agency AC Nielsen Retail Solutions put out in 2004, which reported that the number of brands in the Indian marketplace has grown by around 50% every year for the last five years. This is just in categories like biscuits, shampoos, skin creams, toothbrushes and toothpastes. Factor in new brands being launched in other categories, and new areas that are exploding — telecom, financial services, durables and more — and then work backwards, and the numbers go off the charts. Add to that a media explosion and as Managing Director, Cadbury puts it: "All brand plans today need a 360 degree component to them."

It is this new reality that has driven marketers to rejig their brand management structures. In their glory days, the brand manager was the final word on everything from promotions and media-related activities, to communication and new ideas. With brands growing bigger, rivals becoming more aggressive and decision-making on media becoming more complex, an increasing number of marketers are faced with the problem of managers who are over stretched. 'How exactly is brand management being practiced today?' For starters, most frontline marketers split the brand managers job into two parts. The ongoing day-to-day responsibilities, which include dealing with media agencies, and tactical strategy and promotions, are handled by one manager, whereas long term strategy and brand development are handled by another.

Lets us look at how Procter & Gamble is handling brand management. The brand development takes place across regional and global levels, while brand building happens locally. At P&G each product has a domestic brand manager, as well as a regional brand manager, who routinely exchange information to pick common trends, share key learning, and apply them wherever necessary. It allows to accommodate changes in a market, while also getting benefits of scale, and a chance to apply learning across regions.

Cadbury India has a similar concept but the structuring is slightly different. The innovations are largely the responsibility of a team that is spearheaded by the company's innovation manager. He works with a team of 'insight managers', each of them tracks specific consumer segments and passes these on to brand managers for further exploration. The brand managers are largely working on products that are grouped according to consumer segments.

Hindustan Lever (HLL) has two divisions, called brand building (formerly brand activation) and brand development (formerly brand innovation). Brand development is across regional and global levels and helps manage strategy and equity consistently and coherently. Brand building is local in nature — it's consistent with brand equity but given its very specific task of delivering a brand to a consumer, it happens at a local level.

Besides bifurcation, the other major change is that marketers have been working hard to make brand management more inclusive. No longer is it the exclusive domain of the marketing function and increasingly people from other disciplines are being co-opted.

Making it the responsibility of a single person narrows the window. Company has to train people across various functions in these skills. The training program is held for everyone brand marketing teams, the brand developing teams, brand manager, R&D and sales.

It's something that Cadbury echoes that the insights group is composed of people of diverse functional backgrounds and not merely marketing. Every employee in the organization could have a role to play in the brand development process and has instituted a policy whereby it is mandatory for every employee to go and meet consumers on one day of the year.

HLL too is working hard on inclusiveness. "We have a brand team of cross-functional members from brand development, building supply chain, commercial, manufacturing — everyone is a part of it. It has one formal brand charter that aligns people to specific goals. All the brand teams have regular interactions with the trade and the customer marketing, and interface with front end sales."

Lastly sales, which was often considered an outsider who had to take what brand management gave it, is now coming to the forefront. Each of sales managers is a brand manager as well. At Cadbury, Sales is no longer about covering outlets alone. Managers have to undertake a number of area specific brand initiatives. No one is a 'pure' brand manager — all teams have spent considerable time in sales.

At HLL also there is an active effort to get contributions from the sales side. There is a larger organizational initiative to make people sensitive to consumers and brands called 'Feel the Pulse' in which the employees spend two months in the market speaking to trade, consumers, and understanding HLL brands.

While many things have changed structurally, one thing that has not changed is the skills required for the job. The skills of the past are still relevant — understanding channels, equity management and shopper's insights. Innate qualities that we'd like in a brand manager is intuition, a lot of curiosity and desire to make a difference to what people do and make their lives better. However, one man can no longer deliver the entire solution. Working with teams across boundaries and regions to pick the best is becoming very important. In the end no matter how much brand management changes, it's only the brands that provide more consumer engaging experiences that will win.

Market Campaigns: In America, these days' government, doctors and people are very concerned about the increasing obesity patterns of its population. Market campaigns are being initiated in different forms. Government through its ads and write ups in the Print media and TV are talking to the Public about nutrition and food pyramid, exercise and weight loss programs. Doctors are supporting the healthy way of life cautioning them against risk of obesity and overweight. Schools are being advised to offer only healthy food for lunch and snack and cut down on portions served. Restaurants are being given advisory on nutrition food served, cut down on use of saturated fat and trans-fat in baking and cut down on portions served. Food companies are given advisory on the same lines and also advised not to advertise such food particularly to children. Kraft company and other companies are restricting their fast food ads for children in the age group 6-11 years (2005).

The vending machines are criticized heavily for fatter Americans — kids and adults. The vending-machines companies are launching an anti-obesity marketing campaign to improve its image and fend off efforts to remove machines from schools. A big part of the effort: color-coded stickers on the vending machine items to separate healthier items from those the hungry snackers should choose rarely.

The software in the machine evaluates the nutrition content of the food based on calories, fat, sugar, protein, fiber, calcium, iron and vitamin A and C. A snack is assigned a point value, which then is translated into a color-code. Green is 'best choice', yellow is 'choose occasionally', and red for 'choose rarely' (2005).

Market campaigns focus on the intensity of issues and take extensive measures to inform and educate the audience, the allied industries, marketers, advertisers and media channels, when the campaigns happen to be in social domain as the above mentioned health issues. These types of campaigns for products and services in social domains are very focused, intense and extensive to achieve the objectives. Here the government and the public concerns are the dominant fields. Government, public channels, business and media channels are used to achieve the objectives. The messages are pro-social.

Market campaigns for business products and services also focus intensely on the market segments and consumers, and channels of communications. The primary motive is profits, return on investments through customer satisfaction and market viability. The messages are pro-consumerism and pro-business operations and functions.

SALES OF PRODUCT AND SERVICES

Sale of product and services is the most important function of any business. Therefore, selling power is essential and crucial for business communication. It is the value added sales appeal and not price that activates decision-making in customer. Sales team helps the customer to articulate 'value mission' necessary to sell ideas to management. It shows buyers to calculate accurate and objective return on investment (ROI).

Effective communications: sales talent: Basics of efficient and effective salesmanship lie in effective communication and developing communication skills to achieve that. Since customer is the focus for any sales transaction small or big; the focus for effective communication is creating strong customer relationship and assessing their experiences. The sales person must create easily understood value propositions for the products and successful customer negotiations for them. It is a must to be familiar with the latest technology that might affect the business and products that he is representing and that of his competitors in general. The process of building strong customer relationships and negotiations helps in creating better business acumen and facilitate market expansion and increased profitability.

Effective sales appeal is persuasive but the major appeal is in creating awareness information, knowledge about the value propositions of their own products and services in the framework of market competition.

Potential business is termed as a *Sales Prospect*. Effective communication with the sales prospect sells. Sales is following the persuasion tips. The initial step is, as a sales person, you must map out what you want to accomplish with the customer. Assess whether your customer has a need and desire for whatever you are selling and propensity to purchase. Try persuasion for the product — by making presentations, sending proposals followed by sending information of interest.

Despite your persuasions, effective communicative sales talks, the customer did not buy. Do not give up. Never write somebody off but find new ways to close the deal. Never walk off without planning a follow-on strategy. Be in constant touch by sending relevant information about the product periodically. The skills set to follow-on prospect and stay connected is: determine objectives for your follow-on calls. Call to move the sale forward. If you can't follow up in person make a phone call, use email, or send a letter. Just make sure that the customer knows you care for the business and give a compelling reason for him or her to get back to you. Deliver important information to your prospect about your product and service so as to justify why they should continue to take your calls. Your follow-on call may not make sale but the goal should be to create friendship, rapport and build trust. Since people's attitudes change, the customer may be ready to buy at another point of time. If you are in touch, you are there when the opportunity comes.

The formula for sales success is to adopt fresh innovative approach to improve sales performance. Sales team must identify areas of improvements based on feedback from the market research and analysis team. They should seek variety of solutions for improving by discussing with the market research and analysis team, peer groups, and senior leaders. Prioritize these areas for sales improvements and maximize sales force ROI.

The sales team must get edge over their competition and increase their market share for the product by being aggressive with their sales leads, data bases, direct marketing services and data base marketing services. What distinguishes top sales achiever from run of the mill is their ability to connect to the customer and stay connected?

The basics of salesmanship are: target presentations to key customers. Use a good lead-in to grab their attention. Identify their needs using open-end questions. Define products and services and relate them to customer's benefits. Anticipate objections and respond to them intelligently. Close with agreed upon action. Follow appropriately.

The two key words are *respect* and *empathy* to connect and stay connected. There are ways and communication skills needed to put these concepts into practice.

The communication skills lie in proper goal setting, and execution of those goals solve many problems for the sales people. Once goals are set, they can translate these to positive actions. They should set major goals for doing on daily, weekly or monthly basis as the task demands, such as: productive prospecting, developing and maintaining close contact with centers of influence and getting lead from every person they sell to. They should focus on getting favorable public relation by speaking to periodic sales group or company meetings. Use telephone, email and personal contact with customers to get referrals for more prospects. They should make adequate face-to-face presentations, be in the field making personal calls or even make cold call. The focus can be on increasing the ratio of sales closings. Analyze each attempt to sell, review and study company' sales training methods to understand better and refresh the sales tactics.

The sales call yields better results when sales people are prepared — knowing their customer, knowing their company, and knowing the value of their product and the competition. It is a must to be familiar with the latest technology that might affect the business and products that they are representing and that of their competitors in general. The positive actions regarding their goals and their sales preparation need communication skills (communication skills are discussed in Chapter 8).

Sales personnel do need peer network to help them to overcome business challenges. As Sales Manager, you want to interact with someone else in the other company who has solved the issue that you are facing, you would like to connect with him/her to exchange ideas and know best practices. You can connect with like-minded professionals from variety of businesses that have worked through similar situations. Lessons learned will enhance knowledge and skills. You want to exchange information, because in today's business market place requires you have rapid access to timely and relevant information. Increasingly, managers and executives demand informative learning channels to maintain and extend their competitive advantage.

Sales personnel can acquire new ideas from colleagues from other industries by attending one of their sales meetings. Many of us attend sales training where we interact with people from our own company or own business. Ask one of your customer or prospect — who you know well, to let you attend their sales meeting as an observer. You will have two advantages. One, you will be surprised how important it makes your customer feel when you want to take the time to be present at their meetings. In most cases they will introduce you to the group and allow you to speak for a few minutes. You can take this opportunity to announce your new promotion or do a minute advertisement. It is a great way to promote message to a group of people and solidify a current relationship or establish a new one. Secondly, you get an opportunity to get new sales ideas, tactics and alternate methods for conducting your own sales dealings.

In today's global economy, sales teams in regional midsize corporations have to compete for business with teams from large national and international corporations. Big firms have massive amount of money for advertising to break into regional markets. Smaller firms struggle to position themselves against these and lack the financial resources to go head-to-head. The solution for this is to keep advertising cost low by buying recycle advertising. These are commercial TV clips that can be sold to regional advertisers. These commercials are developed for national advertisers who never used them and the ads can be easily and quickly customized with your own logo and tagline. These are sold at a low price per geo region otherwise they will be gathering dust.

It is easy to think of your customer as sources for your revenue, but customers often provide important information about how your product is performing in the real world. When a customer-support representative helps a customer fix a problem, that solution becomes an asset and that can be used to help other customers and can be folded into the future releases. Even sometimes, customers may come up with their own solutions to problems, solutions that might have real value for other customers. This effort and value can get wasted if there is no way to manage this information and make it more widely available. The solution is to create a feedback mechanism in your customer support environment. Integrating knowledge services directly into customer-services workflows ensures that service knowledge is available where and when it is needed and is contextually relevant.

To forecast sales of specific products and services, the sales team must know about product history, local economy to assess the market situations in general and about particular market segments, and develop business plan based on the market assessment and applications of the products by customers.

Sales teams through their communication skills facilitate customer relationship, customer support services and advertising for selling products, and manage this information and make it more widely available through data bases, direct marketing services and data base marketing services and through feedback mechanism. Sales teams use persuasive and rational appeals through interpersonal communication both personal and interpersonal. It is two-way between the two links in the sales and circular communication among the various sales-customer links. Therein lies the selling power of the Sales.

Christ Paul (2004) argues that continually finding new sales leads is necessary for sales organizations. A number of new technologies have emerged in recent years to help. There are Internet-based technology solutions that can improve lead generation and help create a more targeted and rewarding selling effort. Social Networks, News Alerts, Virtual Tradeshows and Build a Web site are four Internet technologies for improving lead generation.

Internet Social Networks: One of the most interesting new technologies for generating sales leads is through Internet social networks. The premise of Internet social networks is to build friendship circles based on relationships with others within the network. These circles are often built when one person invites another to join. In this way, theoretically speaking, everyone has some connection to everyone else in the network. For salespeople and marketers the network can be a source of highly qualified business leads. Two sites worth exploring are Linkedin and Ryze. Linkedin has a strong upper-management orientation that may be perfect if you sell products and services to that market. The search feature allows users to narrow potential leads by industry, location and other criteria. But making connections may be a little more difficult than other social networks due to a fairly strict privacy policy. Ryze on the other hand makes it a little easier to get started and see results. However, as with any type of open community site, you are more likely to see overt commercialism and abuse.

News Alerts: In many industries the company is the primary source for providing sales leads to its sales force. These leads arrive from numerous sources such as contacts purchased from commercial databases, call centers inquiries and website requests. However, depending on company policy, most salespeople should not limit leads to only company provided information. Instead, salespeople should seek new information sources including news-aggregating sources found on the Internet. For starters, salespeople may want to look at the news services offered by Google and Yahoo. Both allow users to sign up for service that delivers news to an email account if the news contains keywords selected by the user. Another news collector and a newcomer to the news service game is Topix.net. Topix offers news from over 7,000 sources. Best of all for salespeople, Topix segments the news into more than 100 industries ranging from major industries, such as aerospace, to smaller but fast developing industries such as social networking. The site has a strong leaning toward local news as well with information provided from a large number of local publications. Like Google and Yahoo users can have news alerts emailed, though until Topix allows for better search options such news alerts may results in a huge number of emails.

Virtual Tradeshows: A highly successful form of lead generation is tradeshow selling. Tradeshows offer numerous advantages over individual selling efforts including the ability to reach a large number of targeted buyers in one location. Unfortunately, tradeshows are expensive to manage and attendance by potential buyers has declined sharply as corporations tighten travel budgets due to the recent economic downturn, concerns over terrorist attacks and even contagious disease threats such as SARS. Yet the value tradeshows possess for generating leads has persuaded many companies to explore other meeting options including online or virtual tradeshows. Virtual tradeshows employ web technologies such as video conferencing and push technology to satisfy potential buyer's demand for information. Salespeople can answer questions in several ways including online chat session, Internet video or simply calling the customer. Operators of virtual show booths can also use push technology to send selected Web pages to the web browser of tradeshow participants. Virtual tradeshows have been somewhat slow to develop and may never threaten in-person *shows but for some salespeople it may be worth an exploratory look.*

Build a Website: For more technically adventurous salespeople, a productive method for generating leads via the Internet is to build their own website. For those looking in this direction, check out one of the top-hosting firms whose service offerings are both extensive and reasonably priced. Many hosting services offer excellent service plans for less than $10 per month. Good places to begin a search for a web host are HostSearch.com and HostIndex.com, which provide directories and reviews of hosting firms. If you choose to create a website, consider using a content management system (CMS) to build your site. A CMS makes it very easy to create a site and add new information. While there is a bit of a learning curve, the time spent mastering the CMS will translate into a better looking website and one that is more likely to yield more inquiries as a result of good search engine rankings. Another plus is that many of the top web hosting services includes CMS within their service package.

INNOVATION AND PRODUCT LIFE CYCLE

Innovation

Innovation is a continuous process. There are models to guide creativity and innovations for business products, services and ideas. These models are analogous to various business models to guide strategic planning, quality improvement, problem solving, and other activities. Given below are few operative models in the last many years in the business world. Based on these trends, we can suggest a Composite Model operative and more relevant to the present world of globalization and constant cycle of innovative products, services and ideas.

Models for Innovations

1. The Wallas Model for creativity is one of the earliest models for creative process. Graham Wallas proposed that creative thinking proceed through four phases: *preparation* i.e. identifying issue, observation and study, *incubation* — laying the issue aside for a time, *illumination* — the aha moment when the new idea finally emerges, and *verification* — checking it out. The concept behind this thinking is that creativity is a subconscious process, and creative and analytical thinking is complementary.

2. Rossman's creativity model expands four steps of Wallas model to seven steps: *observation* of the issue-need, *analysis* of the issue-need, survey of all available information, *formulation* of all objective solutions, a *critical analysis* of these solutions for their advantages and disadvantages, and the *emergence* of new idea – innovation.

3. Osborn in his seven-step model suggests a theory of balance between analysis and inauguration. There is *orientation* identifying the problem, *preparation* — gathering pertinent data, *analysis* — breaking down the relevant material, *ideation* — piling up alternatives ideas through brainstorming, *incubation* — waiting for the aha moment, *synthesis* — putting the pieces together, *evaluation* — judging the resulting ideas.

4. Creative problem solving (CPS) model of Parns, Isaksen, Trefflinger outlined six steps, *objective* finding, *fact* finding,

problem finding, *idea* finding, *solution* finding and *acceptance* finding.

5. Koberg and Bangnall's model accept the situation as a *challenge, analyze* to discover the 'world of problem', *define* the main issues and goals, *ideate* to generate options, *select* to choose among options, *implement* to give physical form to the idea, *evaluate* to review and plan again.

6. Bandrowski's model for creative strategic planning has five steps: *analyze* the standard planning and insight development, *creativity* leaps strategic connections, *judgment* — concept building and critical judgment, *planning* — action planning, contingency planning, *action* —— flexible implementation, monitoring.

7. Robert Fritz's process for creative model suggests eight steps: conception, vision, current realities, action, adjust and learn, evaluate and adjust, building momentum, completion — living with your creation.

8. Barron's Psychic creation model places great emphasis on subconscious and chance processes in four phases: conception — preparation of mind, gestation — time intricately coordinated, parturition — suffering to be born, emergence of light, bringing up the baby — further period of development. It supports the popular view of creativity as a mysterious process involving subconscious thoughts beyond the control of the creator.

Composite Model of innovation process for products and services suggests that a *Need* is identified and critically analyzed to accept that as a challenge. The critical analysis of the need provides the pertinent information. Based on the pertinent information, and through brainstorming innovators seek for solutions (of possible products and services). A critical analysis of the solutions — of possible products and services weeds out the disadvantageous ones. In current times, there is globalization of businesses. Therefore, products and services (solutions) are sought in the context of national and international business markets and consumers both in terms of applications and reach to the markets. Businesses face challenges of managing

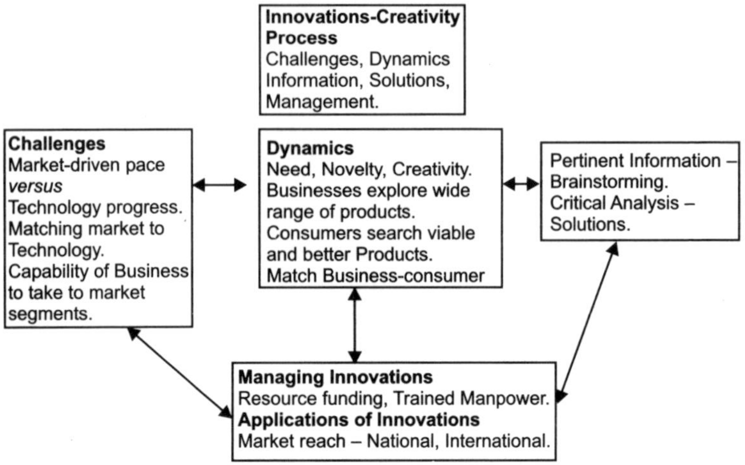

Fig. 4.2. Composite Model of Innovations

innovations in the context of resource funding and manpower at the first stage and subsequently managing business markets and consumers both in terms of applications and reach to different segments of the markets. Businesses face the dilemmas of innovative products and services such as market driven pace of products to match progress by innovative technology, matching markets to technology, and limitations of developing capability of organizations to reach certain segments of the markets and not all markets.

Dilemmas of Innovations: Dilemmas are posed to the technology innovators by the conflicting demands of the Disruptive Technology (DT) and Science & Technology (ST). First, the pace of progress that markets demand or can absorb is different from the progress offered by technology. Consumers driven demands, and technology demands lead us to innovations. Keeping close to consumers is an important management paradigm for handling sustaining technologies; but it may provide misleading data for handling disruptive technologies. Sustaining technologies improve the performance of the established products along the dimensions of the performance that mainstream customers in major markets have historically valued.

There is impact of sustaining and disruptive technologies on product performance — viz low-end and high-end customer expectations and in creating new growth businesses through sustained innovations, low-end disruptions and new market disruptions.

Secondly, managing innovations need resource allocation. Innovation proposals that get the required funding and manpower may succeed. Others lacking resources and given lower priority have little chance of success.

Third dilemma is matching the market to the technology. Successful companies will have the practiced capability of giving sustaining technologies to the consumer in improved versions of products. But this valued capability does not help in disruptive technologies. Disruptive technologies bring to market a very different value proposition that had been available previously.

Fourth, organizations have capabilities to take certain new technologies to certain markets. They have disabilities in taking technologies to market in other ways.

Fifth, the information required to make large and decisive investments for disruptive technologies is not available. It needs to be created through fast, inexpensive, and flexible forays into the market and the product. Failure and interactive learning are intrinsic to the search for disruptive technologies (DT). The mortality rate for ideas for DT is high.

Sixth, companies address different strategies for DT & ST. DT entails first-mover advantages so leadership is important. Seventh, there are powerful barriers to entry and mobility that differ on the type of technology.

Technology Model: You can heat water from 33 to 211 degrees without seeing much change, but raise the temperature just one more degree and you will see the difference — a totally new thing appears. Can anyone forecast such abrupt change? Yes to a degree. Sometimes technology seems to follow a pattern: many small incremental advances followed by an explosion of change. Fads and fashions break out like that.

Tim Fohl's Model of Technology Development suggests that at a constant level of efforts, technologies first advanced slowly — then erupt - like water at the boiling point. After the explosive period they return to slow advance. In other words their progress follows a clear S curve. The model proved so reliable that it could forecast product development cycles.

Dimension	Sustaining Innovations	Low-End Disruptions	New-Market Disruptions
Targeted performance of the product or service	Performance improvement in attributes most valued by the industry's most demanding customers. These improvements may be incremental or breakthrough in character.	Performance that is good enough along the traditional metrics of performance at the low end of the mainstream market.	Lower performance in "traditional" attributes, but improved performance in new attributes - typically simplicity and convenience.
Targeted customers or market application	The most attractive (i.e. profitable) customers in the mainstream markets who are willing to pay or improved performance.	Overserved customers in the low-end of the mainstream market.	Targets non-customers who historically lacked the money or skill to buy and use the product.
Impact on the required business model (processes and cost structure)	Improves or maintains profit margins by exploiting the existing processes and cost structure and making better use of current competitive advantages.	Utilizes a new operating or financial approach or both - a different combination of lower gross profit margins and higher asset utilization that can earn attractive returns at the discount prices required to win business at the low-end of the market.	Business model must make money at lower price per unit sold and at unit production volumes that initially will be small. Gross margin dollars per unit sold will be significantly lower.

Source: V.K. Soni

Fortune at the Bottom of the Pyramid

- Concept development by C. K. Prahalad and S. L. Hart
- Premise: Low-income markets present a prodigious opportunity for the world's wealthiest companies – to seek their fortunes and bring prosperity to the aspiring poor.
- Pursuing the "bottom" forces us to rethink our conventional wisdom about:
  - Technology and business models
  - Scale and profitability
  - Price-performance relationships
  - Productivity and capital efficiency
  - Sustainable development

Source: V.K. Soni

Fig. 4.3. Three Approaches to creating New–Growth Businesses

The results became more interesting and potentially more useful when he plotted additional variable of technology. Though a new technology advances in small steps in the beginning; it does so with big swings in performance between individual successes and failures. It suggested that greater the variations, the steeper the slope of the progress that follows. In other words, the major errors and false starts at the beginning forecast a higher start at the end. Tolerating and encouraging a wider range of possibilities early seemed to nudge a project towards a steeper takeoff.

This model can forecast the course of technology development efforts and find out about dynamics of progress. This modeling technique can be applied to complex social systems like fads and fashions, traffic jams etc. The path is powerfully influenced in the early stages, as consumers explore a wide range of possibilities in search of something viable and better. In a simpler time, one could predict the course of technology (e.g. a man on the moon by the end of decade), but today science bolts from the blue — fashion is born in the street (Narula 2000).

Dynamics of Innovations suggests abrupt change in the product development because of novel ideas. Their progress follows a clear S curve. Novelty, creativity and the need are the dynamics that push for innovative products as consumers explore a wide range of possibilities in search of something viable and better. These dynamics forecast product development cycles and course of technology development efforts. A deeper understanding of dynamics of innovations becomes imperative. Traditional models of innovation show a steep increase followed by diminishing returns — the familiar 'learning curve'.

Customers respond to new products in different ways. Diffusion of innovations theory, pioneered by Everett Rogers, and other diffusion models posits that people have different levels of readiness for adopting new innovations and that the characteristics of a product affect overall adoption.

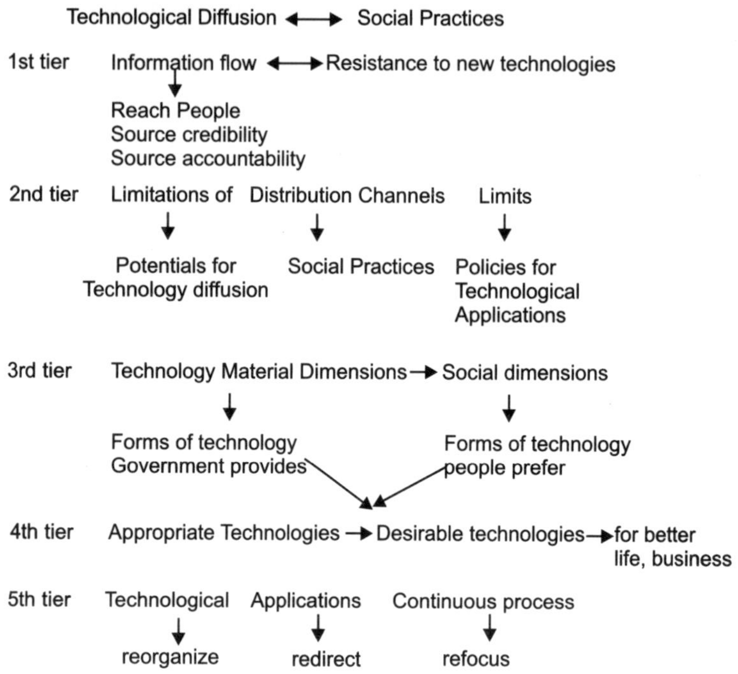

Fig 4.4. Diffusion of Technology — Tiers

Narula (1990) points that the diffusion of technologies and technological change suggest configuration of marketing, policy, control, socio-cultural impact, the effect on educational patterns, government philosophy (policy), and social practice. Along with notions of a new first-time technology entering the culture, as in the case of unique medium such as television, the demand for peripheral technologies and enhanced technologies can also began to grow. Such as videocassette players and tapes, black and white *versus* color system, computerization, enhanced systems of high definition TV and digitalization. Another example is charting the growth from typewriter to a word processor, personal computer, interactive system and so on.

In addition to technological diffusion, the diffusion of social practices is a complementary issue. The role of *information flows* and the concept of *resistance* are of paramount importance in diffusion research. How information about a technology and its capacity reaches the individual, and the credibility and the accountability of the source of the information influences the rate of adoption. If there is resistance to technology and its use, it may not always be uniform resistance. Likewise when we demand an updated technology, the old technology is not abandoned, but rather integrated further into social practices.

When distribution channels are limited, the potential for the diffusion of innovations, social practices, and effective policies for technological applications are curtailed and the adoption process becomes moot.

The material and the social dimensions will determine the forms of technology that governments will provide for its people and also what people would prefer. These two dimensions will set the priorities of applications in terms of appropriateness, desirability and safety of technology that will serve people well and maximize the technologies' contribution for better life.

Since applications of technology is a continuous process; it is necessary to reorganize, redirect, and refocus these two dimensions from time to time to meet the changing demands of people.

Disruptive technology: A disruptive technology is a lower performance or less expensive product or process that gains a foothold in the low end, less demanding part of an existing market, and then successively moves up-market through performance improvements until finally displacing the market incumbents. Disruptive technologies are usually introduced to the market by small startup enterprises. By contrast, sustaining technology refers to the successive incremental improvements to performance that market incumbents incorporate into their existing product.

The term disruptive technology was coined by Clayton M. Christensen and described in his 1997 book 'The Innovator's Dilemma'. His theory is that in certain markets, the rate at which products improve exceeds the rate at which customers can learn and adopt the new performance. Therefore, at some point the performance of the product overshoots the needs of certain customer segments. At this point, a disruptive technology may enter the market and provide a product that has lower performance than the incumbent, but exceeds the requirements of certain segments thereby gaining a foothold in the market. Christensen distinguishes between low-end disruption that targets customers that have been overshot and new-market disruption that targets customers that could previously not be served profitably by the incumbent.

The disruptive technology company will naturally aim to improve its margin (from low commodity level) and therefore innovate to capture the next level of customer requirements. The incumbent will not want to engage in a price war with a simpler product with lower production costs and will move up-market and focus on its more attractive customers. After a number of iterations, the incumbent is squeezed into successively smaller markets and when finally the disruptive technology meets the demands of its last segment the incumbent technology disappears.

There are examples of technologies promoted as disruptive technologies and displacing earlier technologies such as digital cameras from photographic film, mass-market cellular telephony from fixed-line telephony, VOIP, digital telephone systems, ADSL, ISDN from analog and fixed lines, personal computers from mainframe computers. Music downloads and file sharing *vs.* compact discs, e-books *vs.* paper books, e-commerce *vs.* physical shops, open-source software *vs.* proprietary software (for example Linux *versus* Microsoft Windows, although Linux has already largely displaced proprietary Unix), Internet Video on Demand *vs.* Advertising supported broadcast and cable television. Betamax, Laserdiscs, Cold fusion are some of the technologies originally promoted as disruptive technologies but failed.

Not all disruptive technologies are of lower performance. There are several examples where the disruptive technology outperforms the existing technology but is not adapted by existing majors in the market. These occur in industries with a high capitalization sunk into the older technology. To update, an existing player does not only have to invest in new technology but must replace (and perhaps dispose off at high cost) the older infrastructure. It may be simply most cost effective for the existing player to "milk" the current investment during its decline mostly by insufficient maintenance and lack of progressive improvement to maintain the long-term utility of the existing facilities. A new player is not faced with such a balancing act.

Not all technologies promoted as disruptive technologies have actually prospered as well as their proponents had hoped. However, certain technologies promoted as disruptive technologies and displacing earlier technologies such as mobile phones and Internet VOIP are moving ahead at fast pace.

SUMMARY

Business Communication Practices focus on three basic functions — Innovations, Marketing and Communications. The basic objective of any business is to get good, improved return on investment (ROI). Marketing and communications are the two major tools for innovations (products and services). Product life cycle suggests strategies for its different stages and technology life cycle. We need both marketing strategies and communication strategies for marketing products and services, building brands and brand values, targeting segmented markets and targeted audiences and Sales for profitability. Marketing in business is about products, markets and customers. The basic tools of marketing are: marketing strategies, market research and market analysis, pricing policies, supply chain, customer/consumer services and customer/consumer relations. Business organization functions in dynamic environment of marketing. And nothing can be more dynamic than changing consumer profiles, attitudes and behavior. Thus the core of marketing is identifying and understanding the customers. And critical to this intelligence is the ability to update the information in tune with the dynamism of the market environment.

The business practices of marketing products and services and ideas focus primarily on marketing strategies. Communication strategies (CS) are planned to implement marketing strategies. Communication strategies are planned from five angles: characteristics, communication channels, message content, effects, and feedback loops. All marketing strategies not only need support from Communication strategies but rather CS play important role in execution of market strategies at all the four stages. Market analysis and market research are the two major supporting tools of marketing strategies and communication is the essential component in market analysis and market research.

Analysis of markets for its products and services through market research provides objective data to facilitate marketing decision. Various marketing research techniques such as Analytical marketing, Mass media advertising, focused marketing, measuring performance and other variations in marketing techniques provide critical insights into markets necessary for marketing decisions. Market research is multifaceted aspect of marketing. Therefore, we define it from multi-angles. Market research is an effort by business to find useful information that describes the relationship between consumer, products, marketing methods, and marketers through experiments, information search, and processing.

Based on the pertinent information, and through brainstorming innovators seek for solutions of possible products and services. A critical analysis of the solutions — of possible products and services weeds out the disadvantageous ones. Businesses face challenges of managing innovations in the context of resource funding and manpower at the first stage and subsequently managing business markets and consumers both in terms of applications and reach to different segments of the markets. Businesses face the dilemmas of innovative products and services such as market driven pace of products to match progress by innovative technology, matching markets to technology, and limitations of developing capability of organizations to reach certain segments of the markets and not all markets.

The diffusion of technologies and technological change suggest configuration of marketing, policy, control, socio-cultural impact, government economic policies and social practices. Since applications of technology is a continuous process; it is necessary to reorganize, redirect, and refocus these two dimensions from time to time to meet the changing demands of people. A disruptive technology is a lower performance or less expensive product or process that gains a foothold in the low end, less demanding part of an existing market, and then successively moves up-market through performance improvements such as mobile phones, Internet and Internet telephony (VOIP). Not all disruptive technologies are of lower performance. There are several examples where the disruptive technology outperforms the existing technology.

5

Advertising in Business

BUSINESS ADVERTISING

Why do business advertise about their products, ideas, strategies and services and the Corporate itself. They even advertise about their people — their managers, their leaders? For that matter any organization whether social, political or cultural advertise about their goals, ideas, services, leaders and people. Why? One, these are advertised about to create awareness, information and knowledge about them. In short, to create visibility about them. Two, to create acceptance for them and facilitate consuming them now or in the near future. The consumers buy products and use services. They get familiar with a particular company's business strategies and business acumen of its leaders and the people working with them. Innovative ideas, products, services and people when advertised reach people. People may or may not notice it. If noticed, people react by showing interest, accepting or rejecting them or not paying attention.

The social and political organizational advertising stimulates people to go to the second stage of showing interest, accepting or rejecting them or not paying attention. Advertising is an effective tool for both marketing and innovations. This is also an effective tool for creating image and credibility as well awareness and motivation for buying products and services. Advertising through its various channels directly or indirectly creates and enhances the image of the corporate and particular businesses. Consumer behavior is the basis of all advertising.

If we look at the growth of advertising, in early 20s advertisers studied consumer behavior on the basis of their instincts and motives, in 40-50s instead of behaviorism it was the learning theories that mattered, 50-60s brought psychologists to the fore and emphasis was on source credibility, reference group, social class and attitude theory. In the next few decades the focus has been on consumer decision-making and behavior. The focus on consumer behavior is through three perspectives: consumer creation, acquisition, and retention; building consumer trust and loyalty and consumer service and relationship. Since 80s the spurts and innovation in information communication technologies (ICTs) have changed the nature of Advertising — its message presentation, channels and its reception by the consumers. Advertising has changed the consumer behavior. We will be focusing on business advertisement mainly in this chapter.

Seth Godin (2004) points out that the average urban consumer faces a barrage of over a million advertising and marketing communication messages in a day. The barrage starts in the morning when you open your newspaper while having your cup of tea. Then as you hit the road to work, the entire urban landscape is one large canvas of brand messages. You settle down at your desk and boot your machine. Before you can get to the business end of your mail, there's the inevitable spam that you have to wade through. Then those irritating phone calls throughout the day promising you free credit cards with a credit limit that makes you think you are an Arab oil well owner. And as you retire to watch some TV, the barrage continues. As a marketer, if you wanted to reach out to yourself, you'd simply quit.

DIMENSIONS OF ADVERTISING

The main focus of advertising through any channel is visibility, conveying intended meaning. In advertisement, the most important dimensions are message and targeted audience. The channels are selected according to both these components. The channels' effectiveness and appropriateness also depends on these two dimensions. The third most important and essential dimension is the effect of the advertising, which happens to be its main objective. The effects advertising are assessed through quantity of product sales and consumed, utilization of services, acceptance of ideas, people and leaders, and the organization's image. The effects may happen in the framework of present or future.

The effects lend to the credibility of the source of advertisements i.e. the businesses, the social, political, film, and other organizations in general. The source could be the organizations as well as the leaders who lend celebrity appeal to the ads and thus facilitating further credibility.

The communication components of source, message, channel, receiver and effects are essential but when organized in advertisement dimensions, they need to be used and projected in the abovementioned order. *Source credibility* is important for *effectiveness* of the ads with the targeted receivers. The right kind of intended Messages leads to effectiveness. The Ads have wider reach if the targeted receivers have reach to those channels. Therefore, an advertiser will plan the intended message for his/her targeted audience through channels that have wider reach for them. To give credibility to the Ad-messages he/she would resort to different kind of *appeals* — from celebrity appeals to emotional appeals. A film star using Lux bath soap lends celebrity appeal to the product-ad. A long-distance call to parents back home may use emotional appeal by telephone-ad. The important dimensions in business advertising are targeted audience, intended message, appeals, source credibility, channels, and growth of economy. Above all messages through words — jingles, slogans and rhymes etc, graphics, colors, visibles should be eye catching and appealing.

Advertisement Need

Business advertisement message is concerned with connotative meaning. It is a stimulant that provokes image in the head of the consumer though object is in the phenomena. The focus of advertising is two-ways, on consumers and positioning the products and services in the market. The marketers target existing and new users, existing and new market segments, existing and new products and services and using appropriate and available channels focusing on the characteristics of consumers, markets and products. Supply-chain customers, consumers, markets create demands and their demands create advertising in general. Content and brand conscious consumers dictate advertising.

Advertising needs have gone dramatic changes in India and world wise because of well-informed customer and consumers, growth in economy, competition among product brands, and increase in media options. The customers of yesterday have truly become the consumers of today. Far from being happy with what is available, they have fast-forwarded to being very demanding. They have the best of both worlds, access to everything without having to pay a substantial amount to receive the same.

The growth in advertising is mainly because of *growth in economy*. People buy consumer goods both non-durables like food, clothes etc and durables such as homes, cars, and furniture and so on. The quality, quantity and the brand buying of these products and services are according to the spurt in their purchasing powers. With the opening up of the economy, advertising in the Indian market has undergone a dramatic change — from being one of the 'less important marketing inputs', today it has transformed into a key ingredient for brand success. A lot more money is being spent on advertising than ever before — for reasons that are varied but real.

There is intense competition in the market worldwide and in different geographies due to globalization and technology. No single brand, however well placed, can take its place for granted and may lose its position overnight if caught unawares. Different channels on TV will compete with each other for visibility through advertisements; and products and services will compete through advertisement commercials on TV and print ads. Therefore, clients have to focus on immediate as well as long-term means of communication — more advertising being one of the means.

Increase in media options is giving rise to fragmented media usage, leading to less time spent per medium or vehicle. In other words, lower reach per program and lesser time per channel on television; and it is true for press and in addition, press is further fragmented by TV channels. This means the cost of reaching the prospective customer is increasing by the day.

Brand advertising for long-term results and tactical campaigns for short-term rewards are both becoming imperative to outlast competition. With increasing competition, the need to advertise is increasingly higher. The need to advertise at optimum level of spends is becoming critical. This required optimum level is on the increase year after year. Overcoming clutter — through preferred positions and higher frequencies, ensuring roadblocks by being present simultaneously across many channels, and investing in building media properties — which leads to word-of-mouth publicity or long-term cost efficiency, are all pointing towards an increase in advertisement cost.

Advertisers are, therefore, forced to commit a much higher ad spend than they can actually afford. This is because the media inflation index is way above the consumer price index and this increase cannot be passed on to the consumer, thus affecting their bottom line adversely. Understanding the intricate science of determining the level of media presence required against sales or market share objective is becoming an art. In this scenario, clients are now looking for specialists who can help them plan their media spends in the most optimum way as well as buy at the best possible rates for them without compromising in any way.

Advertising Channels are Media, Interpersonal, and traditional performing arts and folk arts channels. The ad messages are conveyed orally, in writing and in gestures. The traditional media channels used for advertisements are Print, radio, TV and cinema. The outdoor channels are billboards placed strategically at different places, road hoardings, cinema houses, market places, trade fairs and exhibitions etc. Internet, cell phones, and even telephone landlines are the non-conventional advertising channels. The interpersonal channels are word of mouth, public meetings and speeches. Performing arts advertising channels are paintings, dance, drama and folk arts and crafts. Even the events, promotions, brand ambassadors are used as media channels to promote products.

Advertisement content is the message through words, graphics, cartoon, picture images, live characters and even blank page. It is framed according to the particular channel of advertisement. The message is brief and focused on products and services, and consumer segments. It may be in rhymes, jingles, slogans etc or indirectly pointing to the message concerns. The settings are modified to be local or global according to the ad campaign need. The content is planned according to the characteristics of the targeted audiences.

MEDIA AND ADVERTISING

For many advertisers and advertising agencies, media, especially in a majority of consumer issues, has always remained a backroom activity. The absolute blitzkrieg in technology development and globalization during the last few years has seen massive changes taking place in both the software and hardware side of media. While technology has created multiple options and new types of competition, globalization has ushered in a new consumer culture — one that edits what it receives. This in its trail has fragmented the attention span of users and has also impacted the process of cumulative reach buildup, message registration and retention of audience. Further, media inflation occurs in geometric progression and has compounded the complexity of the media evaluation, planning and buying process and subjects of media.

How well do we really understand the media effects on people viz advertisement? Marshall McLuhan is the most celebrated among a band of media determinists who believe that media has impacted society much more than the content it carries. And that every medium has its own implicit language through which it effects the viewer. Business advertisers believe that media channels play the primary role in communication. That content is nothing and media is everything.

Media has evolved dramatically. We all know how the media landscape has changed. The media explosion and the resultant media fragmentation has given rise to a new, even more dazzling set of acronyms that the function can befuddle its audiences with. Structurally the function has changed, the business model has changed as have tracking methods. In short, virtually everything has changed. And yet, what this change seems to have accomplished is to push media even more into isolation. It has become a more specialized and has become too complex a subject for generalists.

At commonsense level, this is not new to us. We know that the same message carried in print produces a different effect than if carried on television, and it may be true for other media channels. The question is, how much do we know about these differences? Apart from clichés like 'newspapers' are good for topicality and magazines for retention.

The truth is that our conception of media is that it is a passive vehicle, an inert deliverer of a 'potent' message. Its role is to bridge the distance between the message and the receiver. Its effectiveness is judged on the basis of, to how many people it delivers the message and at what level of intensity and cost. All measurement of media effectiveness relates to how well the message is transmitted and not how well it is received. Media is thus seen as a 'dead' intermediary, a mere postman in the core communication process.

The larger problem lies in our definition of what constitutes media. Again we define the tangible carriers of message as media. What about typography? Typography is, in fact, a medium; choosing one font over another is conceptually like choosing one medium over another. Only here, the evaluation is not based on reach and frequency but on, which font best conveys the intent of the message. Typography is a good way for us to grasp the full conceptual meaning of media. Like all media, a font is a carrier of a message, but one that transforms the message itself. Imagine the Sony logo in a thin elegant typeface; it would forever alter the meaning of that brand, without any change in any other message.

In a similar way, the cartoon is a medium. It has its own language and produces its own distinctive effect. A mouse beating the brains out of a cat is considered funny, for one. A music video is likewise a medium for a similar set of reasons. By the same token, a 30-second commercial is a medium and, that too, one distinct from a 10-second commercial.

When we define media in terms of tangible carriers of messages, we inevitably focus largely on numbers. Since it is assumed that the only effect media has on people is that it faithfully transports a message, the evaluation is quantitative: how many people it reached and how many times. Even the qualitative parameters used — finding a fit between the environment and the message or ensuring that the message is delivered at a time when the receiver is most receptive — are not derived from the transformational role that the medium itself plays. This role is critical.

Walter Ong uses the example of oral culture and literacy to make this point. The medium of writing has profoundly changed the world. Writing allows us to separate thought from action, and logic from emotion. It allows us to not react instantly but to formulate our thoughts and place them in a structure. It robs our reactions of their immediacy and hence postpones emotion. Oral cultures, on the other hand, do not separate thought from action, and respond instantly and with emotion. The oral-written difference is at the heart of the East-West divide in the way each think and what they respond to. The implications of this perspective are quite interesting. Given the fact that India has been an oral culture, what kind of message do we as a people respond to? What narrative styles are we instinctively more comfortable with? The Hindi film structure tells us that we certainly do respond to a unique narrative style. Befitting an oral culture, our films are dramatic and decidedly non-linear, unlike western films. The power of music is another pointer to what we respond to.

The challenge for us is to understand the full scope and power of media and to cascade it back on to the message strategy. Currently, we need to understand how media and people interact for the communication planning. If the medium is indeed the message, why is media planning not at the heart of the communication process? Why is the function of media channels still seen as important but only playing a peripheral role?

We could segment the audience on the basis of how they consume media, how they process information. We know for instance that different children learn differently. Some learn by rote, others by writing, and yet others by analogies. Why not use this understanding in defining audience segments.

This could lead to completely new perspectives. For instance, we could segment the audience not by demographics or psychographics or even in terms of what they buy or watch, but on the basis of how *they consume media and how they process information*. This would conceivably lead to defining people from a true media perspective, which is not from the transmission but at the reception end. It would also take media into the heart of the strategic and creative processes.

We all know that the 30-second commercial is no longer the cornerstone of the communication mix. The brand will increasingly communicate through non-traditional means. Already events, promotions, brand ambassadors are used as media channels to promote products. We must be able to evaluate whether Rs 3 Crore are better spent on a commercial or on roping in Shah Rukh Khan – an Indian top movie star as a brand ambassador.

If the media function stays by its narrow definition of evaluating everything primarily on the basis of numbers, it will find itself addressing an ever-smaller share of the communication pie. The basis for evaluation has to shift to determining which 'medium' produces the best effect. The media strategists of tomorrow must become focused on how people receive messages, regardless of which source they come from. It calls for a radical overhaul of the media mindset, a willingness to acquire new skills and a desire to embrace a new intellectually more challenging role.

Success of India times 8888 has proved that an innovative idea has everlasting value for customers. Indiatimes 8888 is the largest recall short-code in India with 1.8 million requests/messages per day for ringtones, astrological forecasts, news, dating, cricket, jokes, mail, logos and picture messages with over 4 million unique users a month.

Advertising Agencies and Media Planning

Unlike a lot of other services — whether in advertising or in any other field, where the benefits are tangible and visible — media planning offers a whole host of benefits in terms of scientifically planned media usage, innovative ideas, implementation, and monitoring etc. However, more often than not, these benefits are intangible and hence, people find it difficult to accept and appreciate them.

Now the times have changed, the businesses look for a media planning and buying agency as a partner that will respond to their marketing objectives with accountability and an agency that has a hand-picked staff of top professionals so that clients get what they need on time at the best value for them. Usually, what they look for in it is to consolidate its Direct-to-Consumer advertising, media buying and planning, including Internet buys, and to improve efficiency, effectiveness, and return from its advertising.

Businesses want that the hired agency should have experience as a media planning/buying agency on record (AoR), and experienced in buying major media categories. It should apply integration of media and targeting tools for advertising. It should have sound general philosophies and approaches to the media marketplace. Over and above, the staffing plans for the account should have top professionals. When an advertiser contracts a media agency to handle its media investment account, it is called media AoR. The AoR may include both media planning and buying functions or it could be split into two — one planning AoR and the other buying AoR — awarded to two different agencies.

The need, therefore, is to save the advertisers' money to the maximum without diluting the advertising efforts needed for the brand. This is where the specialized skills of these agencies come in. The agency's team of media professionals should be skilled enough to advise on the optimum Ad spend levels, capable of hard negotiation without compromising on the best values. Its right contacts across media would matter and should have access to all relevant tools and technologies, databases, systems and global learning. It is necessary that agency's team is accountable, trustworthy, unbiased and ensures complete transparency, and is service oriented.

The media professionals need to undergo a complete change in mindset — from being a media professional to being a business manager and a service provider. This does require a huge investment in people, tools and technology, databases, systems and in training. Often, this amounts to a three or four-fold increase in investment than that incurred in a traditional media department. To make this investment worthwhile, these one-stop media agencies become independent units to vie for a larger business base that makes them financially viable. Generally all major media independents are part of a worldwide media independent network, having access to the network's learning as well as the latest tools and technology available. This, in turn, makes each a better professional through varied exposure and helps in providing better service to clients.

What is the difference between an ad agency and a media agency? In today's time, the role of an ad agency is generally restricted to creating an ad and media specialist agencies (offshoot of ad agencies) then takes care of bringing the ad to the target audience. With the constant fragmentation of media and complex consumer market, the task of a media specialist is a tough one in ensuring efficiency and value to its client's money.

The Media agency plans and buys advertising space in media on behalf of its clients. In consultation with its clients, the agency decides on how much, where and when to invest. The media specialist agency role is to devise the strategy in terms of investment in media for the advertisers. It does the media planning by selecting media vehicle from a set of options including print, broadcast, outdoor, Internet, direct marketing, cinema etc. to use for promoting the brand. It buys the media space across different media channels as per the strategy. It takes care of the scheduling, frequency and length of the exposure of the brand.

The media agency professionals relies on their market understanding, usage of specific customized tools and models and research reports from different sources to work out a media plan as per the needs and budget of its clients. It places orders with targeted media channels according to the plan. The media houses bills the agency, which in turn bills it to its client. Generally, there are two ways in which a media agency makes its money. Either it charges a specific percentage of commission of the total media buy by its client or it charges a fixed fee from a client irrespective of the quantum of the media investment by its client. Sometimes this variable is also linked to its performance.

An agency needs three things to produce great advertising: a management who wants it, creative teams who can produce it and a client who buys it.

Creative advertising is to know how the consumer thinks and behaves in today's world. There's no denying the fact that brand survival lies in quality advertising. And the only clients that are likely to capture the wallet and heart of the consumer in the long-run are the ones that understand this and who are willing to push creative boundaries and take calculated risks.

It is immaterial how much money one spends on research, on the shoot, on production, on media buying but if your ad isn't noticed, everything else is academic.

If it's not entertaining, involving or attractive, the chances of consumer noticing and remembering the ad are slim or none, if the agency and the client understand this, the brand will stay on the shelf and in the consumer's mind for long.

Advertising Agencies in India

The media scenario in India was very static till early 80s, with very few real options to choose from. Clients also did not demand the same level of involvement from media planning as they did from Creative, and to a much lesser extent from media buying. Advertising agencies were the one-stop shops for all communication needs. They did not want to give up control over media as the same work could be done even without the support of real specialists, without investing much in databases, software, hardware, people and other infrastructure and account servicing people could act as the face of the agency even for media issues.

On one end of spectrum, for advertising agencies in India, there are ample opportunities for growth not only in existing areas of activity, but also in new fields that are opening up thanks to liberalization and globalization, technological progresses and changing lifestyles. At the other end of the spectrum, risks are high for agencies that are not able to identify the critical competencies they need to stay on course and decide how they should build and deploy these competencies, given their current scope and resources.

The multi-Crore advertising industry is becoming globally competitive and presently accounts for 33 per cent of total industry profit in the Asia-Pacific region and ranks seventh highest in terms of contribution to global profit. Global agencies are increasingly getting attracted to the Indian market and now have a share of about 47 per cent of total Indian advertising. In spite of this healthy state of the industry during the mid and late 90s, the uncertainty of the future remains a cause of concern for all agencies, big, medium or small. Developments in the last five to ten years have changed (or are changing) the rules of the industry dramatically.

Let's take a look at some of these developments to identify the opportunities and vulnerabilities of Indian advertising agencies: (i) Clients are increasingly looking for a one-stop communication solution, including direct marketing, event management and public relations. (ii) Emergence of Internet and other new media such as ATM, WAP devices and interactive TV are both exciting and threatening — exciting for fast and first movers in building capabilities and early advantages and threatening for laggards and those basking in past glory. (iii) Interactive divisions of many agencies are now offering online consulting, web branding, web designing and offline advertising strategies. (iv) Concentration in the industry is clearly visible, with the top fifteen agencies accounting for 80% of the billing and the balance twenty per cent being shared by a 100-odd agencies. (v) Opportunities for growth appear substantial. Some of the opportunity areas will be healthcare, insurance, financial services, dot.com, Internet and special communications. (vi) Online advertising will be on the rise and will reach Rs.300 crore by 2005. However, it will change the rules of advertising and will help advertisers to shift focus from broadcasting to narrow casting.

Media planning and media buying has become highly specialized due to the emergence of new media and need for better relating media characteristics with brand and consumer profile. There is a possibility that these two activities will move out of the range of services provided by a traditional advertising agency. Full service agencies will have to focus, how they can add value in such areas as speed, coordination and optimum media plans. Clients will be looking for more comprehensive and also better services with greater speed in delivery and applications across geographically dispersed markets. They will also be increasingly demanding a different remuneration structure (either fixed fee-based or performance-linked) to ensure accountability.

Media planning has become far more complex than before — there are 100-odd channels, more than 400 publications and a plethora of new media that keep coming up every other day. With the rising cost of media and its ever-growing fragmentation, the efficiency and effectiveness of ad spend are now being examined critically more than ever before. Online and offline media-buying companies will be fully integrated and automated. In general, technology will drive initiatives in devising better ways to reach consumers. Faced with increasing media cost and intense competition, many agencies are now trying to scale up quickly to become one-stop solution providers and reduce cost. In fact, the industry has already started witnessing a number of Merger and Acquisitions and strategic alliances.

The decisions taken to reposition the agency in four specific areas of segmentation, scope, scale and capabilities will determine the value proposition that the agency intends to offer to its clients. The uniqueness and sustainability of such value proposition and the ability to deliver such values at a competitive cost will be a critical aspect of an agency's plan to reposition itself.

Segmentation: The choice of segments to be served in the emerging future is the first aspect to be considered in order to reposition an advertising agency in the new competitive environment. It will help the agency to have clarity, consistency and commitment in development of strategy, allocation of resources and identification of critical skills. *Scale:* An agency should examine if it should become a full service agency or focus on one or two specialized areas. A critical issue to be addressed is how big the size of an agency should be. Size will undoubtedly matter if new capabilities are to be built, more value-added services are to be provided and cost to the client is to be reduced.

Building capabilities: One key issue that needs to be considered is what kind of future capabilities an agency should build so that it can have competitive advantages to offer value that is better than its other direct competitors as well as niche players. Second consideration is that more investment will be required in technology, creative people and associated training and development to build capability in number of areas; and applicability of newly developed capabilities across different geographical markets around the world and sectors to be covered (e.g. retailing, distribution, promotions, merchandising, sampling etc.).

Performance criteria: An agency will define a few critical parameters against which it will measure its short-term and long-term performance. Such parameters should be chosen to reflect the importance of both client satisfaction and internal efficiency such as advertiser's business performance, the advertising performance, and performance of the agency vis-a-vis clients' expectations and service standards set in delivering the service and professionalism. Providing values to clients such as research and intellectual inputs to clients in three key areas, viz understanding changes in consumer behavior, developing business insights including making available frameworks for formulating strategic options and crystallizing the brand vision.

Organizing for the future: Against the background of changing environment and the repositioning required to deliver the new value proposition, a key issue the agencies will face is how to organize their activities in future to implement the new direction. While traditional thinking will probably indicate the need to possess all required capabilities and infrastructure in-house, the guiding principle should be to include only those few core activities where the agency has established capabilities or has plans to develop such capabilities. Advancement of information and communication technology can help an agency to have control over its activities.

Let us take an example from Zenith Media in India (2003-04) as a case to illustrate the above points better — how a one-stop media shop provides tangible savings without diluting effort, yet reaches out to the consumer through media in a holistic manner, and assumes accountability for its recommendations and their results, keeping the client's needs and requirements uppermost.

The case study is about a food product used by the entire family, the purchase decision of which is mainly by the homemaker. The product was being distributed in one state of South India in a very competitive environment, and the objective that the company had was to double the sales of the brand in one year. Using various databases for media monitoring, the Zenith team first identified the links between Market Share and Share of Voice, as well as Market Share and Effective Reach (above a certain level of OTS). Thereby, it established clear required targets to double the sales. Using proprietary global models, the Zenith team, along with the brand managers, identified and validated the required frequency levels. Cues were obtained from global learning (using another proprietary global method) and insights through local research to identify the body clock of a typical housewife, her points of contact with media (not only the organized media but with anything that contacts her) and the extent of her involvement with the same.

This helped in the initial screening of media to come up with: (i) the most appropriate time slots/sections in TV and print media respectively when she was most receptive (ii) places/locations for placements of out-of-home sites (iii) additional media to be used for reaching out to her at the kitchen or at leisure. Using the proprietary optimization model, the required share of voice (SOV), reach and frequency was achievable at 35 per cent less, as it threw out all wasteful spots/insertions. Then the buying tools and the Zenith buying contacts were used to buy at the best prices possible. Through this, a further savings of 25 per cent was achieved. Thus there was a total savings of 60 per cent.

To bring further excitement to the brand, innovative ideas were sourced from the worldwide offices of Zenith Media through their global site that contains all innovations from across the world, in addition to creating innovations tailor-made for the brand and the market. Finally, the system matched the sales targets and achievements to the savings and delivery targets. We believe that one-stop media agencies cannot act only as suppliers but as business associates who are accountable and are willing to put efforts for performance.

Types of Advertising. As mentioned earlier, there are varied channels of advertising such as media channels, online advertising, outdoor advertising, indoor advertising and word of mouth and People advertising.

Online Advertising

This new advertising medium brings with it its own distinct advantages and set of rules for success. The Internet, as an advertising medium, scores over the conventional media on two counts: in its ability to provide for interactive communication where the advertiser can establish a two-way communication with the consumer and in its ability to target communication to a specific target segment. It is imperative, therefore, that an advertiser leverages these two advantages to the maximum extent possible. The element of interactivity in online communication is largely a domain for creative planning and execution.

The Internet differs from conventional media because conventional media like press and TV are push and broadcast in nature. All consumers of a particular edition of newspaper or TV channel get exactly the same information. It is then left for each consumer to 'consume' only such information as she/he needs or finds relevant. Thus, the challenge for an advertiser is to choose such editions or channels where most consumers for that particular media vehicle are also target consumers for the advertiser's brand. The emphasis is, therefore, on reducing wastage.

The Internet, on the other hand, is pull and multicast in nature. Each consumer of a website can choose to visit (or not visit) a particular site, and thus the consumer pulls desired information. The cost of consuming multiple vehicles (sites) on the Internet is almost negligible compared to conventional media. Further, it is possible for a consumer to have a personalized view of a particular website i.e. view only desired information in a desired layout. A classic example is a web-based email service. A consumer views only her emails and arranged in a manner (ascending by date or new messages at top) that she chooses. The challenge, therefore, for the advertiser is to ensure that his communication is relevant and part of the information pulled by the consumer.

While planning for advertising on the Internet, planners create two levels of plan. One plan identifies the sites, particular sections within those sites (sports, entertainment etc.) and particular position on pages (top banner, side button etc.). This planning is governed by an understanding of the traffic pattern (e.g. youth, women, NRIs, young professionals etc.) that the site would attract, which is governed by the content type, quality etc. This is pretty similar to the process that is followed while planning for conventional media. Your product offer must be compelling. No amount of marketing budget can sell a product that is bad or not needed. Also, your advertising must be creative and attractive. Boring ads add no value to the brand; in fact, they may actually reduce the value.

However, it is the planning at the second level that differentiates the Internet from other conventional media. Internet plans allow for real-time targeting of communication based on various parameters. These parameters are such that their value can be determined only in real time i.e. as it happens. Some of the parameters that are used for targeting are geography of the visitor (country/city), time of visit (morning/afternoon/late night), day-of-visit (Monday/weekend). The ability to 'read' these parameters in real time and then deliver an appropriate communication is what makes the Internet a powerful advertising medium.

Take a nationwide pizza delivery chain. It may use geography and time of day/day of week targeting very effectively. To start with, advertisements may be delivered only on weekdays as a majority of Internet consumers connect using office infrastructure. Additionally, the highest number of impressions may be delivered during the 11:00 a.m. to 1:00 p.m. time band to catch the 'hungry-and-planning-for-lunch' consumer. The relevance of the communication may be greatly improved if different creative is delivered based on the city of the consumer, so that the base message could remain the same but the 'phone-number-to-call' could be that of the visitor's city.

Internet plans also enjoy the leverage of high levels of course correction that are unheard of in conventional media. Extending the pizza delivery chain example, a quick analysis after, say, the first week of activity may reveal that: Visitors to a certain set of sites are not clicking on the banners. Visitors from City A, C and D seem uninterested in pizza as lunch. Visitors from other cities prefer pizza not only for lunch but also as an evening snack. These observations can trigger course correction for the original plan. Impressions delivered on the 'non-performing' sites and to visitors from City A, C and D are reallocated to increase the impressions delivered to visitors from other cities and increase the number of impressions delivered in the new time band of 4:30 p.m. to 6:00 p.m. Such regular course correction provides for 'better-bang-for-the-buck' Internet advertising plans.

Another Case: A leading portal in India aims at developing the 'learn-at-home' concept. There are two sets of target group: IT-aware i.e. training managers and IT novices i.e. students. The first level plan arrived at a list of websites that were frequented by the target segment. A total of 13 Creatives were served in the first week. The main objective of the campaign was to enable a high CTR. Online planning and course correction led to a dramatic improvement in the CTR over the four-week period, up from 0.83 per cent to 1.63 per cent, an improvement of almost 100 per cent. Correlating various parameters like creative, site content, time band, city etc achieved this.

Certain basic principles of advertising planning apply to all media, including the Internet. One, know your target segment; who it is, why it would want to buy your product and how it would decide on your brand over competition. Two, your product offer must be compelling. No amount of marketing budget can sell a product that is bad or not needed. Three, your advertising creative must be attractive. Boring ads are just that, boring. They add no value to the brand; in fact, they may actually reduce the value. Four, very little advertising spends result in instantaneous purchase. Most of the spend helps build the customer's knowledge about the product category, the brand and its superiority over competition — and hence purchase always lags behind the spend by a finite time. Though the above list seems self-evident, we have advertisers who blame the Internet for the failure of their campaign when the cause of the failure actually lies in not adhering to one or more of the principles mentioned above.

In year 2004 the standard web page banner ad is reformatted for a tiny cell phone screen. This is the latest foray in marketing. This could be enormous new advertising market.

Marketers can reach millions of people with personalized interactive advertisements whose effectiveness can be instantly measured by how many people click on them. Important bonus for advertisers is, they have a consumer's number for future text messages. They are convinced about the potentialities of wireless marketing. The camera cell phone also opens up new advertising potentialities. The cost of producing cell phone ads is minimal. Marketers are feeling their way through issues like people's level of tolerance for screen clutter and their privacy issues. But consumers feel it would be invasion of privacy and they are concerned about privacy issues and scams like telemarketing.

As the Internet makes its presence felt in India, it has begun to attract the attention of advertisers. Various researches indicate that Indians with access to the Internet spend a considerable percentage of their total media consumption time on the Internet. It is thus natural that an increasing number of advertisers are keen to understand the why and how of Internet advertising, and learning in planning and delivering online advertising campaigns.

Research done by Nasscom (January 2001) shows that in India there are 5.5 million Internet users with 1.5 connections. According to IRS 2000, on weekdays the time spent on the Net is 1:30 hrs as against press, which is at 1:13 hrs and TV, which is 2:21 hrs. The level of personalization varies with sites. Some like My Yahoo! (http://my.yahoo.com) provide for a high level of personalization while others like Times of India (http://www.timesofindia.com) provide for minimal personalization. Though the Internet users and the time spent on Internet has gone very high since then.

Google has also attempted to create a network effect in its advertising business with its Google AdSense service. Google AdSense places ads on many small sites, such as blogs, using Google technology to determine which ads are relevant to which blogs. Thus, the service appears to aim to serve as an exchange (or ad network) for matching many advertisers with many small sites (such as blogs). In general, the more blogs,

Google AdSense can reach, the more advertisers it will attract, making it the most attractive option for more blogs, and so on, making the network more valuable for all participants. Google also advertise on its search engines matching the advertisements with the information that consumers want. It also localizes its ads according to the country and that make them relevant for marketing.

Kind of advertising: Businesses target commercial ads at consumers durable and non-durable goods, and industrial consumers. Ads are for products and services. There are classified ads for business services like employment etc. Social ads are for developmental products and services for the society. Civic ads refer to civic organizations, utilities and civic services. Political ads pertain to political communications about the national and international issues by the leaders and civil society. Ads pertaining to elections are important in political communication. Medical ads pertain to medical services, hospital etc, diseases, and medicines. Entertainment ads are for entertainment programs of dance, drama, music, movies, theater, cinema houses, museums, book discussion clubs, weddings and social programs and entertainment in general. Besides telling us about programs, these ads also project celebrity associated with entertainment programs.

Though these different kinds of ads are for their specialized domains but they do overlap and present multidimensional advertisements. These different kinds of advertisements are presented in variety of ways. Many of the conventional ways are undergoing change due to technology and business advancements, and changes in consumer behavior.

Some of these variations in Advertising situations are — dubbing product placements, changing ad pitches, international marketing with modified local pitches, guerrilla marketing techniques, addressable cable technologies, sensitizing employees to company's brands, marketing techniques applied to traditional media like films, and viral marketing through emails etc.

Dubbing product placements: In 2004, Hollywood studios are getting into dubbing product placements. For decades they have been dubbing the dialogues. Digital technology has made it easy and inexpensive to substitute one product plug for another in the domestic and overseas version of the same movie. This gives studio revenue when they can sell product placement rights overseas. The practice actually dates back to the pioneering efforts of 1993 but it was expensive at that time. Though films have routinely featured product placements since 1982 when in picture 'Extra Terrestrial', Reese candy product was used.

Major studios set up units to sell roles, sometimes directly to advertisers, sometimes through agencies that concoct related promotions for the advertisers such as movie themed contests or store displays.

With foreign markets contributing as much as 60% of the box-office take for most Hollywood pictures, the practice of tailoring product placements for international markets is taking off. In some cases, the dubbed plugs are mainstay of a movie's global marketing campaign. If you can take a can in someone's hand and change that from one brand to another, it opens up a tremendous amount of revenues.

The ability to dub in different plugs may give the studios additional marketing clout but some decry the practice since this turns into glorified infomercials. The process has become simpler and cheaper over the years as more special effects agencies offer dubbing services. As digital cameras are shooting more movies, the cost is expected to go down still more.

At present, product dubbing is confined to still shots. Dubbed products are little more than props in the background because dubbing a product frame by frame is complicated. It is easy to dub soap packet so long it is sitting on the laundry counter but complicated to dub when a housewife picks it up and pour in the washing machine. Eventually, movies could digitally alter the appearance of the same product for the local markets. Uniliver may market the same soap product around the world but packaging and color may be different. Some movie stars with approval rights over product endorsements may object to product dubbing. It is often easier when no stars are involved. USA has reached a healthy level for product placement and they are looking for international product-placement sales.

Changing Ad pitches: The marketers are learning that reaching consumers through advertising through traditional means — TV, Magazines, Newspapers is getting harder in the coming years. Consumers are seeking information from broader range of sources and filtering out messages that do not resonate or speak to their specific needs. There is fragmented audience of television because of many TV channels. It is further threatened by electronic ad-skipping devices such as TiVo (video on demand on TV), ad clutter and audience fragmentation. Ad industry needs to reinvent itself. Ad pitches change in 2005. Most likely, there are five areas that the advertisers will face in 2005.

One, *going wireless*. Such things as blackberry, ipod and cell phone are intimate techy devices that have the potential to catch on-the-go consumer at the perfect moment to take buying decision. General Electrical's NBC Universal is already broadcasting 18-20 video news reports designed specially for cell phones customers and it is planning to extend this to entertainment programs. The cell phones are being used by teens for picture sharing and text messaging. As the mobile phone becomes more of a multi-tasker — to surf the web, watch TV and get text information — the distinction between various media platform is blurring. Marketers used to allocate separate budgets to print, television and the Internet but now they have to think differently. They also may seek marketing deals with controllers of electronic devices and designers of software that helps consumers organize electronic media and entertainment choices.

Another hot area in advertising is *addressable cable technology*. It can deliver messages tailored to specific zip codes and neighborhoods. Advertisers can monitor through cable set boxes, the habit of watching on-demand movies and the potential for consumers to skip commercials. They can track who is zapping ads and perhaps figure out ways to get them to stop.

Media buyers believe the set-top boxes have the potential to give more exact audience measurements than consumer panels and sample groups. The marketers are seeking this new way to gather data on the audience for their promotions than to rely on the old fashioned metrics such as newspaper circulation and TV ratings.

Marketers have to use different techniques to reach the audience. The audience is getting more fragmented due to various media options. Marketers need to reach to consumers in individual situations, with ads that are tailored for particular individuals and not the world at large. Mass marketing is not going away but one-on-one marketing is becoming necessary. The key to 'getting to know you' technique with the audience is gathering personal information, which raises the questions about privacy.

Recent (2004-05) problems with painkillers such as Vioxx of Merck & Co and Celebrex of Pfizer Inc show that pharmaceutical ad boom is in danger of going off its *Direct-to-consumer advertising*. Celebrex medicine direct to consumer ads are now embedded in entertainment programs. This kind of advertising for drugs is still in its relative infancy but consumer are chaffing at ads featuring cartoon characters, rhymes and jingles to sell medicine as if it were pizza. Pharmaceutical manufacturers may shy away from aggressive TV ads on these medicines and explore more low-key pitches and pursue subtler approaches such as possible opportunities in movies and TV shows.

Then there is *opt-in-option* where marketing maneuvers engage rather than intrude on the consumers. They make efforts to get consumers to expend energy by engaging them before they get a sales pitch. There are 'invitational' commercials that ask consumers to click to a particular web site, send a text message, or email, offer an opinion or follow up in some other manner that prompts involvement. These moves can be tracked and information they provide can be filed away for future reference.

Comparative Advertisement: When it comes to marketing products and services, comparative advertising is happily tolerated, even enjoyed, by audiences — just so long as it is dished up with a healthy dose of humor. In addition, the claims must be true and documented. For example, attack ads launched for underdog Miller Lite, which had half the sales volume of Bud Light, turned around its decade-long sales decline by focusing heavily on Miller Lite's lower carbohydrate content. They also forced industry leader Budweiser into a defensive posture.

We observe in comparative advertising or even in advertising where the competitors are mentioned and shown as inferior in competition. Watch this ad of courier service: Ad shows UPS and Federal Express vans are rushing to deliver a package to the customer. Then DHL van is shown getting ahead of them and delivering the package. The intended message is that DHL is speedier than UPS and Federal Express. The competitors are conveying what they want to say but by addressing to the public that is shown as their primary audience. UPS and Federal Express companies are not their primary audience though they do get the message.

Another indirect way to communicate with competition is through market and consumers. That is because both the market and consumer will determine whose product works and whose product is successful. Comparative advertising of products and services suggest competitive edge over the two companies directly or subtly.

There is a new McDonald commercial on American TV on weight loss that cautions eaters on chewing down on their 'chicken select'. It compares the fat gram in chicken dish with sweet onion chicken teriyaki sandwich of Subway. The marketers think consumers will embrace the new stance and believe the product spokesman has more leeway for a few new tricks. McDonald retaliated by saying we are always focused on our customers and not on competition. Subway retaliates, any time McDonald wants to talk about our products, we would be glad for them. In this, even retaliation is subtle ways of reinforcing their comparative advertisement stance for their products.

Well-known brand icons are getting in their characters prompting some unexpected behavior such as openly attacking the competition. The ad mascots have indulged in offbeat behavior. For decades, the smiling characters were there to extol the benefits of the product they pitched and little more but they would not deviate from the purity of their image. Such icons were not supposed to dirty their image. But now marketers think of dozens of new ways of attracting consumer attention. These memorable icons have been given long leash for comparative advertising. The reasons why lots of these characters are floundering are because the owners of the characters are not in grip with the fact that audience is more sophisticated. Years ago, it was enough for character to be shill but no longer. The consumer sees the playful pitch for people for what they are — salesmen. Making these characters interesting makes people give more attention to them and also to ads. Characters are also eager to appear for other products (with or without conflict of interest).

Another type of subtle comparative advertisement is Product-placement in the ads. The products are placed in the characters of the show. It is shown being used by them, such as a particular brand of car, furniture etc. TV networks and advertisers are finding that product-placement campaigns need to be constantly reinvented and keep coming with new ideas.

'Spoofing' ratchets up the Ad wars: Marketers employ mimicry of rivals — spoofing to attract notice, but this tactic can spark backlash. "You have to assume if you are going to spoof your competitors advertisements in the marketplace, then your competitors will look for a basis to challenge you." NetZero runs a near-copies of commercials from America online's current campaign, 'want a better Internet?' All this back and forth only emphasizes that marketing world has become a rough and tumble place as more advertisers are taking pot-shots at rivals to boost recognition and market share.

Some spoofs have caused rancor. In 1999, an ad promoting 'Good Morning America' on Walt Disney's ABC, imitated the style of ads used to promote GAP. When the retailer complained, some spots were pulled. Spoofing strategy has multiple risks. "if you are the challenger, upstart you have the license to poke in the eye of the enemy." Others think you are responding to an enemy you should be ignoring. Mentioning a rival typically takes a marketer off its strategy but some of these ads also reveal that advertisers go a great length to stand out in the crowd.

Hoax marketing campaign for a Sega video game in 2003 (by Ty Montague an Ad expert) typifies new guerrilla marketing techniques. He hired a man to spend part of his day leaving voice mails for game developers complaining that Sega's ESPN and NFL football games cause him to lose control of his emotions. The man even created fake blogs to spread the word about the 'dangers' of video games. Mr. Montague and his team produced an hour-long film on boxing championing Roy Jones Jr to promote NIKE. Mr. Jones is Nike's pitchman and during the film he wore company's Jordan apparel — such as Nike's knit caps featuring the Nike jumpman logo. David Lubars in 2003 for Publicis Group's agency did campaign for BMW that attracted huge attention for a series of short films aired over the Internet. You need new fangled marketing techniques to sell products. The non-sexy formulaic advertising does not attract any longer.

Ads for Seniors: An advertising campaign is being run to change attitude of advertisers towards aging consumers. In 2005, Association for retired persons (ARP) is running the campaign in trade publications to highlight the advertisers lack of concern for older people. They seek advertisers respect for persons over 50. "Whenever you see ads, they are selling drugs or something medical to the seniors. It will be nice to see an older person in the ad who is at least shown active". Their campaign messages are: 'these days doctors do not pronounce you dead. Marketers do'. Another message, 'According to most marketers, 10000 people die everyday. Still another, 'the power of you and us'.

The aging population is growing due to longevity; they have money to spend so why not target them for other consumer goods? But the ads are fixated on wooing the young on the theory that they will be the customers for years to come. Most advertisers ignore senior citizens. Many of them assume the ads targeted to young will also be seen by the seniors. Others take seniors for granted.

Senior citizen market is a big market to be targeted both for products and services and need not be bypassed. Among mainstream consumer product companies, only a few smart one advertise for them. By taking the 50 plus market for granted, the marketers can lose a big chunk of the market. Seniors, the mature customers are not looking for flash but they want quality and integrity and the brand that they can trust. The advertisers have to be honest in their advertising with older generation. These people have seen it all; you cannot pull wool over their eyes.

Health clubs and fitness centers gear marketing to younger but statistics show that most of their members are 50 plus and they are regular and loyal. So should they not target the seniors in their ads? A few advertisers are talking about ads for seniors, 'should we use the word old, people are afraid of word old, should we say it visually, strategically'. Best is to word it, 'they may say this is my age. I feel good, I feel healthy, and I want to stay that way'.

Brands visibility happens due to unpredictable ways of ads. Cellular companies are constantly talking of new ways to increase their visibility. Now they have started putting up signages on restaurants too, the erstwhile preserve of the cola giants. Hutchison Max Telecom's cellular services brand Orange has been sponsoring various restaurants across the country. Chief marketing officer, Orange explains: "We have been putting up our signages on restaurants because we feel it's a good place to get brand visibility, apart from the conventional method of branding at shops and other retail stores" (2004).

Sensitizing employees to brands is a good way of word-of-mouth advertising. If they are not sensitized about the brands, employees end up undermining the expectations set by the company's advertising, either because they don't understand what the ads have promised or because they don't believe in the brand and feel disengaged or, worse, hostile toward the company.

International strategy for marketing advertising — one global message would ring in many markets. Nokia corporation, the world's largest cell maker is going global with its advertising to create a stronger more unified identity in the tough cell-phone branding war. The corporate campaign carries the slogan, "1001 reasons to have a Nokia imaging phone," is rolling out across Europe, Africa, and Asia and soon in USA showing up in television, print and online ads. It aims to send one message in all countries where Nokia is sold, a strategy that departs from past approaches that used different images and messages in different countries.

The campaign bolsters a continuing debate among marketers: should advertising be local or global. As companies and cell phones in particular battle each other for brand awareness. It is critical for consumers to get a consistent message wherever they travel. With online advertising and even TV ads being downloaded and shared over the Internet, ads are spreading faster and with less control.

Marketers are also pushing for global campaigning because, if done correctly, the lead advertising firm achieves economies of scale. It can spread production costs across markets, and small markets benefits by having the same quality, slick and creative ads as richer and bigger areas. Yet a global strategy has some risks. One-size-fit-all approach could translate into bad business, if consumers misunderstand the nuances or cross-cultural differences.

To combat concerns of losing local flavor, Nokia is making tweaks for different cultures. The current campaign will employ actors from the region where the Ad runs to reflect the look of the local population, though they will say the same lines. Local settings are also modified when showcasing the phones, such as using a market place in Italy or a bazzar in Middle East.

Nokia can now more easily advertise globally because most regions of the world use the same cell phone technology, allowing it to rollout the new products across the globe simultaneously. Until 2003, it would launch different products in different regions at different times, so it could not use a unified ad. However it did a one shot global ad for its N-gage games in 2003 because it sold the game console around the world (2004).

Negative Ad Tactics: Can marketing campaign through negative ads such as accusations, mudslinging, name-calling, and counterattacks have positive results? Sounds like a bad way to run a marketing campaign but all those negative ads may have a more positive result than you think. What many of us call "negative" or "attack" ads are termed "comparative" ads by those in the industry, and the bottom line is that they appear to work.

"They're very effective," says Rick Farmer, Ph.D., an assistant professor of political science at the University of Akron in Akron, Ohio, who has studied the impact of comparative ads. Farmer, other researchers and campaign consultants agree that negative ads are more memorable than positive ones, provided they reinforce a belief and remain relevant to the central issues of the marketing campaign. In political campaigns, comparative ads work because "people have a cynical view of politics and tend to believe the negative very quickly," says Farmer.

Though many Americans say they don't like negative political ads, research by faculty members at the University of Georgia found that not only are attack ads initially effective, but their impact increases over time, perhaps because they produce an emotional response. And positive ads used to counter them are not as effective because they're ultimately less powerful than the opponent's attack ad.

Negative ads featuring direct comparisons can successfully educate and motivate target audiences, such as the way TV spots for Total brand cereal humorously demonstrate its benefits by showing how many bowls of another brand you'd have to eat to equal the nutrition in one bowl of Total. But before you undertake this type of campaign, it pays to know its risks.

While attack ads cause audiences to experience negative feelings about the company being attacked, negative impressions also go up for the attacker. So while a two-company fight launched by the underdog may prove successful, if there are multiple companies vying for dominance, launching a negative campaign could give lesser competitors an advantage and the opportunity to leap ahead of you.

If you're the market leader, launching attack ads may actually give your lesser-known opponent name recognition. When No. 2 soup brand Progresso went on the attack against No. 1 Campbell's, the leader responded by placing a blue can resembling Progresso's next to its own to describe the differences — which some believe only served to help consumers remember the challenger.

When making a direct comparison, the tone and execution of your campaign must expertly sidestep any possibility of being considered mean spirited or unlikable, to avoid having your campaign backfire.

A safer route is to skip the attack ads altogether and use implied comparisons. Avis doesn't directly attack Hertz, they simply "try harder." Wendy's legendary "Where's the Beef?" campaign never directly named McDonald's or Burger King but humorously implied that other burgers were smaller. In response to Kmart's campaign exhorting female customers to clip coupons, Wal-Mart adroitly ran spots showing busy women who had no time to clip coupons enjoying the convenience of low prices every day without them. No mudslinging necessary — just build a campaign around the comparative benefits of working with you, and your customers will make all the right connections.

People Marketing: Mercedes-Benz has been running ads featuring photographs of customers with their cars — the automaker received more than 1,000 snapshots when it solicited submissions earlier this year. KFC held a contest last year asking its customers to devise commercials for the chicken chain and ran the winning spot nationwide during prime time. More recently, Coors Light had a similar contest in Canada.

The magazine *Look-Look*, put together by the well-known Los Angeles trend-spotting firm of the same name, is made up entirely of contributions by amateur artists and only accepts advertising from sponsors, such as Virgin Mobile and Pepsi, who are willing to let members of that same contributor base design their ads.

In perhaps the best-known case of this, the political organization MoveOn.org organized a contest that solicited anti-Bush TV ads from its user community. Not only was the response enormous, but also the quality of many entries was surprisingly polished. As was the case with MoveOn.org, some of these ad-making contests are clearly geared toward people who are trying to break into the marketing business. The Coors contest, for example, was aimed at film school students. But that does not fully explain what some experts see going on here — or what it might mean for owners of brands large and small. More companies, it seems, are letting their most loyal customers dabble with creating and defining their brands. And even more surprising, perhaps, is that many companies' loyal consumers are eager to get in on the branding game.

What's driving this? As the CEO of ad giant Saatchi & Saatchi, Kevin Roberts is in a position to know a great deal about the relationship between consumers and the brands they choose, and he has recently published a book about where he sees that relationship heading. 'In Lovemarks: The Future Beyond Brands', Roberts argues that the best brands "are not owned by the manufacturers, the producers, the businesses." Rather, "they are owned by the people who love them." A related website, Lovemarks, is jammed with postings from people evangelizing for the products and services they love, from Lego to Post-it Notes.

Another take on the people's marketing notion is in the forthcoming book Brand Hijack by Alex Wipperfurth, co-founder of San Francisco marketing firm Plan B. Wipperfurth, whose clients have included Napster and Pabst Blue Ribbon, believes that companies need to embrace brand "cocreation." By that, he means that marketers should invite consumer subcultures to help shape a brand's ideology, use, and persona.

"The real hook is to have everybody selling their experience as consumers." The West Coast, In-N-Out Burger chain has done this exceptionally well, by developing a "secret menu," designed via customer suggestions, whose offerings are not on the official menu but are on the cash registers at its outlets. The accommodation helps create a kind of insider club, letting its members think about and discuss the brand in their own unique, unfiltered way.

Also extending this concept is Obtainium.tv, a Boston-based start-up. Motivated partly by their disgust for overbearing corporate marketing, the pair made a series of half-minute digital videos highlighting some of their favorite products — Puma sneakers and Schlitz and Pabst beer — and posted them at www.obtainium.tv. The concept evolved as they came to believe that there were more people like them, who had pent-up desire to promote the brands they love. "The real hook," Buckley says, "is to have this kind of peer-to-peer advertising, where everybody is selling their experience as consumers."

So far, Obtainium.tv is essentially a group of online forums featuring Blair Witch-style ads. You'll find nothing that would spark job offers from Madison Avenue, but in a sense that's the whole point — not to join the ranks of ad auteur but to give examples of (and encourage) what anybody can do with today's widely accessible technologies. "They're not ads," Mack says. "They're conversations about brands, in 30-second bits."

So far, the pros whose brands have been adopted by Obtainium have been fairly supportive. Pabst may link its website to an Obtainium microsite, for example. The experiment makes sense for the beer, says Pabst brand manager, because its recent resurgence was basically the result of a grassroots consumer phenomenon.

It's unclear whether there's a real business here (payment

for that Pabst deal is in the form of free cases of beer), but the bigger question for the rest of us is whether its founders have correctly discerned that we're at a cultural moment where marketing is democratized. And if we are, does that mean that some companies will be able to get customers to produce good advertising for them for free?

The Obtainium founders see the concept as inherently scalable: It doesn't have to be, as with MoveOn, about something as critical as the leadership of the free world. It can work for a big national brand or an intensely local one — the catch being that you have to give up a fair amount of control. "If you're going to let them participate, you have to let them participate on their own terms," Wipperfurth warns. According to Buckley, it boils down to this: "It's not necessarily being passionate about the brand. It's being passionate about your life, and the products you choose to incorporate in your life."

Marketing (Advertising) the Films: Bollywood, the film industry in Mumbai, India, has been booming. With no other entertainment option available to the public, movies experienced a golden age, at least commercially, with audiences flocking to the halls over long time spans in the earlier decades. With the advent of TV, video, DVD and other increased entertainment options apart from films; consumers have fixed amounts of time and resources allocated towards leisure activities. The film industry is experiencing that an added effort is needed to market the films both at home and abroad.

The marketing function of the film is not one of simply the "launch planning" of the film, although the launch plan is the most crucial. A well-developed marketing research and feedback system can be beneficial to a film throughout the entire process of a film, from idea generation all the way to the product post-release. But the "launch plan" of a film is the most noticed and easily recognized of the tasks. It is necessary to explore the importance of positioning, targeting and communication during that period. For a product such as a film, whose success is at least partly defined by peoples' perception around it, meticulous targeting and proper communication ensures that we say the right things, to the right people, and get more for less.

We construct rational and emotional quality for the film. Rational quality is dependent on the quality of its components. Hence the rational quality for a movie would be production house, actors, technicians etc. Emotional quality constitutes the more intangible aspects of a movie — how it is presented to the audience and with what emotional appeal. These two aspects put together give the "perceived quality" of the product (movie). Once the product is consumed, "actual" quality is compared to the earlier perception. The disparity between perceived quality and received quality leads to the level of satisfaction or dissatisfaction with the film.

Therefore, the communication should try to accurately portray the overall quality of the product so as to incite a buy-in, and be sure of being able to deliver on it to create creditability. At its core, a film is simply a concept, and its marketing is akin to being a "prototype" of that concept. Like prototypes, movie promotions and publicity try to tell the consumer what sort of quality and attributes the final product will have, and hopefully extracts a "promise to buy". It competes with prototypes of other films in the customer's mind space. There are two fundamental risks, no one buys into the prototype, or there is a mismatch between the promises of the prototype and the final product, leading to dissatisfaction.

Focus on two key tasks when creating your prototype: create a prototype that is exciting enough to get a buy-in, and then deliver on that creditability. It is as important to know your targeted audience as about your product (movie) that you're selling; hence the importance of proper targeting and communication. If you fail to target the right people, then you may not get a buy-in at all. Give them the wrong messages, and you may get a buy in, but word-of-mouth will ensure that your film falls flat. Typically, a film sees the highest viewer ship and revenue in the opening weekend. This then remains constant, or immediately starts to decline based on word of mouth and its overall "quality".

"Watching movies" however, is one of the most common hobbies amongst the people. People don't necessarily watch movies because they are "marketed" to them — they watch them for the entertainment value they offer. Therefore, it becomes relatively easy to evoke interest as least compared to some other product categories. After all, most people are already interested. If you can manage to reach that tipping point, from there you can move from *feeding information*, to providing *content* to an eager audience. The cost per communication falls as people actively search for information. At that point, media channels start to cover a film, not because of a film's public relation, but because the information is important to their consumers. A way of doing this is by ensuring that the targeted people are getting the right messages through targeted channels of communications.

Research conducted by the Maritz Marketing Research Group shows that, in Hollywood, 53 per cent of moviegoers decide on the movie they will watch, based on recommendations from others. Although there is no clear research for Bollywood, the figure surely indicates that a large proportion of the potential audience will be affected by the opinions of others i.e. word of mouth publicity. Add to this the popular adage that "nothing travels faster than bad news", and the fact that the movie viewer is in most cases a group and not an individual, it becomes apparent how potent word-of-mouth can be. Proper Communication of a film's idea serves two equally important purposes, to generate interest, and not to disappoint. The "expectations reduce joy", and the wrong expectations can totally backfire against the film.

There is a very important group among the targeted audience who needs to be familiarized about the quality of the film. For this group, watching films is either a passion or a preferred hobby. They define themselves and others partially by the depth and recency of their knowledge of Bollywood. We've seen such people in our everyday life — not only in films, but in books and music as well. This is a very important psychographic segment, one that defines the opinions of others around them. In word-of-mouth parlance these people are the "connectors", the product diffusion curves could call them "innovators or early adopters". Brand managers call them "spokespeople". Why target them? Since they are the people to whom, others turn for information, and they try to convert people around them to match their own opinions. There are some other key sets of people that we need to address: for example, women who have the power of negating the choice of an entire group of family, and youngsters (14—25) who make up the bulk of moviegoers and popular opinion.

One statement often made is that "this film is for everyone". Although, ideally, a film is made to appeal to the largest possible audience, it does not take away in anyway the importance of segmenting the audience. Targeting key psychographic segments can help our communication be accepted faster, while helping create champions for our films. Some other demographic segments (women especially) must also be targeted as they have a lot of say in the consumer behavior of the group. Meticulous communication is an opportunity to endow a film with certain attributes hence reducing "risk" to the consumer.

Advertising in the emerging markets: American and European consumer goods companies have hit a wall in their home markets; competition is fierce and growth minimal. But as these companies enter the fast-growing emerging markets of Africa, Asia, and Latin America, they face an equally harsh reality. The time-honored techniques that have made them leaders in developed markets — expensive brand building, frequent product enhancements, and sophisticated marketing are ill suited to the vast, but price-sensitive, middle and low ends of emerging markets. A study of 23 product introductions in such regions illuminates the operational and organizational approaches most likely to succeed there. The brand-name products will always capture their share of affluent consumers. But in the low-end of emerging markets, companies should take their cues from local competitors: keep local managers in place, adhere to local standards of quality, and maintain the autonomy and the cost efficiency of local operations.

BPO (business process office operation) ***as marketing channels and advertising***: BPO segment is fast emerging, as the new-age marketer's creamy layer demographic. It's a huge captive audience, and a young one that's ready to experiment with new things. Also, many of them are setting up new homes. We see in it an opportunity, not just to sell numbers, but to expose the brand as well.

In India, the BPO audience shows interest in products such as GSM phones and microwave ovens, and it could help influence purchases in bigger categories like plasma TVs as well. Huge discounts are offered on items as varied as luggage, watches and lifestyle apparel to special schemes on cell phones and services, credit cards, car finance and even on FMCG items. These products are being advertised in a big way with flashy ads, through different channels targeted to the youth segment (iGen generation) that is earning well and is ready to experiment with new and changing life style.

"BPO's have immensely augmented opportunities in institutional sales and they have emerged as a new captive channel that is experiencing robust double-digit growth year-on-year. For example, in Gurgaon (India) alone, 10-15% of our institutional sales come from BPOs" (Pepsi). Companies like Amul have identified the BPO sector as a "key institution", setting up parlors in all Wipro and Infosys campuses across the country, says a company official. That's not surprising, given that the company's milk sales in Mumbai city alone have jumped, thanks to the BPO demand for endless cups of tea, coffee and milk shake.

Take Wipro Spectramind, whose14000 employees are the target of some concerted marketing efforts from brands as diverse as LG Electronics and ICICI (for two-wheeler loans). Says Head, infrastructure and facilities: "It's one more measure to facilitate employee welfare and so it's open to any product that's relevant to them. A couple of days ago, there was a sale of Kashmiri shawls and stoles. Garments, cosmetics, credit card companies and mobile phone services have been the most common items over the last 15 months."

Accenture, which offers its 10,000 employees a range of schemes, covering everything from two-wheelers and cars to ice-cream, as part of its HR strategy. Says Head-HR, Accenture: "Popular brands such as Lee, Hero Honda, Nokia, Maruti, Kwality Walls, Philips, Hutch, HDFC, ING Vysya and ABN Amro have engaged with our employees to offer their products and services." For BPO companies, this is yet another HR carrot to battle the industry's high attrition rates. Says Accenture's Head: "We know how important it is for our employees to strike a balance between their work and personal lives. As part of our strategy to be a great place to work, we have undertaken several initiatives and we offer a basket of conveniences for our employees to have a work and life balance, be it in the form of flexi-timing, work from home using the latest technological innovations or even shopping for home while at work."

Nor is the marketing carrot restricted to discounts alone. Many marketers are now using the BPO segment to build loyalty programs. Says COO of Mumbai-based Epicenter Technologies: "What we encourage are extended warranties and gifts. For instance, Lifestyle has given membership cards and discotheques and other entertainment house discounts of 5-20% to employees on producing their I-cards" (2005). A large number of BPOs with huge market segment for variety of products and services is challenge for advertisers to capture this market.

ADVERTISING MODELS

Information Processing Model is the basic advertising model projecting how information is processed through different types of ads and in different segments. There are other models projecting the specific dimensions of advertising through ads and advertisers. These specific models focus on consumers and advertisers perceptions and behavior.

There are specific consumer oriented models that focus on consumer behavior and personality types, consumer involvement in processing of ads and the factors that affect the buying decisions of the consumers — acute need factor, ego-satisfaction, rational or emotional satisfaction, or just by habit or when emotional needs are fulfilled by buying brands that are visible to others. There are other models that focus on effectiveness of the ads viz short-term, long-term memory and optimum frequency of ads, and buying decisions of the consumers. There are models that focus on the advertising perception, the role of advertising — to inform and to persuade. The risk orientation of advertisers, global and local advertising, and global and local responsiveness of advertising agencies, and how they broker advertising knowledge efficiently. Some of these specific models are presented through the salient research section.

Information processing model is a rationalist model focusing on how individuals process information through information messages (ad messages). The information input is stimuli .... mass or personal. The selective information processing components of the advertisement messages are: Selective exposure to the message and its channel and selective attention given and perception by the consumer to the ad messages.

Selective exposure to the ad itself which is a part of the larger system depends on cluster and clutter in ads i.e. positioning and placement of ads. Selectivity factors such as psychographics and demographics, life styles of audience, ego involvement of the consumer with the ad, or his/her dissonance with the ad effect. Product exposure, attention paid to it, its perception and retention are selective and necessary components for processing information given in the ad messages by the consumers.

The consumer will acquire the information by selective exposure to the ads and will selectively attend to the messages, as what the consumer has been looking for. Consumer will interpret it within his/her framework of meanings (having utility). This will be selective perception of the product. If the consumer finds the ad message relevant and useful, it may be retained in his/her short-term memory. This is selective retention and will be able to recall the message or retrieve the source selectively. So the information process through ad message is not random but selective from consumer point of view.

Selective attention depends on the external factors of figure-ground relationship, physiological monitors such as noise, sound, contrast, and velocity etc. In the ad creating figure-ground relationship is necessary because of synergistic effect and the need to differentiate the relationships in ad message. Clutter or cluster of ad messages for a product does not catch attention. The intensity of the exposure of ad message can be affected by physiological monitors such as noise, sound, contrast, and velocity that is louder and brighter with increased movement to attract attention and more repetition to a point of greater selective attention to create impression.

The internal attention depends on the physiological ability to hear and understand what is being conveyed through the ad, i.e. is it within the range of consumer's attention span, and whether the consumer is mentally receptive to pay attention to the message.

What is relevant is retained and stored. The senses register the visual and auditory. The information can be retrieved from short-term memory and message can be recalled. The messages may not be recalled after a long gap in the ads. That is why ads have to be frequently repeated and reinforced.

Level of processing information is hierarchical according to the complexity and importance of information. The flow of information is initiated by activating a piece of information from the reservoir of memory and by activating the brain.

Motivation triggers the behavior and thus behavior is the function of motivation. Motive is strong and persistent internal stimulus around which behavior is organized. We all have similar central needs but different peripheral needs because of different uses such as social needs, rational or emotional needs. Motivation will differ according to peripheral needs. Therefore, consumer decision to buy is not always rational it could be emotional. The market researchers identify market segments for the product according to the primary motives of the consumers.

Feedback from the marketers to management is necessary

to reexamine and correct the advertising message. Communication requires overlapping perceptual i.e. field of experience. Marketers communicate about their products using symbols, signs, words and graphics etc in the ad message to evoke the intended meaning in the consumer. Meaning is in the individual's perceptual field and not in the environment though it is learned by social environment. It is different for everybody according to one's perceptual field. Meanings can be denotative i.e. there is object-sign relationship. It is connotative suggesting that relationship between sign, object and person is perceived. It is structural when connecting signs to express thoughts and understanding we get from sign to sign-relationship. It has contextual meaning when understood in certain contexts.

Some salient Research Studies in Advertising

These studies highlight the advertising perception, risk orientation of advertisers, global efficiency and local responsiveness of advertising agencies, sales promotion budgets, how to broker advertising knowledge efficiently, consumer behavior and personality types, consumer involvement in processing of ads, optimum frequency of ads, and the factors that affect the buying decisions of the consumers.

Advertising perception: for each of several areas, including account management, creative work and media service. According to the survey, an advertiser's top-of-the-mind awareness (TOMA) of an agency for one or more client services is that agency's differentiating competitive advantage with respect to this potential client. Studies confirmed that the Creative Dimension (CD) of an agency is more important than the Account Management Dimension (AMD) in driving preferences and, consequently, market share. Using this idea, management can swiftly realign its competitive advantage. *"An assessment of advertising agency service quality", Journal of Advertising Research, May-June 1999.*

Risk orientation of advertisers. Advertiser risk orientation is viewed in the context of the propensity of advertising managers to engage in risk-taking. Findings based on a survey of top advertisers in North America measured by advertising expenditure suggests that taking an advertising risk is not something that happens in isolation. Risk-taking is inextricably linked to the confidence and outlook of companies, and this has important implications for the development and acceptability of risky creative work by agencies for clients. Surveys revealed that risk-seeking advertisers differ from risk-averse advertisers in their attitudes towards creative and media decisions. The major difference between the two groups is that risk-takers are more confident about their selection of creative strategies and their choices of creative execution, and are more willing to try out different market segments, creative approaches and media and to react to market changes. — *West, Douglas, Sargeant, Adrian, 'Advertiser risk-orientation and opinions and practices of advertising managers', International Journal of Advertising, Vol. 18 1999.*

Agency strategy: global efficiency & local responsiveness. Globally Integrated Marketing Communications (GIMC) is a system of promotional management which co-ordinates global communications across countries and promotional disciplines, regardless of whether a standardized or adaptive strategy is employed. A survey of GIMC perceptions and practices among US-based executives of large multinational advertising agencies reveals that agency perspectives differ and are broadly subject to organizational as well as market contingencies. The findings confirmed and amplified the need to seek a balance between global efficiency and responsiveness to local conditions, which is necessary to achieve the desired degree of horizontal and vertical communication and coordination. The respondents indicated that coordination was not necessarily associated with centralization. It was reported that the creative function was the most coordinated of the promotion disciplines while media-buying was the least, which suggests that the media function is perceived in more localized terms than the creative function. The study suggests that not only agencies should think in GIMC terms but they should also integrate and share that thinking with their clients and use it to establish their own usefulness and competitive strategy. — *Gould, Stephen J.,*

Dawn B., Lerman, Grein Andreas F., 'Agency perceptions and practices on GIMC', Journal of Advertising and Research, Jan-Feb 99.

Ad and sales promotion budgets: An in-depth study based on 21 interviews, highlighting the practices of companies that are pro-actively coping with budgetary pressures, indicate that protecting advertising spending is more likely to happen when they: Tolerate the uncertainty associated with advertising spending. Allocate funds based on forward-looking objectives rather than historical precedent. Use more experienced brand managers who can balance marketing research information with intuition. Remain focused on brand equity. The factors affecting advertising and sales promotion budgetary allocations can be grouped into three main categories: (i) the good practices which managers felt contributed to an effective decision process: encouraging risk in an organization, combining quantitative models with judgment, focusing on brand differentiation, (ii) the bad uncontrollable practices which are the frustrating realities of the decision process: retailer power, short term focus, top-down influence, (iii) the ugly......correctable flaws or problems in the decision process: political sales force influence, historical inertia, ad hoc changes. — *Low George S., Mohr Jakki J., 'Setting advertising and promotional budgets in multi-brand companies', Journal of Advertising Research, Jan-Feb 99.*

Brokering advertising knowledge efficiently: To tap into, manage and exploit their intellectual capital and to make a mark as creative knowledge brokers, it has become essential for advertising agencies to adopt Advertising Knowledge Management (AKM) strategies which consists of codification and personalization. In codification, explicit knowledge is carefully classified and stored in databases ready to be accessed by anyone. This enables lots of people in the firm to retrieve data without contacting the originators. Personalization strategy is based on tacit knowledge that requires learning by trial and error, leading to the build-up of skills. Rather than being codified, tacit knowledge is tied to the person who developed it and is shared by direct person-to-person contacts. A personalization strategy concentrates on the belief that the most valuable knowledge exists in people's heads and can be augmented and shared via interpersonal interaction or social relationships.

The primary drivers pushing the application of AKM to communications are: accountability, time pressures and information overload, technology, reduced margins and leaner organizations and globalization. AKM will enable leading ad agencies to offer cheap 'commoditized' advertising services, especially over the web. Speed will be of the essence in such services. The first successful AKM systems will prove themselves and gain the confidence of clients, and will come to dominate the market. Interactive commoditized AKM products will potentially generate even more knowledge and a stronger market position for the agencies concerned.

A strong and unified corporate vision is a prerequisite to building a learning framework and developing AKM. Decisions need to be taken simultaneously to flexibly integrate and lever learning within the agency. While the starting point for AKM is to consider the skill and knowledge of the agency, the organization needs to do the following: develop rewards, recognition and career opportunities for specialists. Create a unified vision in an organization of specialists. Devise a congenial management structure to organize task forces. Ensure the supply, penetration and testing of top management. — *Ewing Michael T, West Douglas, 2000, 'Advertising knowledge management: strategies and implications', International Journal of Advertising, Volume 19.*

Consumer behavior mirroring personality types: A total of 100 adults — 55 female and 45 male, belonging to the age group 22 to 57 participated in a study over a course of three weeks, which indicated that individuals preferred images and advertisements that were consistent with the information-processing styles that characterized their personality types. On the basis of how one prefers to take in information and becomes aware of his/her environment, people were divided into two categories: *Intuitive*, they tend to focus on possibilities rather than the concrete. They enjoy solving new problems, dislike repetitive tasks and tend to focus on future possibilities. *Sensors,* they need hard objective facts coupled with an attention to details. They dislike new problems unless there are standard ways of solving them. The study revealed that images and advertisements that are perceived as realistic, concrete and informative will be evaluated more favorably and will elicit higher purchase intentions by individuals with sensor typologies as compared to ads that are perceived as imaginative, conceptual and abstract. The latter will find more favor with individuals with intuitive typologies. — *LaBarbera Priscilla A, Weingard Peter, Yorkston Eric A, 'Matching the message to the mind: advertising imagery and consumer-processing styles', Journal of Advertising Research, Sept-Oct 98.*

***Low-involvement processing of ads*:** Recent studies indicate that consumers regard the most reputable brands as performing similarly, and do not think learning about brands is very important. Brand decisions are made more intuitively than rationally. Most ads are processed at very low attention levels, using low-involvement processing which is a cognitive process using very little working memory, i.e., it is poor at interpreting messages or drawing conclusions from ads. It simply records and stores everything as an association with the brand. The long-term memory works in such a way that the more often something is processed, the stronger are its links with it. Thus, it is these associations, repeatedly stored through low involvement processing, which tend to define brands in our minds and influence intuitive brand decisions. Creativity does enhance the attention paid to ads. But it is hardly powerful enough to initiate the sort of high-involvement processing needed to interpret and store complex messages. It, however, does strengthen linkage between associations and the brand. —*Heath Robert, 2000, 'Low-involvement processing — a new model of brands and advertising', International Journal of Advertising, Vol. 19.*

***Exposure continuity rewarded*:** The notion that a single exposure is not enough to create the desired effect is so pervasive that most media-planning models assume an effective frequency of three exposures a week, and that advertisers would rather plan to be off-air than to expose their advertising at frequency levels below the targeted three. However, studies show that being off-air, as required by the much-prevalent pattern, is equivalent to being out of stock at the point of sale. Researchers conclude that continuity of exposure is rewarded and that the off-air weeks penalize a brand. — *F. Von Gonten, Michael Donius, James F. Journal of Advertising Research, July-August 97 Medium, message and time in advertising.*

Advertising is Double Helix: According to the newly proposed Double Helix model, advertising is non-linear, multi-dimensional, and achieves its effect over time, within limited parameters of medium and message. The model points out that the time span over which media and message interactions occur is an important variable in the advertising environment and central to the current debate about effective frequency. According to this model, the exposure to the advertising may result in attention, sometimes in interest, desire or action, but not in a linear sequence as AIDA.

The helix structure is a useful metaphor for understanding brands with one strand forming the physical and functional virtues and the other strand forming the emotional values of a brand. Brand extensions are offspring that inherit part of the parent brand's genetic material. Ad effects are presented in this model as part of a continuous process rather than a series of steps oriented towards an end game of purchase or adoption.

This model suggests that one ad, one exposure, even one campaign cannot communicate the compound of signals attached to the brands to create perceptions of value. The model challenges account-planners to develop more conclusive methods of measuring effectiveness and suggests that the thrust should be on how much advertising should be applied at each stage of persuasion process. — *Huey Bill, 'Advertising's Double Helix: A proposed new process model', Journal of Advertising Research, May-June 99.*

Six factors that shape buying decisions: Factors like the nature of the target audience, the purchase motivation and the importance of the decision to the consumer can dominate the consumer decision-making as explained in the six-segment message strategy wheel. It primarily consists of two halves: the 'transmission view' or the rational approach and the 'ritual view' or emotional approach. The transmission view of communication deals with imparting information. The ritual view conceptualizes communication as constructing and maintaining an ordered, meaningful cultural world that serves as a control and container for human action. Those within the industry adhered to a transmission view while advertising could be more readily understood under the ritual view.

The factors influencing our decisions in the ritual view are categorized in the following segments: According to Freudian psychoanalytic model, the consumer's emotional needs are fulfilled by brands that are ego-related. Purchase decisions are emotionally important to the customer to allow him to make a statement to himself about who he is. According to Veblenian social-psychological model, emotional needs are fulfilled by brands that are visible to others. Appeal can be directed to gaining social approval through product consumption. Sensory factor Products provide consumers with 'moments of pleasure' based on any of the five senses: taste, sight, hearing, touch or smell. The Cyrenaics strategy, that considers pleasure to be the sole end of life, seems apt in this segment.

The factors influencing our decisions in the transmission view are categorized in the following segments: According to Marshal economic model, consumers are assumed to be rational and deliberative individuals. Their desire for product information is high. Appropriate strategies include generic, pre-emptive, USP and positioning. The role of advertising is to inform and to persuade. Acute need factor, the consumers are driven by an acute need to buy a product. They desire information, but time limits the amount of information that can be gathered. According to Pavlov learning model, consumer decisions are made on the basis of rational buying motives, but consumers do not invest large amounts of deliberation time, and buy according to habit. Advertising provides a cue to how the needs of the consumer can be satisfied by an introductory brand, once the habit is formed, ads remind the consumer to continue buying. — *Taylor Ronald E., 'Six-segment message strategy wheel', Journal of Advertising Research, Nov-Dec 99.*

Can consumers be manipulated? Consumers possess the ultimate sovereignty in a consumer society. Though the silent majorities cannot change the way things are drastically, they are endowed with the supreme power to take the system to its extreme self-defeating logic; they can tear things down as quickly as they can build things up, if they so desire. The masses, which react to advertising on a mediated 'knowing' level, can never be manipulated with the disarmingly 'fooling' ads. Perhaps they have always known more than advertisers gave them credit for. The people in the advertising business ought to remember that as image-makers, they are not shadowy manipulators but the very conscience of the new society. — *Boutlis Paulie, 2000, 'A theory of post-modern advertising', International Journal of Advertising, Vol. 19.*

SUMMARY

Business enterprises advertise about their innovative ideas, products, services and people. Such information reach different segments of audience. People may or may not notice it. If noticed, people react by showing interest, accepting or rejecting them or not paying attention. Since 80s the spurts and innovation in information communication technologies (ICTs) have changed the nature of Advertising — its message presentation, channels and its reception by the consumers. Advertising has changed the consumer behavior.

In advertising, the transmission view of communication deals with imparting information. The ritual view conceptualizes communication as constructing and maintaining an ordered, meaningful cultural world that serves as a control and container for human action. Emotional needs are fulfilled by brands that are visible to others. Appeal can be directed to gaining social approval through product consumption.

The role of advertising is to inform and persuade. Consumer decisions are made on the basis of rational buying motives, but consumers do not invest large amounts of deliberation time, and buy according to habit. It is not always a rational choice, emotional appeals effect also. Advertising provides a cue to how the needs of the consumer can be satisfied by an introductory brand, once the habit is formed, ads remind the consumer to continue buying.

Advertising is non-linear, multi-dimensional, and achieves its effect over time, within limited parameters of medium and message. The advertisement models point that the time span over which media and message interactions occur is an important variable in the advertising environment and central to the current debate about effective frequency.

We could segment the audience on the basis of how they consume media, and how they process information. The important dimensions in business advertising are targeted audience, intended message, appeals, source credibility, channels, and growth of economy. Advertising needs have gone dramatic changes in India and world wise because of well-informed customer and consumers, growth in economy, competition among product brands, and increase in media options. The advertising techniques to position products vis-à-vis consumers and markets have changed accordingly. Advertising in global markets, and particularly in emerging markets for global brands calls for different techniques to position the products and services, and more so for the targeted local low-end audience in emerging markets.

The conventional advertising channels are Media, Interpersonal, and Traditional performing arts and folk arts channels, and outdoor channels. The ad messages are conveyed orally, in writing, in graphics and in gestures. Internet, cell phones, and even telephone landlines are the non-conventional advertising channels. The Internet, as an advertising medium, scores over the conventional media on two counts: in its ability to provide for interactive communication where the advertiser can establish a two-way communication with the consumer and in its ability to target communication to a specific target segment.

Advertising agencies should reposition themselves in the fast-changing business and advertising world. The decisions taken to reposition the agency in four specific areas of segmentation, scope, scale and capabilities will determine the value proposition that the agency intends to offer to its clients.

6

Public Relations

CORPORATE PUBLIC RELATIONS: BUSINESS, PRODUCTS AND SERVICES

Public relation signifies relationship of an organization — business, social, media etc with its 'publics'. A business organization has relationships with its Internal and External links. Thus it deals with internal and external publics. Public relation promotes understanding among its various publics through planned and organized activities to gain favorable response for its products, activities, policies and human relations. PR is the process of providing salient information about the business activities and subtle persuasion for gaining public support. A corporate PR responsibility is to explain its corporate policy and objectives to the public and creating a favorable opinion and trust about its products, services and top-management or owners. The effectiveness of PR depends on the attitude and support of the top-management. It is a communicative channel essential for the success and visibility of any business enterprise — big or small. Bigger companies have separate PR department since they have expanded business activities to cover under PR. Even these or smaller ones may choose to outsource business public relations to PR firms to get specialized counseling and services.

PR functions, Strategies, Focus, Channels

Corporate Public relations efforts through its specialized teams focus on three functions: building images, projecting images and sustaining those images. Three functional images are of corporate business culture, products and services and its top-leaders and management in general. Three PR strategies are used in the context of these three functions: build public opinion, create visibility, create credibility, and do active publicity. PR has five primary focuses: Public as consumers, Supply chain customers, Media, Government and employees. Interpersonal and media communication channels are used for public relation activities.

Initially, the efforts are towards *building* the positive image of the company and in due course to maintain that image as well to upgrade and enhance it. Along with it, PR teams concentrate on building positive image of the products and services and creating brands and brand loyalty. The public image building of the corporate is through media, public relations and business focused conferences. The Public relation (PR) team interacts with the consumers and customers both directly and indirectly, through interpersonal communications with the clients, press, seminars and conferences. Various media channels of print, television and even Internet are used to facilitate it. Certain media technologies are used to further it. The major objective is to create positive visibility for the company in general, its top-leaders and management in particular and for its products and services. Companies focus on building its image through communicating via advertising, public relation activities, by the quality of its products and services itself and by its business culture. It builds the image through relations with media, financial communities, and local and regional markets. If it deals with global products, projecting image in global contexts is equally important.

PR teams make efforts to *project* public image of the company and its products and services. They project its public image through photo and press releases, interviews and group discussions on various media channels and interpersonal group forums on wide range of subjects and as focal point for all company's publications including annual reports and newsletters.

Building and projecting the right image takes continuous immense efforts and it is important for the success of the corporate, its products and services. Sustaining the positive image through prominent public visibility needs equal efforts, time and importance. Corporate needs to put more sustained efforts when they go through the phase of 'Negative Image' for one reason or the other.

Sometimes companies take Ad blitz to create good image and change its negative image as a harsh employer, which might be hurting the business. For instance, Wal-Mart Stores of America has often been praised for its low cost innovative approach to retailing. In recent years its image has been smeared by accusations that it is insensitive to communities where it seeks to expand. It is ignoring social costs created by its mega stores. It is accused of hiring overworked and underpaid workers, low wages, no benefits and high turnover, hiring illegal immigrants, and sex-discrimination.

Last year to improve its image, it initiated a new wage structure and created a 40 persons compliance team to ensure that labor laws are adhered to and corporate diversity goals met. It has been using TV ad spots targeting mainly consumers, to respond to image problems. Last year it tested the effectiveness of launching a Print Ad 'image' campaign on a smaller scale by taking out full-page ads in the Newspapers in California, after voters in Inglewood have rejected its plan to build a super center.

In 2005, it has taken Public advertising as a major part of its defense strategy. Wal-Mart launched an aggressive campaign to bolster its image. Its negative image is being projected with allegations of gender bias and unfair labor practices. In Jan 05 it has given full-page ads in the 100 Newspapers nation wide and in daily and minority publications in 15 major markets. The ads are showing Wal-Mart workers with a five paragraphs letter from the President and CEO and a list of positive points about its labor management in an attempt to set the record straight in labor issues.

The ads points, "when special interest-groups and critics spread misinformation about Wal-Mart, the public deserves to hear the truth. Everyone is entitled to their own opinions about our company but they are not entitled to make up their own facts". "It is becoming clear that we have to be more aggressive in telling our story. The purpose is to be more proactive and initiate debate".

Retail marketing specialists are of the opinion, such an aggressive image campaign is rare and not always cost effective and Wal-Mart image problems will be changed at the store level only through customer's experience with a healthy sales staff.

Some public relation firms are analyzing blogs on the Internet for some companies to know what is being said about them and their competitors.

PUBLIC RELATIONS AND MEDIA

Media is powerful creator of positive or negative images. Therefore media visibility, use, has significant impact on businesses. Business has to plan media strategies for PR. PR managers are in touch with editors of daily and weekly newspapers, trade journals, head of advertisement divisions and freelance writers for Media relations. They would help in positive publicity or justified in counter the negative publicity by explaining facts, issues etc. Business enterprises buy time in electronic media, space in print media and position its material whether as ads, news brief, news item, interview with top-leaders or management at top levels and even projecting image through employees and consumers.

PUBLIC RELATION AND GOVERNMENT

Public relations will gain its rightful place only if the government were to utilize this powerful medium for meaningful communication on matters of critical importance. Exploiting the power of professional public relations to carry the message of public health programs, education initiatives, water supply and sanitation programs, infrastructure development, etc. For we all know that a successful government program can turn overnight into a perceived failure if it is not communicated right.

Government PR has three functions: building images, projecting images and sustaining those images. Three functional images are of government — its leaders and functionaries, its programs and services, and its rules and regulations. The function of government PR is to inform, educate and motivate general public and business groups in particular about its programs, and to abide by its rules and regulations. Four PR strategies are used in the context of these three functions: build public opinion, create visibility for the programs, create credibility for government — its leaders and functionaries, and do active publicity or propaganda in these contexts. PR has four primary focuses: Public and Business groups, Public relation agencies, Media, and Government functionaries. Interpersonal and media communication channels are used for public relation activities.

PUBLIC RELATION STRATEGY: SELF-PROMOTION IN CORPORATE

Having the right skill set, attitude and focus makes a great combination to succeed at the workplace. It is also essential to be able to project oneself in the right light. With marketing having become an essential part of new-age living, success at the workplace demands that one is able to sell one's talents well. In this instant age, with packaging having assumed important proportions in all parts of existence, the workplace is no exception. Growing competition in business world demands that professionals put their best foot forward in all spheres, which will help them emerge winners.

Overall, the job market has witnessed a tremendous surge in the last decade. Competition has forced professionals to get much more people-savvy. Public relation for self-promotion has become essential. Traditionally, self-promotion has negative connotations. Earlier most professionals will not talk about their achievements and capabilities with élan and confidence. However, with globalization, corporate culture has undergone vast change.

Self-promotion is no longer associated with conceited, arrogant and egotistical behavior. Over the years, it has become more about an exercise in conducting self-PR as many realize that it has become a crucial element to finding a job, scaling upward, negotiating a raise and ensuring that you draw attention for the right reasons.

Some views about why self-PR is useful "Marketing oneself is as essential as possessing the right skill set. If you can convince your boss about skills, then execution is not a problem. But in order to convince, sometimes you may have to talk big". "Self-promotion is simply enlightening people about your achievements, which, in turn, can help you to seize better opportunities and set yourself apart from competition." "Sometimes it can help professionals secure the dream job that they have been looking for." "Often, while meeting prospective employers, many people who can pitch themselves well often sail through as the confidence and assurance impresses the interviewer."

Public Relation Agencies: The new business practice is to promote public relations through Public relation agencies. Public relation practitioners counsel top-leaders and top-management in companies on PR matters particularly about their image, image of the company and its business culture. They counsel management in dealing with government, media and public. Thus these PR practitioners counsel, manage and organize PR activities for the companies at different levels and particularly with external links and publics. The larger companies have their in-house PR divisions that mainly counsel, manage and organize PR with the internal links and coordinate with hired public relation agencies and Public relation practitioners in providing relevant and salient information about business matters — issues and facts. Smaller businesses may outsource PR work through public relation agencies or Public relation practitioners depending mainly on their Public relation focus and priorities.

Public relation activities focus is on preparing and releasing news reports, features, brief notes to the media channels either through space bought or through courtesy of media channels.

The focus is on preparation of booklets and brochures for company's products and services; and preparation and issue of promotional material to improve the image of the company and top leaders. Issuing endorsement statements by top leaders supporting, rejecting or debating government public policies particularly economic policies; and issuing endorsement statements by them about their business competitors or business competition form part of their thrust areas. PR managers help provide matter and help prepare speeches of its management and leaders for public functions, seminars and conferences. They organize video press conferences for the management and participant groups.

Normally, and usually, in-house divisions handle PR with the internal links i.e. employees of the company. The focus is on facilitating professional development and training programs for them. They co-coordinate and resolve conflicts among employees, human relation division, and management. PR teams plan and organize welfare programs; and help execute them for the welfare of the employees and their families. These are efforts towards promoting and building employees job and work environment satisfaction.

They edit special reports for shareholders and gather shareholders opinions and suggestions. Issue bulletins for customers, and information sheets for public. Facilitate maintaining relations between large-scale investors and management. In a small company they may even share prepare advertisement matter or revise such matter prepared by ad agencies.

They prepare audio and video, and photo material on company's special activities for limited release in conferences, seminar, and trade shows. They organize press conferences, special meetings, exhibitions, annual functions, competitions, conferral of awards and honors. Eminent guest speakers and experts are invited for talks on special interest to the business activities and its training programs. The PR managers select, invite and follow on such programs.

PR teams can play significant role in managing crisis in the company whether it is due to natural disaster, strike by its workers, financial problems or negative image. They need to handle the crisis by handling public, its stakeholders and shareholders, media employees and government.

Public relation research is important and necessary component of PR. Research and feedback on its PR activities focus on credibility, acceptability and effectiveness of the messages that are sent to its publics.

The abovementioned activities are the major thrust areas for PR. According to the company's policies, Public relation agencies or in-house divisions or by both may handle these activities. The PR team should be experts, with amenable personality traits, and professional and social networking to facilitate PR programs.

SUMMARY

Public relation activities are essential and important for business enterprises in promoting the corporate image and its business culture, its top-leaders, and management and employees in general on one hand. On the other hand the public relation focus is on promoting its products and services. Promotion is through Corporate Public relations efforts through its specialized teams who focus on three functions: building images, projecting images and sustaining those images. Three functional images are of corporate business culture, products and services and its top-leaders and management in general. Three PR strategies are used in the context of these three functions: build public opinion, create visibility, create credibility, and do active publicity. PR has five primary focuses: Public as consumers, Supply chain customers, Media, Government and employees. Interpersonal and media communication channels are used for public relation activities. The thrust areas for Public relation activities for PR teams are varied. Public Relation Agencies, independent Public relation practitioners, and in-house PR divisions of business enterprises handle these activities according to Corporate policies.

7

Communication Skills

> *The gratitude stimulates the brain's left prefrontal cortex, where hope, optimism and appreciation reside. This in turn tickles the limbic system to release feel-good endorphins. When it is the right neocortex, people feel worried, pessimist and frustrated. The habit of thinking what is right is so non-ingrained that people think of it when asking what is wrong.*
>
> —M.J. Ryan

EFFECTIVE COMMUNICATION

Effective communication is important for the success of business practices. These practices may relate to dealing internal and external links, marketing the products and services and use of technology. Thus a variety of communication skills are necessary for effective communication. The important point is these are to be acquired as well develop both in formal and informal settings. Such formal setting is training program through workshops, seminar, business conferences and coaching; and informal settings are social and business Networking. In business, skills are required to communicate effectively, and confidence, ability and language are needed to conduct oneself in business environment effectively. The emphasis is on the four skills needed for effective communications – speaking, listening, writing and reading and over and above an ability to work with others both in and out of the organization and those associated with it.

The main focus of effective communication is the Individual employee in the organization at various levels and across functions. A number of basic and advance skills are needed for him/her to acquire as well develop to use effective business practices in the organization both with the internal links and external links to make organization progress. Various levels also demand different communication skills. Some of these are time-management skills.

INTERPERSONAL COMMUNICATIONS

Interpersonal communication is the major channels for corporate communication both for internal and external links. It is necessary for the employees to be adept in interpersonal communication skills and learn more about them and develop them to be successful. Learning and development can be through training and development programs aiming at particular skills. Further, a person can develop strong communication skills by practice and experience.

From a communication standpoint — an inner world, outer world, relations, means of expressions are not only product of prior communicative processes, but require enactment to function in any particular context. This treats actions as real, pivotal events rather than as transitory states of preexisting entities. That is, the events and the objects of the business world exist because of patterns of actions that have occurred previously and because actions are being performed now to bring them into being. That is the identities of the persons and the reality of the institutions are accomplished by patterns of interaction rather than being objects. This requires us to think in terms of interaction patterns rather in terms of atomistic units.

The dynamics of human interpersonal communications is grounded in three universal aspects of human condition: persons interpret their environment and experience; they interact with their fellows, and they remind to themselves that there is more to business reality than the immediate moment and the process of interpersonal interaction continues. Thus interpersonal communication is a process. *It is a continuous reflexive process of creation and maintenance of business realities.*

Interpersonal communication gives us unique ways of understanding ourselves, our relationship with others, and the situations in which we find ourselves, that is, our business world. *We can have understanding of our business world from First Person Perspective or from Third Person Perspective.* We communicate interpersonally orally, through non-verbal cues including body language, listening, in writing, and even reading. These are basic communication skills that are needed and should be well developed for good business practices in all areas.

GETTING YOUR MESSAGE ACROSS IN BUSINESS

The purpose of communication is to get your message across to others. This is a process that involves both the sender of the message and the receiver. This process leaves room for error, with messages often misinterpreted by one or more of the parties involved. This causes unnecessary confusion and counter productivity. In fact, a message is successful only when both the sender and the receiver perceive it in the same way. By successfully getting your message across, you convey your thoughts and ideas effectively. When not successful, the thoughts and ideas that you convey do not necessarily reflect your own, causing a communications breakdown and creating roadblocks that stand in the way of your goals — both personally and professionally.

Getting your message across is paramount to progressing. To do this, you must understand what your message is, which audience you are sending it to, and how it will be perceived. You must also weigh-in the circumstances surrounding your communications, such as situational and cultural context.

The communication activity is a process. The essential elements are: there is interaction so there is sender/s and receiver/s within a context. There is a message to be conveyed through a channel. The objective of the interaction is to have intended or unintended effects on receivers (targeted audience), to assess the effectiveness, their should be loops of feedback to the sender and receiver. The need for communication channels, messages and audience for the focused issues are varied and are developed overtime.

The human effort is to discover nature, essence, and dynamics of communication to learn what communication is and how it works and to develop means of communicating more effectively. The messages in a shared environment could not only be oral, written, non-verbal, visual or olfactory but these could also be laws, customs, practices, ways of dressing, gestures, buildings, flags, gardens, exhibits, etc. Language and body synthesizers that are culture specific are essential components of messages. People in communication define the various types of society, sub-society and groups. Their characteristics depend on the modes of communication they possess, media exposure, rituals and personal relationships.

Basic Communication Model: Business Functions

This has five basic elements of sender, message, receiver, channel and channel noise, effects, and feedback.

Sender: To establish yourself as an effective communicator, you must first establish credibility. In the business arena, this involves displaying knowledge of the subject, the audience and the context in which the message is delivered.

You must also know your audience (individuals or groups to which you are delivering your message). Failure to understand who you are communicating to will result in delivering messages that are misunderstood.

Message: Next, consider the message itself. Written, oral and nonverbal communications are effected by the sender's tone, method of organization, validity of the argument, what is communicated and what is left out, as well as your individual style of communicating. Messages also have intellectual and emotional components, with intellect allowing us the ability to reason and emotion allowing us to present motivational appeals, ultimately changing minds and actions. If your message is too lengthy, disorganized, or contains errors, you can expect the message to be misunderstood and misinterpreted. Use of poor verbal and body language can also confuse the message.

Channel: Messages are conveyed through media channels, with verbal including face-to-face meetings, telephone and videoconferencing; and written including letters, emails, memos and reports and through media channels about the company, products and services.

Receiver: These messages are delivered to an audience. No doubt, you have in mind the actions or reactions you hope your message prompts from this audience. Remember, your audience also enters into the communication process with ideas and feelings that will undoubtedly influence their understanding of your message and their response. To be a successful communicator, you should consider these before delivering your message, acting appropriately.

Effects: Can be assessed in terms of creating awareness, knowledge, attitude and behavior change through relationship between communication channels, targeted audience and society. Interpersonal communication effects persuasion through personal influence. Media Effects address the dependency of audience on media. It is key variable in understanding why and when media will change their beliefs, attitude, and behavior and maintain a sense of connectivity with business reality.

Feedback: Your audience will provide you with feedback, verbal and nonverbal reactions to your communicated message. Pay close attention to this feedback, as it is crucial to ensuring that the audience understood your message (in later section we have discussed communication skills in giving feedback).

Context: The situation in which your message is delivered is the context. This may include the surrounding environment or broader culture (i.e. corporate culture, international cultures, etc.). In 80s, the communications contexts widened its scope three-way: society specific context, specific–society context within global context, and global context of communications. The global context has assumed importance as a context in itself and also for consideration of development of communications in a particular society.

Communication barriers: To deliver your messages effectively, you must commit to overcome the barriers that exist in each of these stages of the communication process. Communication barriers can come up at every stage of the communication process (which consists of sender, message, channel, receiver, feedback and context) and have the potential to create misunderstanding, confusion and negative returns.

To be an effective communicator and to get your point across without misunderstanding and confusion, your goal should be to lessen the frequency of these barriers at each stage of this process with clear, concise, accurate, well-planned communications. Barriers in context tend to stem from senders offering too much information too fast. When in doubt here, less is oftentimes more. It is best to be mindful of the demands on other people's time, especially in today's ultra-busy society. Once you understand this, you need to work to understand your audience's culture, making sure you can converse and deliver your message to people of different backgrounds and cultures within your own organization, in different segments of society in your country and even abroad.

The above basic model presents a linear view of communications but that is not true with business realities. We have circular communications because the main objective is to make the customers and consumers understand what the businesses want to convey about their products and services; let their internal and supply chain understand their business culture and policies, products and services. All elements of the model are operative in business environments.

Planning Business Messages

The business documents, written requests, messages, reports, presentations memo, letters, newsletters, print ads etc. need to be organized according to the objective and targeted audience. The effort should be to build effective communication skills in all of these areas. Appropriate communication channel: oral, written, electronic should to be selected.

Written communications through various business documents can be effective if it is clear and concise and should convey the facts and information to the point. The business letters, the memo or other written message circulars whether to the outsider or within the organization should be straightforward and to the point, giving no chance for misinterpretations. Does it raise unanswered questions or fail to make the point you need to get across?

Is your written communication well organized? Does each idea proceed logically to the next? Make sure your written communications are easy to read and contain the necessary information, using facts where needed and avoiding information that is not relevant. Again, outline the course of action you expect, such as a return call or visit. Close appropriately, making sure to include your contact information. While this may seem obvious, it is sometimes overlooked.

Technology has enhanced the business connectivity. Mobile telephones and other telecommunication means have facilitated the interpersonal quick communications on business matters and with business associates. E-mail as written communication gives good and instant connectivity to people both within and outside the organizations.

Even instant messaging (IM) may become the primary business communication channel. First taken up enthusiastically by cell phone toting, SMS-savvy Web users who enjoy chatting real-time with text dialogues within a network of chat-buddies, IM has evolved as a nifty corporate person-to-person communication tool. It may even overtake email as the preferred means of rich online communication because of exciting content, its immediacy and versatility. For example, with some of the latest IM products, such as MSN Messenger, you can send and receive IMs, streaming audio, and streaming video all in the same window. IM is a "real-time" medium, in contrast to the send-wait-receive asynchronicity of e-mail messages. A key feature that makes IM for business acceptance is on-line presence of other party. IM has had "chat buddy lists" as a central feature from the start, letting you know who is online, and giving you the option to accept or refuse messages as you wish. Since the exchange of presence information creates an "open" channel between users who are online, IM accommodates more of a free form, loosely structured style of conversation than the phone.

COMMUNICATION IN ORGANIZATION

To ensure successful communications within your organization, it is best to start with the very basics: first one should be at ease and even adept in verbal and non-verbal communications. In the workplace, these types of communications are continually exchanged, oftentimes without much planning or even the thought that such communications are taking place.

Non-Verbal Communication is important. It is not always just what you say. It's also how you "say" it – taking into account your eyes, your posture, your overall body language, even your appearance at the time the communication is exchanged, and the voice in which you offer the exchange. In verbal communication, an active dialogue is engaged with the use of words. At the same time, however, non-verbal communication takes place, relying on nonverbal cues, such as gestures, eye contact, facial expressions, even clothing and personal space.

Nonverbal cues are very powerful, making it crucial that you pay attention to your actions, as well as the nonverbal cues of those around you. If, during your meeting, participants begin to doodle or chat amongst themselves, they are no longer paying attention to you. Your message has become boring or your delivery is no longer engaging.

Once again, you need to be considerate of cultural differences when using or interpreting nonverbal cues. For instance, the handshake that is so widely accepted in Western cultures as a greeting or confirmation of a business deal is not accepted in other cultures, and can cause confusion.

While eye contact, facial expressions, postures, gestures, clothing and personal space are obvious nonverbal communication cues, others strongly influence interpretation of messages, including how the message is delivered. This suggests paying close attention to your tone of voice, even your voice's overall loudness and its pitch. Be careful about your own nonverbal cues, as well as the nonverbal cues of those around you. These can enhance your communications.

Body gestures can both compliment and contradict your message.

Eye contact is an important step in sending and receiving messages. Eye contact can be a signal of interest, a signal of recognition, even a sign of honesty and credibility. Closely linked to eye contact are facial expressions, which can reflect attitudes and emotions. Posture can also be used to more effectively communicate your message. Good posture indicates confidence and reliance. Clothing is equally important. By dressing appropriately for your job, you show respect for the values and conventions of your organization. A well-dressed person creates good working ambiance around him/her. This inspires self-confidence, organization, and work motivation; and work inspiration for others around you also since they are attracted by these qualities.

Give people their personal space when communicating. Do not invade their personal space by getting too close and do not confuse communications by trying to exchange messages from too far away. This is very important in international business dealings. Some cultures like to sit or stand close to each other while talking, while others like to keep a short distance between them. There are other niceties in this respect which one should be careful about.

The dynamics of business communications in employee – management relationship are in the context of performance, productivity and human relations.

We reiterate as mentioned earlier in Chapter 2 about corporate communications with internal links, 'Internal communication is mostly interpersonal. This channel is used both for formal and informal interactions. It is both vertical and horizontal interpersonal communications encompassing employees' interaction and management interaction within the different business divisions and facilities of a corporate. Feedback is important component in the interpersonal interaction process. There is technology support to interpersonal communication also. People at all levels communicate with each other by telephones, emails, intranets through computers, formal presentations and after question hours to clarify their doubts and also through informal interpersonal interactions.

The informal internal communication is facilitated in staff lounges, lunchroom, cafeterias, around the vending machines and water coolers, and people interact and exchange information and views informally even when they are walking through the office corridors. These social operating mechanisms help to get to know the office happenings, informally exchanging both positive and negative views about people and products, and sharing new ideas and knowledge effortlessly and inadvertently.

Open interaction strategies, operating group dynamics help the leaders to promote healthy interpersonal communication among people in the business at all levels. The interpersonal communication is important, for the people at all levels of business organization from top-leaders to other levels of employees. Such communication process helps in surfacing the business reality, finding realistic solutions and implementing them. Some salient communication interpersonal channels including organization culture facilitate the communication process. The characteristics of the communicator are important in this process. Further, appraisals as communication tools help in getting the right person for the right job.

But these above mentioned business communication nuances need communication skills to handle it deftly with positive results. We will discuss what kind of skills helps in general. These are discussed under the sections: 'Developing communication skills' and certain other salient techniques helpful in developing these skills under section 'Practical techniques'.

DEVELOPING COMMUNICATION SKILLS

Communication skills, including written, oral presentations and technology oriented, as well as an ability to work with others, are the main factors contributing to job success. In spite of the increasing importance placed on communication skills, many individuals continue to struggle with this, unable to communicate their thoughts and ideas effectively – whether in verbal or written format. This inability makes it nearly impossible for them to compete effectively in the workplace, and it stands in the way of career progression. Lack of good interpersonal communication both with internal and external corporate links aggravates it further.

Particular Communication Skills are needed in different business areas and functions. People are hired with befitting communication skills by businesses. Further, such skills may be enhanced through on-job training and development programs and exposures to seminars, business conferences and in-house workshops focusing on the particular skill areas.

The business communication skills focus on development of individual and the organization; skills needed to communicate with internal and external corporate links, and with leadership for business functions.

We discuss communication skills development for business practices under four heads: General communication skills, special communication skills, practical techniques to develop communication skills, and training programs to develop communication skills. These divisions are purposive to facilitate discussions, they may be overlapping and a few are highlighted to familiarize the reader with communication skills development.

General Communication Skills in Business Practices

Communication skills for giving feedback, Networking, making Business Presentation, managing effective meetings and work-outs are discussed under this head.

Communication Skills for Giving Feedback

Feedback to corporate internal links — employees can be both written and verbal. Verbal is preferred and is more effective. Written feedback in the form of warning, reprimand, explanation may sound more officious and harsh for improvement. Create Positive Feedback. To give constructive feedback to your employees (subordinates) needs communication skills and diplomacy. The most frequent feedback is confirmatory and corrective. Confirmatory feedback ascertains the moves and actions of the employee.

Corrective Feedback needs more communication skills. First, it should start with a positive note that shows appreciation of what has been done and understanding of the current situation. This makes the participant more alert and receptive to the message relayed. Secondly, set up good rapport. If he/she is convinced that the boss is not biased and has his/her best interests in mind, he/she will not turn hostile and receive the feedback in right spirit. Thirdly, empathize to understand why he/she is behaving in a particular manner, not only at the time of communicating feedback but throughout the interaction. Such understanding builds and improves relationship.

Clarify the agenda for feedback to the employee before discussing. It can antagonize him/her if there is no clue about the issue being talked about. The purpose of the corrective feedback should be spelt right at the beginning. Focus should be in giving specific examples that need correction. "Your behavior really upsets me" does not convey much. Re-phrase it, 'I could not submit the research report in time because of your inability to work on research project efficiently. The end result is we have no further funding for the time being'. Positive reactions result with this kind of feedback. Not only the employee realizes that he/she is at fault but he/she is also made subtly aware of the gravity of consequences. Further, specific instances concerning slips and errors in performance should be mentioned to make feedback specific and precise. This would add to the gravity of the interaction. Finally, the communicator must ensure that feedback intentions are understood rightly. If the intentions are misunderstood then the purpose of feedback is defeated.

Networking

Business Networking is necessary channel for communication about business trends and practices both for personal and professional visibility and feedback. The objective is to socialize with the like mind people in the business to talk about the business trends in general and exchange ideas about particular trends. They aim to develop business contacts and opportunities to be availed of later at mutual advantage.

Networking clubs, business associations, exhibitions or conferences are business Networking channels for most of us.

There are certain groups that attend networking events, new businessperson, amateur, professional, and the seasoned Networker. The seasoned Networkers stand in a group, always watching what goes on around them. The motto for them is to 'come away with at least one more contact' in every networking session. Usually he/she has a successful business, and enjoys being at networking events for the buzz, and of course for the opportunities. With networking after a while, they know most people in the event venue and in approaching a newbie, quite likely they would think about the business leads that this new contact may give. They will look after the newbie, introductions will follow and will also offer a bit of mentoring (as they probably do all day long in their own business).

How to approach fellow Networkers at an event with justifiable reason? Some events have lost the principal objective of meeting new business opportunities. Quite literally, the tighter the group at an event, the harder it is to get yourself in. If you see a group of Networkers talking and there is a reasonable space between them, there is a reasonable chance of joining that discussion.

Those who network do so because they want to be there, they want new business, they want to meet new contacts and they understand the initial pressures of joining a group. With this in mind you should approach one of the key organizers and ask for their help in pointing out possible sources of business, or one better, get them to introduce you to them. Organizers are there for this purpose (or they should be).

Your responsibility, when introduced, is to say something interesting about something you know both of you have an interest in. If you are in marketing research and the target has a advertising business, you would say something like, "have you seen the latest product placement in the movie and TV serials." You would then be able to both talk about the same thing and get a feel for each other. Remember this is not a sales pitch, but common ground to start conversation. You might end your conversation by talking about other trends in advertising and a suggestion to talk more about it from the market research perspective at his business premise when you pass by. May be there is an opportunity for a market research project. Experienced Networker love saying to business contacts, "I know someone who can do that for you, I'll have a word with them and see what we can do": being able to say this adds value to their own services, it's the next best thing to getting the work themselves.

Keep your initial comments limited and work your way in over a number of events. If you have something really worthwhile to add, suggest but never make promises you cannot keep. It is easy to try and please in this environment. No harm in saying that you will try to do or get something done but do not lose credibility.

The prospects of social networking that focus on business development are promising. Business Networking makes business connections, and make new contacts and friends. Networking among business associates of different companies has become imperative today. As competition peaks, the corporate world has become the survival of the fittest. With high-stress jobs becoming the order of the day, most professionals are realizing that it takes more than simple good work to be able to climb up. Networking, building the right image and trying to portray an image of self-assuredness and confidence have also become important criterion.

For networking, one must target the right person, at the right position, in the right division. Discover background information and personal connections that can give you an advantage. Initiate contact through mutual acquaintances that can make a warm introduction. Nurture existing relationships, cultivate new relationships, and organize them.

A CMO for marketing the products has to focus on an array of marketing outlets from Internet sites to Cable TV, movie theater advertising, to store promotions in order to reach global consumers. At the same time they must justify the quick returns of their campaigns to their companies. CMO of different companies may promote different products yet they do share many of the same challenges in a job that has become complex and risky. They feel if they network with other CMOs of different companies they may be able to share their work challenges far removed from the office politics. Because marketing options and product pricing are getting more complex, and consumers are getting busier and harder to reach as well to figure out. In this context many are joining seminars and non-competitive groups — with just one executive from a particular industry.

In such groups, CMOs get chance to build network and relationships, and exchange ideas with the peer groups from other big global companies. They also try to figure out their common problems and challenges. They get a chance to know ideas that they can use and that their competitors may not know about. They gain perspective on different marketing tools used by their peers. The gatherings may help them to improve their ability to work collaboratively since to succeed they have to work across functions in the company with many business unit leaders. Thus Communication skills for Networking is important for business development.

Making Business Presentations

Presentations are becoming more and more important in business scenarios. It may be to strike a new business deal, propose some changes in the work process, to discuss business strategies with specialized internal teams, or a presentation to the board of director or to the human resource manpower committee. Basically, the endeavor is to sell an idea by expressing across your viewpoints on the subject-matter optimally to the audience. How forcefully you are able to move across your ideas depends on the effectiveness of your presentation.

Preparation is one of the most important factors in determining your communication successes. Set presentation time well in advance, thus allowing yourself the time you need to prepare your communications. Think about the entire communication process and its components sender, message, channel, receiver, feedback and context. To give presentations is an art. There are some general rules to follow for forceful presentation:

Before delivery of presentation

1. What do you wish to communicate? Know your topic well and research it before presentation. Structure it, and highlight the salient points, the way you would like to present them. Your message should be clear, simple, natural and vivid. Be concise and to the point. Where appropriate, support these with short, easy-to-understand examples, which help demonstrate your message.

2. Know your targeted audience well and research about it (the objective focus). What are their interests, presuppositions and values? What do they share in common with others and how are they unique?

3. Rehearse your presentation, use video and audio rehearsals to improve on your body language, voice modulations, and delivery of words and emphasis on the important points to be made.

During presentation

1. How best can you convey your message? Language is important, so are the nonverbal cues. Choose your words and your nonverbal cues with your audience in mind. Develop a sense of timing, so that your contributions are seen and heard as relevant to the issue or matter at hand. In order to convert audience into listeners, you need to know why they should listen to you. What disposes them to listen? That implies that you know yourself why you are seeking to communicate the value or interest of what you are going to say.

2. The beginning and the climax of the presentation should be forceful. Your introduction should attract participant's attention and explain your objectives, clearly defining the main points of the presentation in logical sequence. These should flow well. Your climax should summarize the presentation clearly and concisely.

3. The presentation should be interactive. You should ask questions to the participants and be open for discussion during presentation or after presentation depending on the objective of presentation. A dash of humor always helps loosen up people.

4. Do not concentrate on one intelligent section of the audience. Distribute you attention. Do not side track from your topic. Remain focused on your objective.

5. Always use visual aids in your presentation. You may use transparencies, flip charts, slides etc. Make your visuals colorful and attractive. Use of graphics is recommended. The visual aids should be easy to read and easy to understand. They should synchronize with the points you are trying to communicate and should be easily visible to the audience.

6. Always ask for feedback from the audience about the presentation wherever it is plausible. This would help you make your future presentations better. Follow-on discussion after presentation to the board meeting or team meetings is in itself feedback. This helps you to plan action.

7. Dress attractively, nicely and groomed appropriately to give professional look and effusing confidence among the audience.

Pose self-confidence to attract audience attention to your presentation.

After presentation

After business presentation, be ready for discussions, explain wherever discussants needs more clarity, more facts, and more inputs. Welcome both positive and negative suggestions since they are healthy criticism. Incorporate them for subsequent meetings and actions.

MEETINGS — GIVING PEOPLE TIME

Setting aside a specific time for meetings and regular communications is a great idea. This allows time for everyone involved to prepare. Also, keep in mind that listening is oftentimes much more productive when working to communicate effectively, and can very well be more important than talking. Allow everyone involved the time they need to communicate effectively. Keep your messages short and concise. This means preparing in advance whenever possible. And for the impromptu meeting, it means thinking before you speak.

Running Effective Meetings: Business meetings are wonderful tools for generating ideas, expanding on thoughts and managing group activity. This face-to-face contact with team members and colleagues would need adequate preparation and leadership. Designate a meeting time that allows all participants the time needed to adequately prepare and ensure that all from the team are involved. If you are the meeting leader, make a meeting agenda, complete with detailed notes. In these notes, outline the goal and proposed structure of the meeting, and share this with the participants before hand. This will allow all involved to come prepared for the meeting and ready to work together to meet the goal(s) at hand. The success of the meeting depends on the communication skills displayed by the meeting leader. To ensure the meeting is successful, the leader should:

- Generate an agenda to all involved in the meeting
- Start the discussion and encourage active participation
- Work to keep the meeting at a comfortable pace – not moving too fast or too slow
- Summarize the discussion and the recommendations at the end of each logical section
- Circulate minutes to all participants

These will make your meeting productive and well received. There are other important areas that need to be considered to make sure your meeting and negotiation skills are fine-tuned and ready to take to the boardroom.

Managing a Meeting

Choosing the right participants is key to the success of any meeting. Make sure all participants can contribute and choose good decision-makers and problem-solvers. Try to keep the number of participants as a small group. Make sure the people with the necessary information for the items listed in the meeting agenda are the ones that are invited.

If you are the leader, work diligently to ensure everyone's opinions and ideas are heard. Guide the meeting so that there is a free flow of debate with no individual dominating and no extensive discussions between two people. Summarize the debate on that agenda item and move on the next item on the agenda.

When an agenda item is resolved or action is agreed upon, make it clear who in the meeting will be responsible for this. In an effort to bypass confusion and misunderstandings, summarize the action to be taken and include this in the meeting's minutes. In the Minutes, record the decisions of the meeting and the actions agreed. They provide a record of the meeting and, importantly, they provide a review document for use at the next meeting so that progress can be assessed. This is a useful technique to discipline individuals' performance and non-performance of agreed actions. And it gets high visibility.

The style of the Minutes issued depends on the circumstances. In situations of critical importance and where the record is important, you may need to take detailed Minutes. Where this is not the case, then Minutes can be simple lists of decisions made and of actions to be taken (with the responsible person identified). Generally, they should be as short as possible and as long as all key information is shown. The leader should issues Minutes on the same day.

Special Communication Skills

Time Management Skills, project management skills, Practical techniques for problem solving, Decision-making and Creative solutions are discussed under this head.

Time Management Skills are important to maximize your effectiveness in any business. These are some of the most important career skills that one must learn. Time Management skills are essential for successful people. These are the practical techniques that have helped the people in businesses and public service. By applying the skills you can optimize your effort to ensure that you concentrate as much of your time and energy as possible on the high payoff tasks. This ensures that you achieve the greatest benefit possible with the limited amount of time available to you.

These skills help you to become reliable and effective. It shows you how to identify and focus on the activities that give you the greatest returns. In this context, goal setting is a vitally important skill for achieving what you want to achieve with your life and profession. Learn how to set realistic goals, generate a life plan and leverage all of the opportunities that life has to offer. The following Time Management Tools facilitate these skills:

Time Management Tools

- Costing Your Time — Finding out how much your time costs
- Activity Logs — Understanding where you lose time
- Small-Scale Planning — Action Plans
- Prioritized To Do Lists — Doing the most important things first
- Personal Goal Setting — Planning to Live Your Life Your Way
- Professional Goal Setting — Planning by your career objectives
- Scheduling Skills — Planning to make the most of your time
- Time management resources.

Scheduling skills is most important: It is the process by which you plan use of your time. By scheduling effectively, you can both reduce stress and maximize your effectiveness. You need an effective system to schedule efficiently. This can be a diary, calendar, paper or electronic organizer, PDA. Scheduling is a five-step process:

- Identify the time available.
- Block in the essential tasks you must carry out to succeed in your job.
- Schedule in high priority urgent tasks and vital "house-keeping" activities.
- Block in appropriate contingency time to handle unpredictable interruptions.

- In the remaining time, schedule the activities that address your priorities and personal goals.
- If you have little or no discretionary time left by the time you reach step five, then revisit the assumptions you have made in steps one to four.

At the heart of time management is an important shift in focus: concentrate on results, not on being busy. Many people spend their days in a frenzy of activity, but achieve very little because they are not concentrating on the right things. This is neatly summed up in the Pareto Principle, or the '80:20 Rule'. This argues that typically 80% of unfocussed effort generates only 20% of results. The remaining 80% of results are achieved with only 20% of the effort. While the ratio is not always 80:20, this broad pattern of a small proportion of activity generating non-scalar returns recurs so frequently as to be the norm in many areas.

Project Planning & Management Tools

As you progress in your career, you will face more and more complex and difficult challenges. These may involve the coordination of many different people, the completion of many tasks in a precise sequence, and the expenditure of a great deal of time and money. You need specific skills to run these projects successfully, helping you to complete them successfully and with minimum wastage of resources. You must have good interpersonal and analytical communication skills for analysis of stakeholders in your business and managing their support for your projects.

Management Tools

- Estimating time accurately
- Scheduling simple projects
- Gantt Charts — scheduling projects with dependent Stages
- Critical Path Analysis & PERT — scheduling complex projects
- The Planning Cycle — A planning process for middle-sized projects

- Planning Large Projects & Programs
- Stakeholder Analysis — working out whose support you need
- Stakeholder Management — communicating to win support for your projects
- Project management resources.

PRACTICAL TECHNIQUES

Other useful communication skills are Problem-Solving Techniques, Decision-Making Techniques, and Creativity Techniques. These are essential skills for different levels of employees in the business organizations to communicate about the core competencies, processes and people.

Problem-solving Techniques are important and prerequisite for decision-making process for any area of business or its functions.

Problem solving Techniques are multi-step techniques:

- Identify the problem/s
- Extract most information from facts available
- Break down problems into manageable parts
- Cause & Effect Diagrams — identifying likely causes of problems
- Systems Diagrams — understanding how factors affect each other
- SWOT — analyzing your Strengths, Weaknesses, Opportunities & Threats
- Cash flow forecasting with spreadsheets — analyzing whether an idea is financially viable
- Risk Analysis
- Porter's Five Forces Analysis — understanding the balance of power in a situation
- Complexity Resources

Taking the right decisions related to diverse business activities and functions is important for good return on investment. Decision-Making Techniques help us to make better decisions when we have grasp on the problems through problem-solving techniques. These facilitate making the best decisions possible with the information available. With these techniques you will be able to map out the likely consequences of decisions, work out the importance of individual factors and choose the best course of action to take.

Decision-Making Techniques are multi-step techniques:

- Pareto Analysis — choosing what to change
- Paired Comparison Analysis — working out the relative importance of different options
- Grid Analysis — making a choice taking into account many factors
- Decision Trees — choosing by valuing different options
- PMI — weighing the pros and cons of a Decision
- Force Field Analysis — analyzing the pressures for and against change
- Six Thinking Hats — looking at a Decision from different perspectives
- Cost/Benefit Analysis — seeing whether a Decision makes financial sense
- Decision-Making Resources

Creativity Techniques

Develop creative solutions to the problems you face. You can use a wide range of techniques to come up with creative and imaginative solutions to the challenges you face. There are three systematic approaches to creativity. These are important lateral-thinking based approaches, which can be used to come up with original solutions to problems.

One approach is to be creative in improving products and services. A second approach is about generating new products and services. Applied creativity is third approach to solve problems and create growth opportunities. It is not just creating new ideas, but making them happen! Applied creativity combines imaginative and analytical thinking. Creativity is not just about generating a lot of ideas that never see the light of day and is only for the "creative types" in R&D and advertising. Applied creativity is the key to gaining and maintaining your organization's competitive edge. It recognizes everyone's ability to be creative. It is finding and defining new problems and opportunities, and implementing workable solutions. It is experiential learning with on-the-job problems.

Techniques for Creative Solutions

- Morphological & Matrix Analysis can be used for creating new products, services & strategies.
- Brainstorming helps in generating many radical ideas.
- Reframing Matrix facilitate looking at products, services & strategies with different perspectives
- Concept Fan — widening the search for solutions
- Random Input — making creative leaps
- Provocation — carrying out thought experiments
- Implement — a simple process for creativity.

Technology Oriented Skills

In businesses today the employees at all levels have to be computer literate and trained. Different expertise in computer related technology is required at different levels. Communication through emails, use of Internet for database and searches and use of Intranet and net conferencing etc are the basics. Use of Software packages for different business functions would require software competencies. Businesses in Information technologies would need higher technological competencies. These communication competencies are upgraded all time since the pace of technology is changing fast and businesses have to keep pace with them.

TRAINING AND DEVELOPMENT

Training for different levels of employees is planned to raise the levels of skills, productivity and performance. Training should be developed relevant to the operational skills of the employees. Training need assessment methods are planned through three dimensions of search analysis — emotional, rational and empirical. In emotional dimension, the training considerations are not rational i.e. training is imparted for the sake of training. In rational dimension, the employees themselves or the supervisors determine the need for training. Empirical approach decides the need for training through performance evaluations, job-analysis and for upgrading the information and knowledge about business practices and upgrading the communication skills.

Training programs focus on either upgrading employee/s particular capabilities to fit in a specific assignment. Or they may aim at general professional development of the capabilities. *Coaching* is intense training of a person for developing his/her weak points to fit in the assigned work. It aims at upgrading specific capabilities in particular and professional development of the person in general.

A few techniques are used for identifying the training needs: Direct one-on-one discussion to upgrade the skills — this is problem approach to correct problems in the individual or groups through training actions. Management requests, team conferences suggest responsibility approach to narrow down individual/team training needs and identify the appropriate training module. Observations on job, job or activity analysis, performance ratings and appraisals, personnel records, business and production reports identify training needs and specific modules. Long range organizational planning will focus on training modules helpful in training personnel needed for business operations in the long-terms. It is a kind of building people's potentialities. On the other hand self-appraising questionnaire, and psychological tests are also used to identify the training needs.

The context of training is the frame of reference within which the training will occur either to solve problems, change behavior and upgrade business practices through communications skills, information and knowledge. Analytical and diagnostic tools, intervention strategies and evaluation of impact of intervention, team development for empowerment, communication skills-development training techniques are used.

Workshops are organized having different focuses. We present examples of five focuses for workshops.

Focus 1

- A workshop is organized based on the training needs, context and using appropriate training techniques.
- Identify the key issues. Use tools of case-work, group exercises, individual exercises and real life and business situations.
- Develop skills to diagnose problems, propose strategies for intervention and problem solution and develop skills of intervention specifications.

Step 1 & 2 are presented through lecture sessions and participatory interactive sessions and practicum exercises.

Practicum exercises: Every group participant develops an intervention strategy based on identifying the key issues and problem diagnosis. All intervention strategies are presented for group discussion to highlight key issues, technical issues and generic issues related to the business.

Evaluations of the training program both individually and by group as a whole are done.

Focus 2

Second type of *in-house workshop* is focused primarily to increase awareness, information and knowledge about ongoing business practices. Outside experts are invited to apprise the participants about the recent developments in their work areas including innovations in techniques and technologies in related businesses. (in-house workshop are discussed in detail in Chapter 2).

Focus 3

- Development of Self workshop: SWOT Analysis
- Workshop focus is on knowing about self. Knowing oneself can serve as solid base for exploring ways to become better leader when dealing with conflicts, interacting with difficult people and motivating others.
- Swot analysis is needed both at personal level and at organizational level.

- Swot analysis at individual level is the basics of people process. Swot Analysis is done to improve their capabilities through assessment of their strengths, weaknesses, opportunities available and grabbed, and training needed.
- Organizational SWOT can identify the strength, weaknesses, opportunities available and threats of the organization.

Self-assessed people are ready to make use of their strengths through opportunities available, and through demand. They demand training programs to develop their weaknesses into strengths. This is excellent for human talent development programs.

Organizational SWOT can identify the strength, weaknesses of the organization. This pertains to both the core competencies and the people process of the organizations. Strength of core competencies of the organizations can help them to develop business opportunities. They can improve the weak core competencies or drop them depending on the business requirements rather than wasting business resources on them. These two together create good business opportunities for them. Weaknesses can create threats for business, therefore they should be focused well.

Business can assess the strengths of the employees through dialogues and appraisals and give them optimal job fits and thus creating opportunities for people as well as the organization to grow. They can further develop employees' weaknesses through training and coaching programs and giving them more opportunities to grow.

Focus 4

***Problem-solving workshops through training facilitators*:** Facilitators use various problem-solving methodologies to develop problems — critical problems.

- Develop problem-solving skills in a wide range of users for rapid resolutions to complex and critical problems.

- Bring value to organizations by creating a structured environment where people can think together. People have different, often competing perspectives. Due to the close link between ego and knowledge, differences of opinions and perspective can become quite personal. Facilitators create a third point of common focus.
- This technique rapidly creates an environment of fact-based, cooperative reasoning.
- The customers have demonstrated repeatedly that when people think together, problems are rapidly and innovatively solved.

Problem-solving Tool is used in the meetings. It is the quickest and easiest way to break through difficult business issues. The system structures interaction between team members in a way that allows them to truly solve complex problems.

Focus 5

Workshops for leadership training

- The program begins with discussion of good and bad leaders, and difference between good/bad leadership. Self-assessment tests are given to identify personality type and indicate propensity to problem solving and decision-making. Leadership style is assessed ranging from Command, Control, Delegate and Empower leadership styles through LEAD tests.
- TIP test assess the way mind focuses on thinking patterns. Tests are given to determine participants' orientation to conflict.
- A 360 degree behavior feedback — a popular tool in government and business, focuses on specific elements of successful behavior. The participants are asked to submit names of people who have good knowledge of their behavior. These could include peers, bosses, employees, clients, friends, and family members. They rate the participant suggesting improvements, which then he/she can compare with his/her own self-assessment of behavior.

- Through group and personal coaching, self-defeating behavior can be improved.
- Such a feedback can provide the participant — whether he is not a good listener, whether his/her sporadic temper derails employees from focusing on their mission so on and so forth. Over time his dialogues with his boss and team became more open and honest. Change in his behavior improves his performance and morale.
- Since the results of these tests are only for the participant, they can be honest about it, and true to oneself and then can prepare themselves for the challenges of leadership both in public and private sectors.

Executives realize that they work in a rapidly changing work environment. They also realize being unaware of oneself and oblivious to others can be costly. Real progress can result from honest dialogue. This enhances their ability to work efficiently with others. Being able to encourage candor and risk taking requires self-confidence, which is inevitably result of self-awareness. Power of situation is important. The situations in which we find ourselves exert a very strong influence on the way we behave. The kind of job we have, particular employers and the co-workers and the work environment shape our actions. This is equally true of family situations that influence to mold the behavior, integrity, and short-term and long-term actions.

HOW PEOPLE ARE HIRED IN BUSINESS: RIGHT PERSONS IN THE RIGHT JOBS

Businesses look at competencies of the individual while hiring. Competencies are defined for each of the roles. There are two kinds of competencies they assess while hiring — technical/functional, behavioral and leadership competencies. Qualification, experience and communication skills generally form part of and contribute to technical/functional competency. Team player and individual ambition (achievement-orientation) form part of behavioral and leadership competencies. They also look at culture-fit and value-fit of the employees. All these three aspects are equally important.

Team Player Vs Individual Ambitions: In business interdependence is a greater virtue than independence. Being a team player is critical to success. Hence, team player quality is of very high importance. Team players would score higher over people who are solely individually driven. An ideal person would have a mix of both team and individual ambition.

From a hiring managers' point of view, what should be the key highlights in a resume for a mid-management position? At the mid-management group, one should look at education and experience and while doing assessment one should look at culture and value-fit, competencies and leadership qualities. Individual achievements and training and examples of situations where the candidate positively changed the way the earlier company conducted its business are valued. They also consider examples of how the candidate influenced their peers and management on a key activity outside the scope of their current job requirements and exposure to multiple levels of responsibility and growth.

There are some jobs where communication skills are very critical to do the job. For such jobs good communication skills will be considered. If for the target job/role, communication skills are relatively less important, businesses may go by the job requirements initially; keeping in mind current training capabilities, and trainable communication skills. Businesses do work with the employees on refining their communication skills.

Companies have difficult choice between new tech savy new graduate to implement fresh technologies and to retain middle level managers to ensure continuity and consistency and experience. They need upfront technologies. It is a challenge for them to coordinate. In such situations, either managers take e-learning technologies while earn and continue working while upgrading themselves with upfront technology. Many organizations develop in-house e-training modules to assist their managers' upgrade their skills. Some may provide complete interactive online forms of experts from various fields for the mid-career enhancement.

Communication Skills for Salespersons

Ray Dreyfack suggests communication skills for salespersons to connect and stay connected with the customer. The two key words are respect and empathy to connect and stay connected. There are ways and communication skills needed to put these concepts into practice:

- Value customer's time — do not waste it.
- Define the buyer's communication preference. Buyer A may be bottom-line oriented and wants to get down to business. Buyer B enjoys bit of light banter first.
- Pin point and address the customer's priorities — do not be focused on your own.
- Be up-to-date about your products and services and the competition as well.
- Act professionally in word, deed and appearance.
- Define the buyer's personal and professional objectives. Make them your own goals as well.
- Probe and help meet the challenges the buyer faces.
- Strive for simplicity and understand the difference between nice-to-know and need-to-know.
- Put yourself in customer's shoes.
- Finally spend as much time and effort in staying connected as you put in getting connected.
- Avoid the annoying behavior.
- Do not talk at length about your product without listening to the feedback from your prospect. Not listening can also exhibit itself through arrogance being overly demanding and monopolizing conversations.
- Are you still pushing your agenda even if someone asks you to stop?
- Old time style of sales being pushy and aggressive is gone. Understand the style and personality of the buyer before the meet.
- Observe how the sales person interacts with the clients, and if there are things you think annoy the clients, coach the salesperson.

- Role-Playing exercises, watching video presentation about making sales pitch help Sales people to act in the proper way to make a sales pitch.

Communication Skills Training programs for Media campaigns and Market research surveys.

It needs communication skills to conduct Media campaigns and Market research surveys. Appropriate training programs and workshops are organized to develop and enhance the variety of task oriented communication skills among those associated with these functions.

Media campaign needs the skills for planning focus area both thematic — products and services, and geo area for specific Campaign. Skills required for Media planning and communications channel planning and the skills to deal with the targeted audience and market segments. Further skills are needed to reinforce the campaign message and strategies according to the feedback. Market research needs the same types of skills. In addition, they need the research skills and good knowledge and training in research and analytical techniques.

Micro-inequities Training

New awareness of micro-inequities improves business relationships. The focus of the training is to handle micro-inequities and steer clear of inflicting them on co-workers. It is group training. Ask the participants to:

- Recount the work situations where micro-inequities occur. Describe factually the offensive behavior, how you felt, how it affected your relationships with the boss and co-workers.
- Recount the work situations where you sent micro-inequities. Looking back what made you do it and how you felt the relationships were affected.
- Devise skits to illustrate exclusionary situations. How these situations should be handled: (a) ignore slights, (b) retaliate with anger, (c) say firmly I want to be part of the team, (d) suggest and work out other alternatives.

- Pair the participants to widen their perceptual lenses so that they could see beyond associates' age, gender, ethnicity, accent, rank, tenure, likeability or other factors that might cause their colleagues to be ignored.
- Analyze five people you overlook consistently; you will discover ways to turn their differences into advantages. Enlist why you overlook them. Enlist the kind of advantages turned from those differences.
- Suggest best ways you can act inclusively at work (read more about Micro-inequities in Chapter 2).

CROSS-CULTURAL TRAINING: COMMUNICATING INTERNATIONALLY

With more and more companies globalizing, employees in various international locations now have day-to-day communications with each other. Given different cultural contexts, this brings new communication challenges to the workplace.

Even when these employees speak the same language (for instance, correspondences between English-speakers in the U.S. and English-speakers in the UK), there are some cultural differences that should be considered in an effort to optimize communications between the two parties. In such cases, effective communication strategy begins with the understanding that the sender of the message and the receiver of the message are from different cultures and backgrounds. Of course, this introduces a certain amount of uncertainty, making communications even more complex.

Communication and cultural exchanges are preconditions for global culture. New Information technologies, Media exposure, and Information society are the influencing factors for preserving both cultural and multicultural identities.

Without getting into cultures and sub-cultures, it is perhaps most important to realize that a basic understanding of cultural diversity is the key to effective cross-cultural communications. Without intently studying the individual cultures and languages, we must all learn how to better communicate with individuals and groups whose first language, or language of choice, does not match our own.

Learning the basics about culture and at least something about the language of communication in the host country are necessary. This is necessary even for the basic level of understanding required to engage in appropriate greetings and physical contact, which can be a tricky area inter-culturally. For instance, kissing a business associate is not considered an appropriate business practice in the U.S., but in Paris, one peck on each cheek is an acceptable greeting. And, the handshake that is widely accepted in the U.S. is not recognized in Asian cultures.

While many companies now offer training in different cultures where the company conducts business, it is important that employees being thrust into communicating across cultures practice patience and work on their own to increase their knowledge and understanding of the different culture. This requires the ability to see that a person's own behaviors and reactions are oftentimes culturally driven. Perhaps a genuine interest, paired with patience and understanding, is the best solution.

In these training programs, at the basic level, the participants learnt and practiced skill sets such as: Introductions, making an entry, making an exit, handshakes, business card protocol, magic words, the importance of apologies, compliments, criticisms, personal *vs.* professionalism, timeliness and cell phone etiquette. There are lessons including correct pronunciation of American States, how to gather information professionally on the phone, understanding British/US accents, e-mail etiquette, body language and general knowledge. This kind of training is necessary for call center and BPO employees. Different training modules are needed at higher levels.

SUMMARY

Communication skills are required for business practices. People associated with businesses at different levels learn them according to need specifications. Learning and development can be through training and development programs aiming at particular skills. Further, a person can develop strong communication skills by practice and experience. Effective communication is the basic and essential skill to make things move in any business. Effective communication skills can be both written and oral. Interpersonal communication is the major channels for corporate communication both for internal and external links. Getting your message across to business links in the right perspective is important and so is the planning of business messages through written, oral and electronic communication channels.

Developing communications skills including written, oral presentations and technology oriented, as well as an ability to work with others, are the main factors contributing to business success. Developing communication skills can target general communication skills in business practices such as Communication skills for giving feedback, Networking, making Business Presentation, Managing effective meetings and work-outs. Special skills development such as Time Management Skills, Project management skills, Practical techniques for problem-solving, Decision-making and Creative solutions are discussed.

Further, technology oriented skills such as computer expertise at different levels to software applications are required in businesses. Communication through emails, use of Internet for database and searches and use of Intranet and net conferencing etc are the basics. Use of Software packages for different business functions would require software competencies. Businesses in Information technologies would need higher technological competencies. These communication competencies are upgraded all time since the pace of technology is changing fast and businesses have to keep pace with them.

Training and development programs at different levels of employees are planned to raise the levels of skills, productivity and performance. Training programs focus on either upgrading employee/s particular capabilities to fit in a specific assignment. Or they may aim at general professional development of the capabilities. The context of training is the frame of reference within which the training occurs either to solve problems, change behavior and upgrade business practices through communications skills, information and knowledge. Analytical and diagnostic tools, intervention strategies and evaluation of impact of intervention, team development for empowerment, communication skills-development training techniques are used.

Training Workshops are organized having different focuses. Training programs are discussed for Communication skills for business hiring, Skill development for Salespersons, Micro-inequities Training, training for SWOT and Intercultural training.

8

Communicating Through Technology

TECHNOLOGY AND BUSINESS

Technologies are advancing the processes of products and services for business. Various types of information communication technologies are further facilitating them. Both types of technologies — hardware business technologies and ICTs have created multiple options and new types of competition. Computerization through both its hardware and software has expanded businesses. Both hardware and software of computer has become an industry in itself. More than that, the computer software is offering business management, information, operations and manufacturing solutions in various areas of businesses. They have become the basics for all progressive businesses. Computerization is supporting telecommunication, and other ICTs for businesses.

Sustaining technologies improve the performance of the established products along the dimensions of the performance that mainstream customers in major markets have historically valued. Disruptive technologies bring to a market a very different value proposition that had been available previously.

Christensen (1997) advocates a theory that in certain markets, the rate at which products improve exceeds the rate at which customers can learn and adopt the new performance. Therefore, at some point the performance of the product overshoots the needs of certain customer segments. At this point, a disruptive technology may enter the market and provide a product that has lower performance than the incumbent, but exceeds the requirements of certain segments thereby gaining a foothold in the market. Christensen distinguishes between low-end disruption that targets customers that have been overshot and new-market disruption that targets customers that could previously not be served profitably by the incumbent. There is impact of sustaining and disruptive technologies on product performance viz low-end and high-end customer expectations by creating new growth businesses through sustained innovations, low-end disruptions and new market disruptions.

In (2005) on the anvil is a computer language of business reporting called XBRL. It is going to change how stock investments are done worldwide and therefore contributing to the stability of the economy. The day when stock investors scan corporate results with computer software to make immediate buy-and-sell decisions may be close at hand. After agonizingly slow progress, XBRL appears to be on the verge of wider adoption XBRL could have major implications on the speed at which hedge funds and other investors make trading decisions, making accounting shenanigans more readily apparent and potentially increasing stock price volatility. XBRL, which stands for extensible business reporting language, is a language derived from the code of the World Wide Web. It consists of thousands of "tags" that correspond to items on financial reports, including balance sheets and income statements, making the filings understandable by a computer.

Telecommunication — telephones: landlines, cell phones, Internet phones, Internet in its various modes of connection from dial-up, DSL, Wi-Fi, broadband have become ubiquitous and change the way information is being handled, businesses are being done and consumers profiting by such modes. The applications of Internet such as emails, search engines, e-commerce, online advertising are some of the instances how business dealings have changed.

Diffusion of cell phones has created a unique experience in the social-personal and businesses of lower strata of people and rural people; particularly in developing countries where landline density was low in urban areas and nil in rural areas. India is a case worth mentioning. In India millions of phones are being owned and consumed by self-employed lower level businesses like carpenter, plumber, electrician, construction worker and vegetable-fruit vendors. It gives them independent and fast connectivity to their business clients and boosts their business and better time management. In addition cell phones give them both personal and social connectivity and even entertainment. Cell revolution resembles the transistor revolution of 50s. Rural people are also having both personal and social connectivity and even entertainment through cells as well landlines. Even in their farm businesses, they have fast connectivity and reach to their markets.

Expansion of multiple modes of telephony and to distances within countries and at international levels has further boosted the businesses, and has created innovative ways of doing business. Computerization is featuring in almost every way of our lives. Innovations, remodeling, adding new features in this area are further boosting life and business.

ICTs are playing a significant role to reach out to consumers in business contexts. More and more of information is being created, and shared every moment both in business and personal lives — in fact people feel there is information overload and even it overwhelms people. Data storage systems are handling the information overload and newer options both physical and technological are being innovated for businesses. Hitachi (2005) said it is seeking to push the limits of data storage with smaller stamp-sized disks for handheld gadgets and vastly higher-capacity drives that can store up to 100 films.

Consumers need access to products and services anytime. With the development of new interactive media like, email, web, SMS, ATM kiosks and now even Interactive television, it is possible for consumers to react to marketing communication immediately and short-cut their way through the actual transaction process. For the marketer, if the business end of the population is tech savvy, it is easier to move ahead. While technology has created multiple options and new types of competition, globalization has ushered in a new consumer culture — one that edits what it receives.

Does technology play a role in reaching out to the customers, especially in the Indian context? Take for instance, earlier, in India when we talked about booking train tickets, something usually get associated with touts and long queues in smelly stations. And what can be a more clinching argument than the figures quoted by IRCTC for their online railway ticket reservation system. Visa Asia rates it as their second most profitable e-commerce site in Asia. True, it would take long for all the billion Indians to get tech savvy.

A quick look at some very interesting statistics given below will highlight that technology of mobile phones, PCs, Internet, and other business software is leapfrogging in the life of the Indian consumer and that is going to facilitate the businesses directly or as support systems.

End of March 2004, there were 33.7 million mobile phone subscribers compared to 43 million fixed line subscribers. In the last calendar year, the number of mobile subscribers has increased by 20 million while fixed line subscribers have grown by just 1 million. The number of Internet subscribers (ISP accounts) is 4.55 million with about 0.2 million broadband subscribers. Include people who browse from offices, colleges and cyber cafes and you easily get 5 times that number (Source: TRAI).

World wide the mobile ring tone market is worth $13 billion. In India, while no figures are available, there are a dime a dozen ring tone providers including music channels like Channel V.

A leading bank in India offers a special bank account product that can be operated only via ATM or over the Net or phone. You cannot operate it through branches, Launched five years ago in one city, today across four cities, it has an account base of more than five lakhs.

As we note, innovations in computers and its applications, telecommunications and its applications, broadcasting — TV, radio, satellite, video technology and their applications, and allied accessories and upcoming technologies in these areas are growing beyond our imagination every day, but as we get used to the old technologies, we take them for granted and as way of life. Another important dimension is that not only these support the other businesses but the very businesses of computer, telecommunications, broadcasting and other ICTs are growing globally and have competitive global markets in hardware, software applications and consumer demands. Thus they play a significant and important role in the growth of market economy by playing the dual role of creating the business itself by their growth as well playing supportive roles for other businesses.

The automated teller machine or a mere cash dispenser has not changed much since then, at least functionally except for maybe in sheer numbers. But the next generation is here and happening. With personalized service becoming the benchmark for retail banking, cash dispensers are getting intelligent and more connected. It greets you when you walk up, offer updates on personalized information while transaction is being processed, inform your FD expiry or point out the high balance in your account. Or pop up with details on retail products — car loans, home loans or special festival offers while you wait for the transaction slip. New ATMs will be doing everything that a traditional human teller may have done in earlier days and more. The banks are moving with the times even in developing countries. Indian banks are offering very good automated banking experience to its clients and adding more and more technological features.

Magnetic card stripe technology is used for 'credit/debit cards' that are ubiquitous as a plastic currency in many countries including India. This technology is also being used for other smart cards for various other transactions such as medical, aviation and hotel rooms etc. These are used for electronic payment and identification.

Bio-metric technology is used for identification by touch of fingers or retina scans. It is being used for physical access control to let employees in security regions, identification of travelers at the airports and employee attendance/ identification in many factories.

Marketers use technology enabled market tools for market research. *Video miners* spy on the sales floor. It checks who is buying and who is browsing. It can analyze video images without relying on the human eyes. Video miners (cameras) take no face images. But this technology is capable of matching indirectly photo with credit card transaction. Video miners are different from security cameras, which spy for shoplifting. The marketers use these in addition to them. Then there is *shopping monitoring system* through monitoring retailers and consumer databases, loyalty store credit cards and other in-house programs.

The *computer-vision technology* monitors consumer preferences in retail stores, restaurants etc. For example in McDonalds restaurant, it may monitor about a new salad appeal and liking from face reactions, glimmer in the eyes and shapes of the face when looking at the Menu, ordering and eating. Visions give breakdown of gender, race, age group, length of time spent in looking at menu before ordering, length of time spend in queue and reactions while eating.

Shopper track technology videotapes consumers in the store (without their knowledge) facial images to assess, what percentage of consumers buy and what percentage browse only. The technology further compare the number of people who entered store with the store transactions to get the number of people who only browsed. They also assess how much is spent and on what item and further aligning it with age group, gender and race. It's high-time we get the guesswork out of marketing and take advantage of modern sophisticated analytics and customized marketing to figure it out.

Electronic Commerce or e-business refers to the general exchange of goods and services via the Internet. It is a term for all kinds of business that are established electronically especially over the Internet. This includes both electronic sale (Internet shops) and B2B transactions, i.e. business between two companies and the conducting of business communication and transactions over networks and through computers. However, e-business also includes all inter-company and intra-company functions such as marketing, finance, manufacturing, selling, and negotiation that enable commerce and use electronic mail, EDI (Electronic Data Interchange), file transfer, fax, video conferencing, workflow, or interaction with a remote computer. Electronic commerce also includes buying and selling over the World-Wide Web and the Internet, electronic funds transfer, smart cards, digital cash and all other ways of doing business over digital networks.

E-commerce (or electronic commerce) is any business transaction whose price or essential terms are negotiated over an online system such as an Internet, Extranet, Electronic Data Interchange network, or electronic mail system. It does not include transactions negotiated via facsimile machine or switched telephone network, or payments made online for transactions whose terms were negotiated offline. It refers to the growing retail, service and business-to-business industries on the World Wide Web. E-commerce websites facilitate the buying and selling of goods and services over the Internet. Email is by far the most popular activity on the Internet. E-mail technology makes it possible to send and receive electronic "letters" almost instantaneously over the Internet. Encryption is the process of scrambling transmitted data over the Internet, it usually refers to the scrambling of an e-commerce transaction in which credit card information privacy is assured.

Existing laws about the sale and supply of goods and services, consumer protection, credit card fraud and so forth apply in e-Commerce. In addition, there are special laws about electronic signatures and the interception of communications. The global nature of the Internet poses difficult legal problems.

Christ Paul (2004) argues that continually finding new sales leads is necessary for sales organizations. While this task is often a painful struggle, a number of new technologies have emerged in recent years to help lessen the burden. In particular, those involved in selling may find Internet-based technology solutions can improve lead generation and help create a more targeted and rewarding selling effort. The four functions facilitated by Internet-based technology solutions are: Internet Social Networks, News Alerts, Virtual Tradeshows and Build a

Web site. Considerable opportunity exists for businesses of all types and sizes to take advantage of un-crowded, cost-effective, and highly targeted local Internet marketing solutions. There are many low-cost, low-maintenance, and high-performance marketing solutions designed to drive local customers to your business.

E-Retailing enables businesses and merchants to create, manage and run full-fledged online businesses. They can establish online storefront to sell products and services online. Customers will have access to the storefront 24 hours a day, 7 days a week. The Storefront Service in its basic form or as part of a complete package has been carefully designed to accommodate all e-commerce requirements including online payment, security and a range of other options that are a necessity to run e-business. Properly executed, e-retailing has the potential to generate new markets and customers. There are three drivers of e-retailing growth: consumer acceptance, technology advancement and market forces. While it is obvious that market power exists in the online retailing business, especially among the market leaders, the factors that drive that market power have been considerably less analyzed.

Automatic identification: Automatic identification, or auto ID for short, is the broad term given to a host of technologies that are used to help machines identify objects. Auto identification is often coupled with automatic data capture. That is, companies want to identify items, capture information about them and somehow get the data into a computer without having employees type it in. The aim of most auto-ID systems is to increase efficiency, reduce data entry errors, and free up staff to perform more value-added functions, such as providing customer service. There are a host of technologies that fall under the auto-ID umbrella. These include bar codes, smart cards, voice recognition, some biometric technologies (retinal scans, finger touch for instance), optical character recognition and radio frequency identification (RFID). Bar code and RFID (and Cypak's 'contactless technology' that the company maintains can both complement and compete with more traditional RFID systems) are the upcoming technologies that would enhance the efficiency and profitability of the businesses. Therefore, we would be discussing these two at greater length.

Bar Code

Bar-code identification has evolved 20 years ago to identify the business product contents. Bar Code is an automatic identification technology. It allows data to be collected accurately and rapidly. A Bar Code symbol consists of a series of parallel, adjacent bars and spaces. Predetermined width patterns are used to code actual data into the symbol. To read information contained in a Bar Code symbol, a scanning device, such as a light pen (or wand), is moved across the symbol from one side to the other. As a scanning device is moved across the symbol, the Bar code decoder analyzes the Bar code width pattern of bars and spaces, and the original data is recovered.

Bar code systems require three elements: (i) origin, you must have a source of bar codes. These can be preprinted or printed on demand, (ii) a reader is needed to read the bar codes into the computer. The reader includes an input device to scan the bar code, a decoder to convert the symbology to ASCII text, and a cable to connect the device to your computer and (iii) computer System to process the bar code input. These can be single-user, multi-user, or network systems (more details are given in later paras).

Automatic identification or "Auto ID" encompasses the automatic recognition, decoding, processing, transmission and recording of data, most commonly through the printing and reading of information encoded in bar codes. Bar codes allow for rapid, simple and accurate reading and transmission of data for items that need to be tracked or managed. Bar Codes can be printed directly on mailing tubes, envelopes, boxes, cans, bottles, packages, books, files and other paperwork, furniture, cards and many other items for identification.

The emergence of Auto ID systems, including bar codes and the related printers, scanners, decoders and software, has significantly increased the speed, efficiency and accuracy of data collection and entry. Early applications of bar code scanning, which included retail point-of-sale, item tracking and inventory control, have been expanded to include more advanced applications such as time and attendance, work-in-process, quality control, sorting, order entry, document tracking, shipping and receiving and controlling access to secure areas.

These expanded systems have measurably increased productivity by linking production, warehousing, distribution, sales and service to management information systems on a batch or real-time basis. Consequently, opportunities to improve operational efficiencies and customer responsiveness have developed for retailers, transportation and package delivery companies, manufacturers, wholesale distributors and service providers.

The most visible application of this technology is the supermarket industry, where it has been in use since 1970. Bar Code is now the de facto automatic identification technology, for virtually any application. In today's business environment, staying competitive is critical to its success. Bar Code data-collection technology is an effective way to improve the bottom line and meet the competitive challenges that organizations face every day.

Combined with data-collection technology, bar codes provide a rapid, accurate, and efficient means to collect, process, transmit, record, and manage data in a variety of industries. Retail, package delivery, warehousing and distribution, manufacturing, healthcare, and point-of-service applications can all benefit from the use of bar codes.

Bar code is a fundamentally simple technology. There are bar code printers, bar code readers, bar code labels, bar code networking devices and bar code data concentrators. The hardware, labels, the systems and software tie everything together.

Benefits of Bar Coding

Bar code data-collection systems provide enormous benefits for just about any business. With a bar code data-collection solution, capturing data is faster and more accurate, costs are lower, mistakes are minimized, and managing inventory is much easier. Some of the benefits of bar code data entry are: fast and reliable data collection, reduced labor costs, reduced revenue losses, maintain necessary inventory levels, improved management and better decision making, and faster access to information.

Fast and reliable data collection: A bar code scanner typically can record data five to seven times as fast as a skilled typist and 10,000 times better accuracy. Keyboard data entry creates an average of one error in 300 keystrokes but Bar Code data entry has an error rate of about 1 in 3 million. The benefits of using Bar Codes for automated data collection are very simple: speed and accuracy. Time after time, it has been proven that entering Bar Code data is at least 100 times faster and more accurate than traditional manual keyboard entry, which translates into a dramatic increase in efficiency and productivity for any operation. Labor costs are reduced and this is the most obvious benefit of Bar Code data collection. In many cases, this cost savings pays for the entire data-collection system. Revenue losses are reduced resulting from data collection errors. This benefit often surpasses the savings in labor costs. You know that if you make a significant error on an invoice in the customer's favor, you will never hear about it again. However, if the error is in your favor, you will hear about it immediately. In most companies, it doesn't take many errors to amount to a great deal of lost revenue.

Using bar codes is one of the best ways to reduce inventory levels and save on capital costs. Keeping a tight handle on inventory business can save significant amounts of money. Improved Management and better decision-making could result. Although hard to measure, this is an important benefit. In many cases, improved management due to automated data collection technology could be the best benefit of a Bar Code system. A Bar Code system can easily gather information that would be difficult or impossible to gather in other ways. This allows managers to make fully informed decisions that can affect the direction of a department or company. The benefit of faster access to information goes hand in hand with better decision-making. With better information, you can gain opportunities and get the jump on competition.

Origins of Bar Codes: As we mentioned earlier a bar code system must have a source of bar codes — labels and a way to read them. Bar code labels fall into one of the following categories: preprinted or printed-on-demand.

Preprinted Bar Codes: Using preprinted labels is the most economical way to get high-quality Bar Codes. This places some restrictions on you, because the information in the bar codes must be determined in advance. In many cases this is acceptable, but in some it is not. Preprinted Bar Codes are used where very durable, high-quality labels are necessary to withstand the environment (such as on printed circuit boards), or where high-volume packaging or labeling is done. Examples of preprinted bar codes are *Bar Codes on Packaging*, and *Stickers or Tags*. The most common example of preprinted bar codes are the one you see on packaging for retail sale. Grocery stores are the most common application, but the system is gradually working its way up the manufacturing chain. In many cases, you need to identify a particular item as unique. There are several companies that will print stickers, pallet tags, item tags, or other types of very high quality bar code labels in any required sequence.

Either of these systems works very well when you can manage the assignment of codes beforehand. In many cases, you can also use assigned codes by generating a correlation between the bar code and another significant value. For example, you could use a randomly numbered sticker or tag and have the user type in the corresponding invoice number, control number, or other information that goes with it.

Printed-On-Demand Bar Codes: On-demand bar codes are used where the bar code must contain some information that is available only when the bar code is generated. On-demand bar codes can be produced in small quantities for less money than preprinted Bar Codes, and in less time. They can be printed with:

Dedicated Bar Code Printers: These produce very rugged bar codes. Dedicated printers come in several varieties, including thermal and thermal transfer. The best of them can produce bar codes that are not bothered by acids, rain, sunlight, or various other problems. These printers can also print a single tag or sticker easily and remove the label backing automatically.

Laser and Ink Jet Printers: Bar codes printed by these printers are comparable to those printed on dedicated label printers. In fact, the print quality is almost as good as on preprinted bar codes. However, laser printers are not quite so rugged as dedicated label printers, and they print a full sheet of labels at a time.

Reading Bar Codes: Once you have a bar code in hand, you must read it and process the information. Reading bar codes requires three basic decisions. You must decide on the input device, the decoder, and the interface. The input device reads the bar code and transmits the data to the decoder, which converts the data to ASCII characters. The interface is the connection between the decoder and the computer.

Operating Systems: Once you have decided on the scanner technology, you must design the system. These systems can be set up in several configurations. Some applications will work with only one particular system type, but most applications allow you to select the system to meet the best cost/performance requirements. The basic system types are: Single-User, Multi-User, Local Area Network, and Portable System.

Single User: These systems use a single PC with a single bar code reader to process data. These are generally the best type of system to start with, as they give you experience with Bar Code technology without some of the complexities of multi-user systems. An example of a site with a single-user system is a small video store that uses a wand to read Bar Codes on movies and stickers on customer cards. The store might also use a slot scanner for customer cards. *Multi-user*: This was once the most common type of system. It consists of a single computer that is hooked to several bar code readers, terminals, or both. A multi-user operating system manages the data collection.

Local Area Network: These systems connect several essentially single-user systems and a common file server using a network. These are the most flexible systems and currently the most popular. *Portable Systems*: Portables are most often used in conjunction with a computer system for a bar code application. They can be used with a single-user, multi-user, or network system. Each portable has its own operating system and program. To collect item, location, and quantity data, you would need a custom program. Portables are used with computers to keep data current either in real time or in batch mode.

Bar Code Symbologies or Formats

Bar Code systems can use several symbologies. A symbology is equivalent to a language. Each symbology has strengths and weaknesses. Many symbologies are around for historical or political reasons, while others have definite technical advantages. In many systems, you must conform to a company-specified symbology. In other systems, you are given the choice to use any symbology you wish. Choose your symbology carefully.

Different symbologies are: UPC, Code 39, Extended Code 39, Code 128, Interleaved 2 of 5, Code 93 and Extended Code 93 are compressed versions of Code 39 and Extended Code 39.

The most popular Bar Code format is the UPC (Universal Product Code) format, which we find in all supermarket products. Available since the early 1970's this format is known worldwide, and is universally recognized. This is the most popular Bar Code format. The UPC Bar Code is the standard format for items that are for sale to the public. Probably the largest users of the UPC code are local supermarkets. The UPC Bar Code format is used to encode a 12 digits number. The first number is the number system character, the next five are the manufacturer number, the next five are the product number, and the last digit is the checksum character. This Bar Code Format only encodes numeric information and must have exactly 12 characters in length.

For Automatic Identification Applications, however, Bar Code 39 Format is the de facto standard for Government, Manufacturing, Bar Code Industry, Education, and Business applications. The popularity of the Code 39 Format is based on several factors, which include ease of use, ability to code numbers and letters, flexible word length capability (can generate Bar Codes with any number of characters), and universal reading capability (Bar Code equipment from any manufacturer can read this code).

Extended Code 39 is a derivative of Code 39, Code 93 and Extended Code 93 are compressed versions of Code 39 and Extended Code 39.

The Interleaved 2 of 5 Bar Code Format (aka: Code 25) is a numeric only code that prints out a little larger than the UPC Bar Code when ten digits are encoded. The Interleaved 2 of 5 is an excellent choice for numeric only applications, because it has the flexibility of having from 2 to 30 digits. The Interleaved 2 of 5 code requires an even numbers of digits to be encoded. A leading 0 must be added if the digit count is not even.

The 128 Bar Code format is a very compact for codes with all numeric information. Alphanumeric information can also be encoded, but at the expense of loosing the "very compact" benefit. The compact size of the Bar Code printed with the code 128 when using only numeric digits is achieved by using "double density" (two numbers are included in one character width). When alphanumeric data is encoded, however, Code 128 uses "single density", and the Bar Codes are twice as long. This is not a simple Bar Code format to use, as there are several Code 128 subsets, each with specific specifications and limitations. Code 128 also has five special, non-data function characters. These are generally used to set reader parameters or return parameters. Code 128 actually has three different character-code subsets. It has two forms of error checking, making it a very stable bar code. Checksums are not required. If you have your choice, Code 128 is generally the best all-around choice you can use. Those who ship items with UPC codes specifically use this bar code on shipping containers. UCC 128 has automatic checksums.

Codabar is useful for encoding dollar figures and mathematical figures. The EAN/JAN-13 and 8 codes are used for overseas applications where a country code is required. The MSI bar code is used most often in the grocery industry for shelf labels.

Zip+4 and DPBC POSTNET. This bar code is the special code that is placed on the lower right portion of an envelope. This bar code is used to speed mail through the postal service (by automated sorting) and get reduced rates.

2D (Two-Dimensional) Bar Code Symbology allows vast amounts of data on a single bar code by storing data in 2 dimensions. A common demonstration of the technology is a single bar code no larger than a standard UPC bar code that contains the entire mailing address. Some common 2D bar code symbologies include PDF 417, DataMatrix Code, and MaxiCode.

Checksums are additional characters appended to bar codes to guarantee good reads. Checksums are necessary on some bar codes that are prone to errors. For example, Interleaved 2 of 5 is a very dense, numeric-only bar code, but it is prone to substitution errors. One should always use a checksum on this code. Other codes, such as Code 128 and Code 39, are self-checking and seldom require a checksum. Most bar code readers can be configured to use (for more details about barcode symbologies refer Appendix 1).

Examples to Applications of Bar Codes

The following are just a few of the many ways bar codes are being used to improve the profitability and efficiency of businesses. Bar code systems routinely save companies money while improving quality, on-time performance, and other key business factors.

Point of Sale: It is one of the most common segments of the bar code market. Everyone is familiar with the scanners in grocery and department stores. Point-of-sale systems can be used in any retail setting. The grocery industry is the best organized setting, but most vendors in that area are concentrating on high-end scanner/mainframe systems. There are abundant opportunities for PC-based systems in small to medium-sized businesses, such as video stores, convenience markets, and clothing stores. Benefits of bar coding in point-of-sale systems include:

Cost Savings: This is the most obvious benefit. A medium-to-large store can save enough checker time to significantly reduce payroll. You also save direct labor costs through less time spent taking inventories and ordering product. *Customer Satisfaction*: A proper bar code system will speed customer checkout. This will improve customer satisfaction enough to directly increase revenue over time. *Reduced Inventory Costs*: Immediate access to inventory information on a real-time basis can be used to reduce inventory levels. This will reduce costs for a company in a number of ways, including interest, labor for handling excess inventory, and facility overhead. *Automated Reordering:* Accurate stock levels allow for automated replenishment of low inventory.

Better Decision Making: With bar code data-collection you can tell not only what the customers are buying, but also when they are buying it and in what combinations. This can improve business management by suggesting better locations for goods in the store and identifying advertising targets.

Work in Progress: Many manufacturing and other industries have work that must go through several steps to completion. Bar code systems can track material through each step of the work and keep detailed records on each piece or batch. When a problem occurs in the output, supervisors and managers can track the work back and quickly resolve the issue. This is one of the best ways to improve both quality and yield in virtually any multi-step process.

Inventory Control: Tracking inventory manually is a laborious process. With bar codes applied to each item in inventory, portable scanners can be used to track shipping and receiving, and can quickly take physical inventory. The data from portable scanners can be uploaded to a central computer system at regular intervals or portables can update inventory in real-time depending on the system you have chosen. Bar code inventory control provides accurate, real-time inventory updates. This allows a company, the opportunity to reduce stock levels and thereby reduce carrying costs. It also reduces the time taken to collect data for purposes such as annual inventories. With improved efficiency, operating costs are lower. Different modules of the Inventory management software target different applications of inventory control, including fixed asset tracking, inventory management, check-in and checkout tracking, and stockroom management.

Secured Access: A secured access system provides door and gate security by controlling access using encoded employee identification badges. Bar code badge scanners or magnetic stripe readers are mounted at doors and gate entrances, and authorization is provided from a central computer.

Time and Attendance: A time and attendance system uses encoded employee identification badges that are scanned when employees start and stop work. This allows automatic tracking for payroll and eliminates paper time sheets and time clocks.

Quality Control: Bar code systems in quality control can be used to tell a person which test to perform for a given part and where to send it if it fails. Bar code systems can also create permanent records for tracking component and sub-assembly failures.

Packaging: For packaging, a bar code printer is used to generate a label to identify part numbers, serial numbers, and shipping information. This labeling can be used to automatically sort packages for shipment, automate receiving, and greatly enhance package tracking.

Collection of Data from Form: Businesses such as medical and dental practices rely on complex patient forms. Using bar codes, detailed information can be quickly entered in the computer. Bar codes printed by check boxes on a form allow fast accurate data entry by simply scanning the codes by the check boxes. This makes an easy task of gathering large amounts of information for a client. Reduced data collection costs and better service are the results.

Productivity Measurement Systems: Productivity measurement is a practice that can drastically reduce labor costs in manufacturing, warehousing, and most other types of business. A well-managed system will allow supervisors to isolate the problems that may come up so that they can take steps to solve them. Within an organization, departments may have different types of activities, making it difficult for supervisors to keep track of what everyone is doing. Productivity-measurement systems automatically track what work is being done and compare the work to expected output. When the results do not measure up, supervisors can take corrective action. This type of informed supervision and management can typically cut department costs by 15 to 20 percent.

RFID: Radio Frequency Identification

It is another evolving auto identification technology and is being applied for commercial business in the current decade. Radio frequency identification, or RFID, is a generic term for technologies that use radio waves to automatically identify people or objects. There are several methods of identification, but the most common is to store a serial number that identifies a person or object, and perhaps other information, on a microchip that is attached to an antenna (the chip and the antenna together are called an RFID transponder or an RFID tag). The antenna enables the chip to transmit the identification information to a reader. The reader converts the radio waves reflected back from the RFID tag into digital information that can then be passed on to computers that can make use of it.

An RFID system may consist of several components: tags, tag readers, tag programming stations, circulation readers, sorting equipment, and tag inventory wands. The purpose of an RFID system is to enable data to be transmitted by a portable device, called a tag, which is read by an RFID reader and processed according to the needs of a particular application.

RFID tags can be either active or passive. Passive RFID tags do not have their own power supply: the minute electrical current induced in the antenna by the incoming radio-frequency scan provides enough power for the tag to send a response. Due to power and cost concerns, the response of a passive RFID tag is necessarily brief: typically just an ID number. Lack of its own power supply makes the device quite small. There are products that can be embedded under the skin and are commercially available. As of 2004, the smallest such devices commercially available measured 0.4 mm × 0.4 mm, and thinner than a sheet of paper; such devices are practically invisible. Passive tags have practical read ranges that vary from about 10 mm up to about 5 meters.

Active RFID tags, on the other hand, must have a power source, and may have longer ranges and larger memories than passive tags, as well as the ability to store additional information sent by the transceiver. At present, the smallest active tags are about the size of a coin. Many active tags have practical ranges of tens of meters, and a battery life of up to several years.

As passive tags are much cheaper to manufacture and do not depend on a battery, the vast majority of RFID tags in existence are of the passive variety. As of 2004 tags cost from US$0.40. The aim is to produce tags for less than US$0.05 to make widespread RFID tagging commercially viable. However, chip manufacturers' supply of integrated circuits is not sufficient and demand is too low for prices to come down soon. Analysts from independent research companies like Gartner and Forrester Research agree that a price level of less than $0.10 is only achievable in 6-8 years.

There are four different kinds of tags commonly in use. They are categorized by their radio frequency: Low frequency tags (between 125 to 134 kilohertz), High frequency tags (13.56 megahertz), UHF tags (868 to 956 megahertz), and Microwave tags (2.45 gigahertz). UHF tags cannot be used globally as there aren't any global regulations for their usage.

Low-frequency RFID tags are commonly used for animal identification, beer keg tracking, and automobile key-and-lock, anti-theft systems. Pets are often embedded with small chips so that they may be returned to their owners if lost. In the United States, two RFID frequencies are used: 125kHz (the original standard) and 134.5kHz, the international standard. High-frequency RFID tags are used in library book or bookstore tracking, pallet tracking, building access control, airline baggage tracking, and apparel item tracking. High-frequency tags are widely used in identification badges, replacing earlier magnetic stripe cards. These badges need only be held within a certain distance of the reader to authenticate the holder. UHF, RFID tags are commonly used commercially in pallet and container tracking, and truck and trailer tracking in shipping yards. Microwave RFID tags are used in long range access control for vehicles, an example being General Motors' OnStar system. Some toll booths, such as California's FasTrak and Illinois' I-Pass system, use RFID tags for electronic toll collection. The tags are read as vehicles pass; the information is used to debit the toll from a prepaid account. The system helps to speed traffic through toll plazas. Sensors such as seismic sensors may be read using RFID transceivers, greatly simplifying remote data collection.

RFID is not new. It is a proven technology that's been around since at least the 1970s. Up to now, it's been too expensive and too limited to be practical for many commercial applications. But if tags can be made cheaply enough, they can solve many of the problems associated with bar codes. Radio waves travel through most non-metallic materials, so they can be embedded in packaging or encased in protective plastic for weatherproofing and greater durability. And tags have microchips that can store a unique serial number for every product manufactured around the world.

It is an evolving auto ID technology. RFID products and applications for businesses are RFID tag application, tag tracking and integration. The solutions help business to meet short-term RFID compliance as well position itself to benefit in the long-term. The companies can choose the solution that best meets their needs. RFID is real and so is the need for the investment to pay-off. Whether they want to implement it now or choose to do so later, it makes sense to invest in smart RFID products to lower cost of ownership, function in a global marketplace, comply with existing standards and lower IT administration requirements. Customer demand is building, suppliers are moving ahead and a flood of RFID applications is about to inundate the consumer and industrial landscape.

RFID is not new. The innovative companies have been using it for a decade or more in 'closed loop' systems in which information is rapidly and accurately transmitted among the parties within the organization (like in hospital system). Businesses with logistic operations such as automotives, consumer packaged goods, manufacturing, government and retail have been quick to embrace RFID.

Recently, industry giants and US Department of Defense has thrown a new spotlight on RFID. Companies are considering how this technology can be used to transmit information in an 'open loop' to their suppliers, customers and other business partners outside their premises — thereby enhancing product visibility, increasing sales and boosting profits. Therefore, the focus has turned on RFID technology by businesses that value the benefits and the proven benefits. The next step is to gain a better understanding of RFID critical integration and payback concerns.

Since 2004, the demand for RFID products and services has exploded. Chip and tag makers are trying to meet the sales orders. The industry has faced and met a number of RFID challenges and collective knowledge has grown tremendously. The first set of RFID tag standards were finalized in early 2004 by industry consortium EPCglobal Inc, in Brussels. Technology vendors are developing these tags to help companies meet their mandates.

Challenges

Challenges of using RFID effectively are (i) to integrate it into company's existing IT architecture. Experts agree that linking RFID to other auto-identification technologies such as bar-coding is fairly straightforward, connecting it to an enterprise systems is more complex, (ii) hardware issues such as incorporating additional data streams into label printers. Understanding where to place labels and antennae in the products. The source of this challenge is the need to filter and pre-process the huge data by the RFID systems and not to overwhelm the back office business software such as enterprise resource planning (ERP). Even with filtering and pre-processing, the data collected will be staggering. Many ERP solutions are yet unprepared to accept RFID data efficiently. Once accepted, the data must be converted into documents that can be used by business partners such as advance shipping notices in retail. To solve this problem 'middleware' software is specially developed to connect the system with one another. In most industries middleware is new but is maturing quickly, (iii) as companies will expand their RFID systems from simple tag and reader configurations, middleware will become the primary challenge to integrate it with other business systems, (iv) another integration challenge is that companies have yet to determine which practices should be incorporated into RFID systems.

Joe Dunlap RFID specialist in Siemens Corp Ohio, provides RFID technology solutions across multiple industries cites an example; consider the case of a forklift operator who places pallets of products on warehouse shelves. Typically, the operator uses barcode scanner to read the proper location when placing the pallet on the shelf. However if the operator puts the pallet in the adjacent bin, the product will be picked incorrectly or show as out of stocks. This results in poor accuracy, dissatisfaction of customer, and higher indirect labor cost. With an RFID solution the operator would not need the bar code scanner because a mobile reader on the forklift could read the tag automatically. If the pallet was placed incorrectly, the system could recognize the error and notify the operator. If the operator did not make correction, the system would notify the supervisor or even prevent the operator to make additional transactions. Successful RFID compliance depends on readable labels (2005).

Systems could also be configured to accept the challenge and reassign the storage location. In addition warehouse management vendors would incorporate these processes into their software. More time is needed for the user community to decide which best practices should be integrated into the technology.

The hardware issues may be easily manageable with the right business partner but controlling and manipulating the information you receive from these systems, then using it within your enterprise and sharing it with your supplier is harder. Introducing RFID into a company's business processes requires a commitment from the company in partnership with competent technology providers. Suppliers will get only negative ROI (return on investment) if they just put the label and ship. They get positive ROI when they manage tag data and integrate into warehouse management system to allow the distribution system to work more efficiently.

For companies who are willing to extend their RFID implementation to support sales and replenishments, it can be rewarding. First, companies get an understanding of what happens to their products once they leave the facility. Shipments are easier to track, making it easier to be paid for goods and to see where the problems occur in the logistic process. Secondly, companies can take action based on the information received. For example, if product deliveries are delayed, the company can track data to demand better services from the carrier. The data can also be used to improve on-time shipments to customers. Thirdly, RFID system can also show when the deliveries are made providing critical documentation needed to get customer payment. Fourthly, if supply chain shares data, the manufacturers can even adjust their production and shipments based on the retailers' sales by having the right product in the right stores at the right time the manufacturers can boost sales and profits.

The companies are using RFID in stages. For example, Conair Corp is using printers and tags to master cartons of goods, but is not using any RFID stock-keeping units (SKUs) in its own systems. The biggest cost was the internal IT labor hours needed to modify the company's warehouse management software so that it could handle the new technology. Conair did not want to purchase middleware at this point so it made the decision to customize the software internally to handle the RFID requirements.

If RFID has been around so long and is so great, why aren't all companies using it? Many companies have invested in RFID to get the advantages it offers and currently most of these investments are usually made in 'closed-loop' systems, that is, when a company is tracking goods that never leave its own control. Thousands of companies around the world use RFID today to improve internal efficiencies. So far, it has not been used extensively by the companies in 'open loop' i.e. for external supply chains for three reasons. First, because some existing RFID systems use proprietary technology, which means that if company A puts an RFID tag on a product, it can't be read by Company B unless they both use the same RFID system from the same vendor. Second reason is the cost. If a company tracks assets within its own four walls, it can reuse the tags over and over again, which is cost effective. But for a system to work in an open loop supply chain it has to be cheap because the company that puts the tag on case or pallet is unlikely to be able to reuse it. RFID tags are also fairly expensive — 20 cents or more - which makes them impractical for identifying millions of items which might cost only a few dollars. RFID readers typically cost $1,000 or more. Companies would need thousands of readers to cover all their factories, warehouses and stores. The third issue is about standards. There are well-developed standards for low frequency and high frequency RFID systems, but most companies want to use UHF in the supply chain because it offers longer read range (up to 20 feet under good conditions). UHF technology is relatively new and standards aren't established until recently.

Applications of RFID

The most common applications for RFID are payment systems (Mobil Speed pass and toll collection systems), access control, and asset tracking. Increasingly, companies are looking to use RFID to track goods within their supply chain, work in process and other applications. Companies are using the technology's potential in manufacturing and other areas. As the technology becomes standardized, it will be used more and more to track goods in the supply chain. The aim is to reduce administrative error, labor costs associated with scanning bar codes, internal theft, errors in shipping goods and overall inventory levels.

It is being used more and more in all areas of automatic data-capture allowing contactless identification of objects using RF. With applications ranging from secure Internet payment systems to industrial automation and access control, RFID technology solutions are receiving much attention in the research and development departments of large corporations. RFID is a major growth area in auto ID. There is no global public body that governs the frequencies used for RFID. In principle, every country can set its own rules for this.

Examples of How RFID is Being used Currently

Companies are rapidly using RFID in multiple areas and through multiple cross functions. We have its applications in retails, manufacturing and their delivery systems, hospital systems, postal systems, travel and travel documentation, in space centers, tracking cows, sheep and pets, and mental and Alzheimer patients, skiers in ski resorts, and triggering equipment down oil wells. The FDA in US recently (2004) approved the country's first RFID chips that can be implanted in humans. The 134.2kHz RFID chips can incorporate personal medical information and could save lives and limit injuries from errors in medical treatments. The RFID tags are being put in cadavers to control theft of bodies and theft of organs for illegal trade in organs sold for implants. The applications are limited only by people's imagination.

RFID in Retail

Fashion retailer Benetton Group SpA of Italy will soon (2005) start attaching radio frequency identification (RFID) "smart tags" to its Sisley clothing line to help track shipping, inventory and sales in the chain's 5,000 stores around the globe. Retailers see a lot of potential for this new technology. Security is one possibility because items transmit their location. Another possibility is a new checkout system that bypasses the cash register so as to install in-store readers that constantly count what's on the shelves and restock automatically. An RFID tag communicates its location to Benetton's computerized supply chain network, allowing the retailer to learn the status of its inventory at a glance and make restocking decisions quickly. For consumers, retailers envision instant access to product information on the manufacturer's Web site, via scanner-equipped, Internet-enabled cell phones. But when the items leave the stores, the RFID labels will be disabled so that they can't infringe on the privacy of customers.

While there is no indication that Benetton intends to track its customers with the tags, privacy advocates are worried that the technology could lend itself to unauthorized customer monitoring. In fact, a policy analyst at the Electronic Privacy Information Center in Washington said his group has been watching the development of RFID systems and the potential for privacy invasion is significant. Although privacy groups have expressed concern about the use of RFID tags, Benetton said they didn't believe it would create a problem if done openly and with notification to customers. Still, some groups urged that the company's clothing be boycotted.

Benetton is not the only Italian firm involved in this project. This revolutionary product for the world of garment and accessories based on RFID technology has been in fact invented and designed in Italy near Bologna. Located here is the LAB ID headquarters, the first company in the world that produces a complete transponder system: the reader that is the seeking device, the transponder that contains the information and finally the antenna, which permits the dialogue. In this way LAB ID has been able to design and to patent the first electronic tag in polyamide in the world, besides the other five worldwide licenses. LAB ID designs and realizes transponder technologies that are personalized to meet the requirements of industry and public authorities. These range from the intelligent boutique, to the supermarkets of the future, to the library that files information on each of its books, to the census of a forest. The LAB ID philosophy is: "Industry, economy, but most of all culture, will take advantage of items with an attached transponder as it allows inclusion of all kinds of information, from the price of a product to the history of a given work of art. First of all, it enables the user to think and work faster".

LAB ID is in the process of reaching a series of agreements with important international groups in order to apply and spread the new technology to various fields. "Until a few months ago we thought we had a niche in the market – Mauro Benetton concludes — but today we are aware that we can become a worldwide leader in a very promising field and we are valuing offers from several partners interested in financing our development". Italy would lead in this technological leadership.

RFID in Manufacturing

General Motors needed to boost production of its Hummer H2 to meet demand, but its manufacturing facility had limited space for parts. The automaker turned to RFID to keep the plant humming. GE Uses RFID to Secure Cargo. General Electric's Security division is developing a new RFID-based system that can be built into a new generation of shipping containers.

Travel and Travel Documentation

New U.S. passports will soon be read remotely at borders around the world, thanks to embedded chips that will broadcast on command an individual's name, address and digital photo to a computerized reader. The US State Department hopes the addition of the chips, which employ RFID, technology, will make passports more secure and harder to forge, according to spokeswoman Kelly Shannon. "The reason we are doing this is that it simply makes passports more secure," Shannon said. "It's yet another layer beyond the security features we currently use to ensure the bearer is the person who was issued the passport originally." Last week, four companies received contracts from the government to deliver prototype chips and readers immediately for evaluation.

Diplomats and State Department employees will be issued the new passports as early as January 05, while other citizens applying for new passports will get the new version starting in the spring. Countries around the world are also in the process of including the tags in their passports, in part, due to U.S. government requirements that some nations must add biometric identification in order for their citizens to visit without a visa. Current passports (which are already readable by machines that decipher text on the photo page) will remain valid until they expire, according to a State Department spokeswoman.

The RFID passport works like a high-tech version of the children's game "Marco Polo." A reader speaks out the equivalent of "Marco" on a designated frequency. The chip then channels that radio energy and echoes back with an answer. But instead of simply saying "Polo," the 64 Kb chip will say the passport holder's name, address, date and place of birth, and send along a digital photograph.

While none of the information on the chip is encrypted, the chip does also broadcast a digital signature that verifies the chip itself was created by the government. Security experts said, "the U.S. government decided not to encrypt the data because of the risks involved in sharing the method of decryption with other countries."

There are criticisms about RFID technology being used in Passports: "Even if they wanted to store this info in a chip, why have a chip that can be read remotely?" asked Barry Steinhardt, who directs the American Civil Liberty Union's Technology and Liberty program. "Why not require the passport be brought in contact with a reader so that the passport holder would know it had been captured?"

But Electronic Frontier Foundation attorney Lee Tien argues that RFID chips in passports are a "privacy horror" and would be even more if the data was encrypted. "If 180 countries have access to the technology for reading this thing, whether or not it is encrypted, from a security standpoint, that is a very leaky system," Tien said. "Strictly from a technology standpoint, any reader system, even with security, that was so widely deployed and accessible to so many people worldwide will be subject to some very interesting compromises."

Travel privacy expert Edward Hasbrouck argues that identity thieves are not the only ones with an interest in recording the data remotely. Commercial travel companies, including hotels, will capture the data to create commercial dossiers when people check into hotels or exchange currency in order to up-sell their customers, he argues.

While there are no laws in the United States prohibiting anyone from snooping on someone's passport data, Roy Want, an RFID expert who works as a principal engineer for Intel Research, thinks that the possibility of identity theft is overblown. "It is actually quite hard to read RFID at a distance." A person's keys, bag and body interfere with the radio waves, and the type of RFID chip being used requires readers equipped with very large — and obvious — coils to capture the data. Still, he concedes that a determined snooper could create a snooping system. "In principle someone could rig up a reader, perhaps in a doorway you are forcing people to go through. You could read some of these tags some of the time. But overall the chips will help cut down on passport fraud. The problem with security is, there is always a possibility of attack. RFIDs are not going to solve the problem of passport forgery, but people who know about printing are not going to learn about RFIDs."

But civil libertarians and some technologists say the chips are actually a boon to identity thieves, stalkers and commercial data collectors, since anyone with the proper reader can download a person's biographical information and photo from several feet away. (Jan 2005 Wire News service)

Airports are using RFID. When its RFID luggage-handling system goes online in January 05, the Hong Kong Airport expects to lower labor costs, increase capacity and improve security.

RFID in Hospital Systems

Hospitals are planning to use RFID to find innovative solutions for reducing medical errors, increasing patient safety and improving medical processes. They are looking through case studies for practical and first-hand knowledge into some of the key areas to understand how to make today's Auto-ID investment foundations for the future. The focus key areas are: First, how RFID can be utilized to improve patient safety in a variety of clinical applications at the point of care and enhancing the quality of care by instantly having the most current patient information. Second, analyzing and capturing relevant data through RFID systems to improve hospital processes, through RFID tagging for medical equipment, examining real-time asset restocking and replenishment and quickly and accurately filling requests and repackaging individually bar coded products for patient use.

In hospital applications, RFID tags can be used to track and manage equipment such as wheelchair and medical devices, locating them faster for patients and reducing theft. Using tags the size of a pager attached to equipment or beds, clinicians will be able to find the nearest EKG machine or locate nursing staff in patient rooms. Emergency department (ED) staff can also find where patients are by simply looking on the wireless electronic dashboard located in the ED's central core. When medication and dosages are tagged, doctors and nurses can ensure that the right medicine is dispensed in the right amount to the right patient at the right time.

In a hospital an elderly woman dozes quietly in her bed, tucked under layers of blankets. Her physician stops by on his rounds and clicks on a wireless tablet PC that is equipped with RFID reader. The device transmits a signal to an RFID tag in the woman's hospital bracelet, even though the bedding hides it. The tag transmits information to the PC, which is integrated with the hospital's management system. On the display, the doctor sees the woman's name, her previously administered medications, plus her recently collected vital information. The doctor has received the accurate and update information he needs without disturbing the patient or having to check back at the nursing station. The hospital gets 100% accuracy in identifying the patients and an overall savings of clinician's time because doctors and nurses get the patient information they need at the bedside. This enhances patient care, supports safety goals, and enhances the patients experience by limiting disturbances. (Jacobi Medical center in Bronx USA. They use siemens RFID system).

Several hospitals in Boston area are testing RFID potential in the medical arena to track critical equipments in emergency department, to ensure patients are not made to wait too long between tests, or given the wrong medication or blood. They are testing that tags are accurate, nobody could intercept the signals and there is no interference with the medical devices. Mass General hospital, Beth Israel hospital and Brigham and women's hospital in Boston have started using RFID technology in some areas since 2003 and expanding to test in other areas. Privacy advocates are concerned about the vulnerability of a massive medical records database. The more RFID becomes a standard of patient care, the less likely it is to be optional. RFID tags are being used to track Alzheimer patients and patients in mental hospitals. Other applications of RFID are being researched as adaptive technologies for various disabilities.

RFID in space center: NASA Creates Thinking RF Sensors. Low-cost wireless sensor networks developed by NASA can detect environmental changes and take action in response to what they detect. Now RFID is set to make them even more effective.

Security option: Systems developer Icon Nicholson says RFID is already a better security option than existing electronic article surveillance systems. RFID is employed against checking terrorism. Pilots and programs overseen by the U.S. Department of Homeland Security show how RFID technology can speed the movement of people across boarders while reducing the threat of terrorism.

RFID brings Order to the Law: After a national law firm installed an RFID system to track legal files at its Boston location, accuracy in locating files jumped from 35 to 98 percent — saving tens of thousands of dollars in time spent looking for documents. In India RFID tags are being used to track Supreme Court files.

RFID in miscellaneous applications: Soap Maker Cleans Up with RFID. Canus, a maker of goat's milk soap, is deploying RFID to cut distribution costs, keep products from spoiling in transit and meet Wal-Mart's tagging requirements ahead of schedule. Chip Maker tries 'Snack and Trace'. By using RFID to track shipments within its supply chain, KiMs, a Danish potato-chip maker, not only spiced up its sales but also cut the fat from its inventory and workforce. RFID gives Racing a Winning Edge. Using active RFID tags, the Indy Racing League not only times and scores 16 events, it also provides critical data to drivers and race crews, and helps engine, tire and chassis makers develop products. In Australia the sheep stations are quite widespread, the mangers use RFID tags to track the sheep. They insert these tags in the sheep's ear.

Cypak Contactless Technology and RFID

Many products are difficult to track with RFID, but good system design and precise tag placement can overcome most hurdles. Here's what you need to know to tag successfully Smart Packaging, Smarter Cards. Swedish Startup Cypak offers RFID technology that tamper-proofs mail, increases the security of smart cards and helps people take their medicine.

March 3, 2004—Swedish technology startup Cypak has launched evaluation and development kits for its secure 'contactless' technology that the company maintains can both complement and compete with more traditional RFID systems. Cypak joins its own small, chip-based designs with its methods for using conductive ink and adhesives to print electronic circuits and antennas on paper and plastic. According to the company, the resulting contactless data-transfer technology can connect objects to host computers and networks at a fraction of the cost and power consumption of RFID.

However, the company's readers and tags are limited to read ranges of just 5 millimeters. Since some of its customers have asked for longer reader range, the company is developing a tag that complies with the ISO 15963 standard. The company plans to do this by mounting its ASIC (including microprocessor, large memory, clock, temperature and tamper sensors) onto an ISO 15963 antenna, which is longer than Cypak's antenna and enables a greater read range. For close-up high-security applications using low-cost readers, Cypak will mount the ASIC onto its own proprietary antenna. "The ISO 15963 will extend our offering to customers who want to use any of our patented functionality but would like to communicate with standard RFID readers for longer read range or to fit into a current RFID infrastructure," says Ehrensvärd, marketing director at Cypak, which is based in Stockholm. "ISO 15963 is integrated on our proprietary System-on-Chip (ASIC), that will be ready for mass production in Q3 2004."

The company hopes the new kits will entice developers, systems integrators and business developers to use its technology for a range of potential applications. "The best way to understand the potential of our technology is to see it working," says Ehrensvärd. "Our long-term goal as a company is not to manufacture products but to provide our patented technology and license the rights to others to develop applications."

Cypak's has developed a technology to produce printable 13.56 MHz microelectronics tags and sensors that can detect if a package has been tampered with. The company is currently in the process of adding temperature sensors. The company has also developed low-cost readers that can be integrated into flat nonmetallic surfaces such as computer keyboards or cell phones and has also developed the software needed to process and manage the data retrieved from its sensors.

The new Cypak evaluation and development kits contain working samples of Cypak's three key designs for its technology: Intelligent Pharmaceutical Packaging; SecurePak; and Smarter Card. Its Intelligent Pharmaceutical Packaging can be used to build pharmaceutical packaging capable of detecting if a patient is taking medication as prescribed. Cypak's SecurePak solution can be deployed to monitor whether packages have been tampered with, damaged or opened. The Smarter Card design enables a smart card to store and verify a personal identification number (PIN) through memory and a keypad built into the card itself. The company maintains the Smarter Card enables greater security because the PIN is never transmitted, therefore it cannot be intercepted.

The Cypak development kit contains documentation, an application programming interface and professional engineering services. Both the evaluation and development kits are priced at 500 euros ($650) each. Buying the evaluation kit is the prerequisite for buying the developer kit. The cost of Cypak's tags and reader chips—for SecurePak, Smarter Cards, Intelligent Pharmaceutical Packaging or other future applications—will be from 50 cents each up to a few dollars, depending on functionality and volume, according to the company.

Cypak recently won support for its Intelligent Pharmaceutical Packaging (IPP). In January 2005, it announced that it had licensed its IPP technology to Mead Westvaco's Global Healthcare Packaging group. Under that agreement, Mead Westvaco will have exclusive right to produce and market IPP technology in the Americas and a nonexclusive right in rest of the world.

Cypak has also seen its SecurePak solution deployed by the Swedish Postal Service (Posten AB, Koncern Säkerhet) in a trial to track packages. The postal organization is using SecurePak only for its internal use by sending Cypak-enabled smart packages through problem areas in its delivery network to track where and when some employees have tampered with packages. The company maintains that a number of postal and courier businesses have also shown interest in the technology for similar internal deployments. However, the technology will support new customer-oriented services as well. This is a technology that any courier company could use to provide new secure services. Cypak's technology can currently utilize its chip's 32 kilobits of memory to 15 time-stamp when a package is opened, tampered with or damaged. The company says that it will start mass production of its microelectronics tag in spring 05.

Why is RFID Better than Using Bar Codes?

Bar-code identification has evolved 20 years ago to identify the business product contents. RFID is an evolving auto identification technology similar to bar code. This new technology can be considered as the 21st century bar code.

RFID is not necessarily "better" than bar codes. The two are different technologies and have different applications, which sometimes overlap. The big difference between the two is, bar codes are line-of-sight technology i.e. a scanner has to "see" the bar code to read it, which means people usually have to orient the bar code towards a scanner for it to be read, RFID by contrast, doesn't require line of sight. RFID tags can be read as long as they are within range of a reader. Bar codes have other shortcomings as well. If a label is ripped, soiled or falls off, there is no way to scan the item. And standard bar codes identify only the manufacturer and product, not the unique item. The bar code on one milk carton is the same as on every other, making it impossible to identify which one might pass its expiration date first.

RFID technology puts a microchip on retail goods with an antenna that broadcasts its unique 96-bit identifier and location to corresponding receivers. The receiver relays the data to a computer, which decodes the information and processes it according to whichever application is running. The difference between bar code and RFID scanners is that the latter records data from each item at a distance of 4 to 5 ft. away. This guarantees an easier and faster transaction.

RFID offers more generous reading area and tag positioning than optical scanning of bar codes. RFID tags for the distribution chain can be read over a larger variation of placement and orientation than bar codes used in these applications. They can read through many materials, highest reading rates results from approximately line-of-sight between tag and the reader's antennas.

Bar code requires direct line-of-sight between code and the reader, typically with the readers scanned beam perpendicular to the code face and oriented to pass through all the coded lines at the same time. In automated reading applications like reading codes and boxes passing on conveyors, multiple readers may need to be deployed to cover larger variation of placement and orientation of bar codes on packages or pallets, or their position on conveyors. Larger RFID reading areas can be achieved by adding only additional antennas connected to the same reader.

RFID tag reading can be frequently automated whereas reading bar codes automation would be impossible or would require expensive scanning arrays on applications such as reading pallets passing on forklift trucks.

RFID allows for new applications, which is not possible with bar codes. It enables searching areas for taking inventory or searching for specific tags or items within reading range of antennas. Some new RFID applications allow construction of reading areas or storage shelves with built in antennas that effectively inventory the shelves contents by continuously reading the items within the areas or on the shelf allowing the associated system to maintain accuracy.

RFID has reading, durability and higher data content advantages over bar code. The major RFID advantages are increased material handling efficiencies and lower cost from enhanced tag readability over greater tag placement variation. Secondly, increased accounting efficiencies and lower cost from increased data content take place. Thirdly, there are fewer lost packages, there is decrease in out of date losses to identify and use the oldest packages — first in and first out, and enables efficient searches for specific packages in the inventory.

RFIDs possible drawbacks as compared to bar codes: RFID will go through a process similar to bar code technology 20 years ago. Initially people could not afford bar code technology. The payback grew as it became more wide spread. Now it is indispensable to companies in the developed world and even companies in developing countries are fast adopting it. Same way as companies implement RFID technology deeper within their operations, the return will grow and applications will expand.

Will RFID replace bar codes? It's very unlikely. Bar codes are inexpensive and effective for certain tasks. RFID and bar codes will coexist for many years.

SUMMARY

Technologies are advancing the processes of products and services for business. Various types of information communication technologies are further facilitating them. Both types of technologies — hardware business technologies and ICTs have created multiple options and new types of competition. Computer, telecommunication, and other ICTs technologies are changing the way the businesses are developing globally.

Computerization through both its hardware and software are expanding businesses. Both hardware and software of computer has become an industry in itself. Computerization is supporting telecommunication, and other ICTs for businesses. Telecommunication — telephones: landlines, cell phones, Internet phones, Internet in its various modes of connection from dial-up, DSL, Wi-Fi, broadband have become ubiquitous and change the way information is being handled, businesses are being done and consumers profiting by such modes. The applications of Internet such as emails, search engines, e-commerce, online advertising are some of the instances how business dealings have changed. Diffusion of cell phones has created a unique experience in the social-personal and businesses of lower strata of people and rural people, particularly in developing countries.

Expansion of multiple modes of telephony and to distances within countries and at international levels has further boosted the businesses, and has created innovative ways of doing business. Computerization is featuring in almost every way of our lives. Innovations, remodeling, adding new features in this area are further boosting life and business. ICTs are playing a significant role to reach out to consumers in business contexts.

Marketers use technology enabled market tools for market research such as Video miners, shopping monitoring system, computer-vision technology and Shopper track technology.

Consumers need access to products and services anytime. With the development of new interactive media like email, web, SMS, ATM kiosks, magnetic card stripe technology, biometric technology and now even interactive television, it is possible for consumers to react to marketing communication.

Automatic identification, or auto ID for short, is the broad term given to a host of technologies that are used to help machines identify objects. Auto ID is often coupled with automatic data capture. Bar code and RFID (and contactless technology that can both complement and compete with more traditional RFID systems) are the upcoming technologies that would enhance the efficiency and profitability of the businesses.

Some of the benefits of bar code data entry have been fast and reliable data collection, reduced labor costs, reduced revenue loses, maintaining necessary inventory levels, improved management and better decision making, and faster access to information. This is 20 years old technology and has its limitations over RFID, the new auto ID evolving technology.

Companies are rapidly using RFID in multiple areas and through multiple cross-functions. We have its applications in retails, manufacturing and their delivery systems, hospital systems, postal systems, travel and travel documentation, in space centers, tracking cows, sheep and pets, skiers in ski resorts and mental and Alzheimer patients, and triggering equipment down oil wells. Both Bar code and RFID with their advantages and limitations are likely to co-exist for businesses.

9

Concluding Observations : Changing Business Practices

GLOBALIZATION TRENDS: CHANGING BUSINESS PRACTICES

We present our concluding observations about the changing business practices. Globalizations, technology and economic liberalization have tremendously changed the business practices worldwide. These three factors have tremendously changed the consumer profile — consumer behavior, preferences, demands and expectations for products and services from housing to consumer durables and non-durables and as diverse fields as insurance, sanitation and legal systems. Thus consumer is the focus from manufacturing to medical services to education services. There is a Paradigm shift to new business practices in these and many new areas. New business practices can be observed in earlier conventional areas and practices and in the upcoming new segments.

There are upcoming New Practices. Change is a process and there is continuity of the earlier. Earlier change becomes history. What was earlier best practice is no longer so. It is outdated. Nonetheless, we do learn our lessons from the history of change and best practices and move on to bring more change for the better and new. Those who keep pace with the changing do progress, but who do not — they stagnate. Same way, businesses need to change the business practices to match the changing consumer profiles. Globalization and technology make the consumer profiles change rapidly as they are exposed to newer trends. Technology innovates as well re-innovates to set these new trends. Business practices have to keep pace with the rapid technological change to be successful. Best practices of yesterday may not serve the consumers of today, therefore the practices are on a continuum of change — sometimes positive and sometimes negative. Therefore, even the businesses have to be selective and competitive about which practices will give them edge.

Business practices, business models and consumer profiles have changed. There are more *collaborative efforts* in doing businesses. In fact, there is global supply chain whether in setting the fashion design such as supplying clothes, clothes designing, buttons and other accessories, stitching, clothing models and consumers apart from the marketing processes; or for manufacturing the cars or even setting up medical or educational services. Collaborative efforts call for communication, co-ordination (through one-on-one, group meeting, business presentations, conferences and regional or world focused summits.), problem-solving, decision-making and applied creativity to find creative solutions. These days beside the capital development, human capital development both at local and global level is also of utmost importance from the point of globalization of business practices.

The business technology and personal technology is going to change the communication between the customers, consumers and different layers of management. Since the customers/ consumers are getting more and more informed about the business channels, products and services and they would be making in-formed demands, and critic and reject any products and services not up-to-mark. Their preferences and expectations will change fast because of fast exposure to information and that also at global level. The communication styles and message focus among employees at different layers of management and top leaders will go tremendous change due to being well-informed about the changing ways of doing things at business, expected to have different relationship with the customers and services because of changing products and services. The changes will be further supported and upgraded by the business technology both in dealing with the products and services and information for the employees, management layers and top-leaders; and the supply chain customers and consumers.

What is update today in business communication may be redundant and outdated and the search for the new will be ongoing.

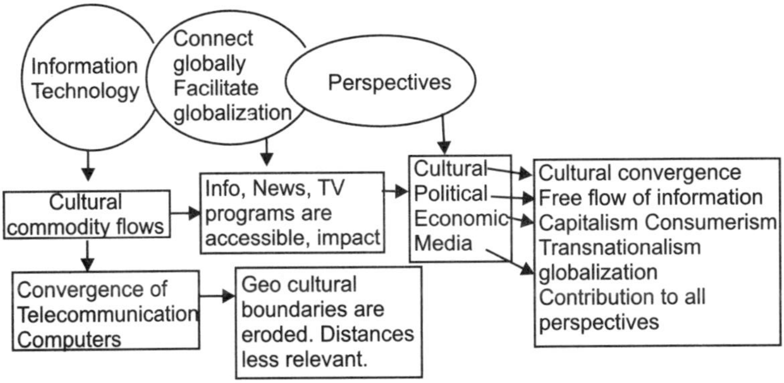

Fig. 9.1. Globalization and Technology

Globalization is a process that creates connectivity and convergence. It is understood from four contexts. One is cultural convergence. Second is political context, which is concerned about free flow of information. Third is economic context focusing on capitalism, consumerism, transnational, and globalization of western economic values. Fourth is media context focusing on media contribution to all the above-mentioned three contexts. In the past decade, rise of market capitalism around the world has contributed to the new economy boom. The third globalization cycle in 2000 onwards is being driven by three factors: high-speed data connectivity pipes between geographies; the proliferation of PCs in all those geographies; and the convergence of software that uses this infrastructure to create a genuine global work platform.

Globalization gives ambitious companies access to the best capital, talent, markets, and resources that the world has to offer. But then companies are essentially competing against the best in the world. the changing landscape will force many companies to reevaluate their strengths and weaknesses. As the pace of globalization accelerates, companies will no longer be able to take advantages or protectionist regulation. Competitors will need to restructure their organizations to match the skills of the world's best players.

As capital markets and markets in goods and services become more international, economies must respond to pressures that are not under the control of nation state. New technologies assist this process, allowing for the integration of production processes and swifter exchange of information. International capital shifts must be seen as of fundamental importance.

In reality, the process of global economic integration — of which offshore outsourcing is a highly visible component — diffuses the best business ideas and management tools, intensifies competition, and sparks innovation. It thereby leads to lower prices and higher wages as well as bigger profits that companies can reinvest in new business opportunities.

The fact that economic integration benefits the global economy as a whole doesn't mean that it benefits all workers and companies. On the contrary, offshoring can destroy the jobs of workers in developed economies, and incumbent companies in developing ones can lose out to more efficient foreign competitors during the transition to modern production methods. Those hardest hit can face major dislocations and a loss of status.

Though such reaction to these hardships might be misguided. Companies and policy makers together have the power and the responsibility to help workers deal more flexibly and painlessly with employment changes. In healthy economies, companies create new jobs — often with higher wages and higher value added to the economy — for most of the people who lose their old ones. Companies can make it easer for their workers to adjust by committing themselves to continual on-the-job learning and retraining programs. Policy makers can assist them by offering tax credits or other incentives for companies that hire and train displaced workers.

The global collaborative model of Social Responsibility of Businesses helps in combating many diseases and health issues. Diseases such as HIV/AIDS, malaria, and tuberculosis claim six million lives annually and have devastated economic growth in some areas of the world. Clearly, no effective long-term response to these maladies can take root without collaboration between corporations and the public sector. Executives must not ignore the risk such epidemics pose, and public-health efforts should welcome contributions from private businesses, which can offer not only money but also marketing and distribution skills, product-development expertise, and intellectual property. Programs that combine commercial skills with public-health objectives can bring private-sector resources to bear on the gravest public-health issues.

Three models of Globalism, Glocalization and Outsourcing in the context of Globalization may profile business practices differently. Globalism discourse is based on three levels: values, knowledge and interests. The focus is on global understanding and global consciousness. *It is the awareness that local events have global consequences and understanding of global impact.* Globalism suggests a global culture of standardization of food, clothes, music, TV programs, films, business practices etc. Global has two meanings. One, is the traditional definition of international, which has messages, data, or people going across or through some kind of barriers, boundaries or constraints, whether it be the encoding or decoding process from one human being to other, or the artificial borders between nation-States. The other definition concerns issues that are common enough to group of people to transcend traditional boundaries.

Glocalization is merging local and global trends. This model operates in two ways: one is adapting and fitting global trends to local ways such as fitting global business practices to local business cultures. There is more localization and picking only the relevant. Second, local trends are changed into global trends. Such as business practices are changed to global practices of doing business.

Outsourcing of manufacturing of products and services and knowledge based industries moved initially from western countries to countries where cost of production is low and professional competency is available as in knowledge-based industries. Profit making is the main driving force for outsourcing. As we will observe in later sections the outsourcing model has changed with times.

Emerging Markets

The emerging economies have boomed because of these three factors — globalization, technology and economic liberalization. Models of *Globalism* and *Glocalization* shape the focus of their business, products and services. In addition, they are competitive and achieve more when they follow a *Collaborative model* of Business Communication practices. Catering to *Low-end Mass Market* is new upcoming business practice in the emerging markets. This model is creating more business within the country. Low-end market is 90% in these countries and they have to focus on competitive affordable low prices, quality and durability, no frill and modest packaging and most of all the efficiency of delivery to the doorpost for this market. This segment's needs were/are treated peripheral by the businesses but now even businesses have created trickle down consumerism as outcome of global player practices in this segment. Thus consumerism created by outside market forces and market forces from within boom the economy and change in business communication practices. Thus booming economies of emerging markets have brought change in their business practices.

Asia is no longer source of comparative advantage based on low cost labor. It is having comparative advantage based on management innovations. Emerging markets are innovating products and processes.

Mexico, Brazil, India and China are some of the emerging markets. We will present our observations about the two emerging markets of India and China in the context of changing business communication practices.

Emerging markets such as China and India have become breeding grounds for new management processes and practices that help companies to maintain or even improve the quality of their products and services while simultaneously reducing prices. The disruptive impact is now confined to developing countries, but "blowback" from this surge of innovation could quickly be unleashed on the rest of the world. To meet the challenge, established businesses must learn new skills and ability to orchestrate complex networks of specialized enterprises. In Asia, managers need to exploit mass markets and compete with best-in-class companies.

The world's two biggest developing countries China and India are taking different paths to economic prosperity. Often it is asked, which is the better one? Who is progressing more? It is an observation that different emerging markets have their business strengths and weaknesses according to their specific models of business communication practices. Some of these are emerging as booming markets as interplay of abovementioned three factors and other additional models but their markets develop according to models of their predominant business strengths. As such China and India are taking different paths to economic prosperity as per their business strengths.

First it was China. The rest of the world looked on in disbelief, as the Chinese economy began to take off in the 1980s at lightning speed and the country positioned itself as a global economic power. GDP growth, driven largely by manufacturing, rose to 9 percent in 2003 after reaching 8 percent in 2002. China used its vast reservoirs of domestic savings to build an impressive infrastructure and sucked in huge amounts of foreign money to build factories and to acquire the expertise it needed. In 2003 it received $53 billion in foreign direct investment, or 8.2 % of the world's total — more than any other country.

India began its economic transformation almost a decade after China did but has recently grabbed just as much attention, prompted largely by the number of jobs transferred to it from the West. At the same time, the country is rapidly creating world-class businesses in knowledge-based industries such as software, IT services, and pharmaceuticals. These companies, which emerged with little government assistance, have helped propel the economy: GDP growth stood at 8.3 percent in 2003, up from 4.3 percent in 2002. But India's level of foreign direct investment — $4.7 billion in 2003, up from $3 billion in 2002 is a fraction of China's.

Both countries still have serious problems: India has poor roads and insufficient water and electricity supplies, all of which could thwart its development; China has massive bad bank loans that will have to be accounted for. The contrasting ways in which China and India are developing, and the particular difficulties each still faces, prompt debate about whether one country has a better approach to economic development and will eventually emerge as the stronger (Sinha Jayant 2004).

Experts view India has entrepreneurial advantage. China has shackled its independent business people. India has empowered them. China has best of all possible models. But China is not an efficient market, and India has relatively little investment funding. For many corporations, India and China are two sides of the same coin. This is understandable. After all, India's economic potential and the challenges it faces do look very much like those of China.

The talent drain is hardship for poor countries, from which many of these workers emigrate. It could have lasting economic repercussions for the developing world, depriving it not only of the skills of these workers but also of their influence on the productivity of others. For most countries, tackling the fundamental cause of the talent drain will take years. Comprehensive economic reform is needed in place of the hodgepodge of regulatory and fiscal incentives emerging markets have generally offered to lure emigrants back home. Meanwhile, a strategy that encourages the participation of emigrants in the economic development of their home countries can mitigate the effects of today's brain drain.

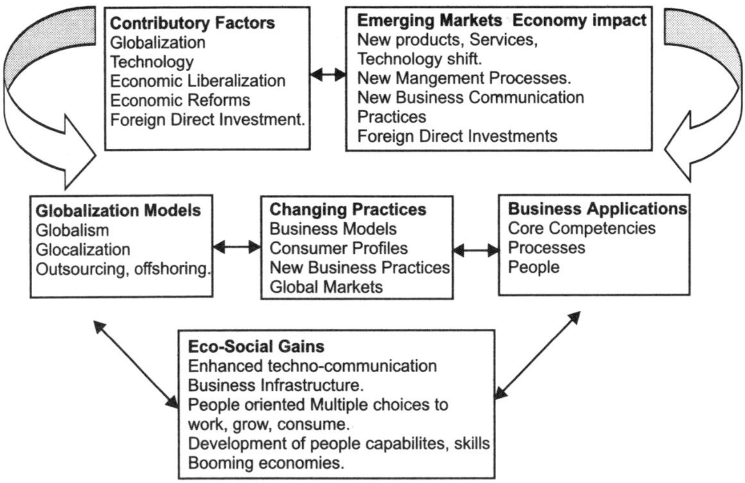

Fig. 9.2. Impact of Changing Business Practices

Emerging Markets of India

Globalizations, technology and economic liberalization and economic reforms, economic policies allowing foreign direct investment (FDI) in Indian enterprises have tremendously changed both business, and business communication practices in India. India is exposed to global business practices through technology and other channels facilitating globalization.

The Models of Globalism and Glocalization are operative in this context. In 90s India was getting conscious of the fact that local events such as outsourcing and IT hubs will have global consequences and impact. It did value those business propositions, it did create interest among the business community for its economic potential and developed knowledge-based capabilities in the IT areas. Thus Globalism has helped India's exposure to global business practices in the context of global offshore outsourcing and accepting them in their business models and in consequences getting global business partners. It modeled these outsourcing business services on Glocalization model by employing the local capabilities and human talents. It further enhanced the capability and appropriate communication skills of the personnel by utilizing local training professional services.

To set up the infrastructure for these services; they did utilize the foreign funding but it was developed and built by Indian professionals. Thus Glocalization gives Indian businesses chance to cash on their strengths and business cultures. They had strength in IT software applications and development, so they are encashing on that strength and have not so far got into hardware manufacturing of IT that is not its strength as yet. They further strengthen their weakness; such as they needed the foreign funding to set up update infrastructure for outsourcing business.

India's outsourcing model focused on three areas: Customer care through call centers, BPO for back office professional services and applications, and development of Information Technology services. India has the advantage of graduate, English speaking huge manpower of youngsters who are ready to join call centers after being trained by the local professional trainers. There is huge pool of appropriate professionals such as chartered accountants, medical technicians, radiographers etc. for BPO services. India has well trained IT professionals for outsourcing services in IT areas. The good point is India is delivering efficient services in these areas to the global partners and creating potential for getting more outsourcing.

Such business practices have created higher employment, higher wages, core competencies and business processes. People have been the main focus and through this process they have gained economically, in competencies, and better life styles promoted through more purchasing power and consumerism with high spend. Interestingly, these growing businesses practices are communicating different lifestyles, economic and social values to young growing generation — the iGen.

The wealth generated by India's fast-growing information technology and business-process-outsourcing industries shows that the country has started living up to its economic potential. By contrast, most sectors of India's economy remain shielded from global competition by high tariffs and restrictions on foreign direct investment and are thus woefully uncompetitive. Although some might argue that removing these barriers would threaten social objectives such as the protection of jobs and incomes, a robust economy would be more likely to realize them. If India is to replicate the success of its IT and outsourcing industries elsewhere in its economy, its leaders must lower barriers to trade and encourage foreign investment in other sectors.

India's $1.5 billion outsourcing business in 2004 illustrates how foreign investment and trade have benefited the country. Along with IT and software, business-process outsourcing is perhaps the most open sector.

Without early investments by multinational companies, the outsourcing industry probably would never have emerged. The success of these companies demonstrated to the world that the country was a credible offshoring destination. The multinationals trained thousands of local workers, many of whom transferred their skills to Indian companies that sprang up in response. Although Indian outsourcing firms now control over half of the intensely competitive global IT and back-office outsourcing market, all of the leading ones started as joint ventures or subsidiaries of multinational companies or were founded by managers who had worked for them.

For many companies, offshore outsourcing is about little more than saving costs on low-skill, labor-intensive activities. Yet the leading offshore outsourcing companies offer their Western clients superior performance in high-skill business operations as well. Computer industry players such as Dell, HP, and Gateway demonstrates that offshore outsourcers can even be used to launch attacks on adjacent product markets. Offshoring is no longer just about call centers and assembling products it is about Western companies using the sophisticated design and management capabilities of their partners in the developing world to go where they can't go alone.

Economic reforms since 90s in India has changed business practices as well how they are communicated to the Indian people and society. There is greater focus on promoting healthy consumerism. There are more protection and safety clauses built in for the low-end consumers. For instance, through economic reforms, the bank loan and mortgage system, and hire-purchase system is worked out. Many middle class people including the younger generation could now buy cars and houses on easy loans and instalments for which earlier they have to wait for years to save, and could have enjoyed those facilities only at the fag end of their lives. Such a changed business practice has communicated to the people — zest for life and higher standard for living. This practice has boosted the automotives businesses and Real Estate businesses. Economic reforms in Stock Market controlled the scams which earlier had ruined the investors. Steps were also taken to protect the low-end investors.

Economic liberatization focused on the relaxing restrictions on import and export of products and services, technologies, and experts and expertise. For example, manufacturing facilities were upgraded in many sectors through such imports and through foreign collaborators. This created better consumer products and services for the domestic consumers at competitive prices and promoting domestic markets. At the same time the manufacured goods were allowed to be exported. This helped in balancing the manufacturing capacity and prices.

It is evident in the sector of cars, now we have variety of cars in the market from utility to luxury cars. Other sectors such as cement, steel, oil and gas exploration, telecommunication equipment and services also benefitted from opening of markets. Many Indian food products like meat products and vegetables, canned pickles etc. are being exported to neighbouring countries and same way the other food products be it chocolates or special cheese or Pepperoni required for Pizza for the Pizza hut are allowed to be imported. Higher level of global expertise is sought in setting up in new hospital services such as Max, Wockhardt have been set up through collobration with Harvard medical group Boston.

Following the glocal model, the Indian partners in joint ventures have created local employment, upgraded the business expertise and learnt and applied some of the best business practices. By exporting goods and services to outside markets not only they are utilizing their market capacity, creating exonomic gains but also created global visibility and competition for their products and services. Joint ventures also created global visibility and scope for further businesses.

In India, over the decade the economic liberatization is done cautiously and gradually to safeguard domestic industries and consumers, and economy of the country. The political factor and business groups lobbying have also influnced it time and again.

Opening of markets through economic liberalization has allowed Indian businesses to have joint ventures with foreign companies. Allowing foreign direct investment (FDI) has been another factor that boosted joint ventures.

New research by the McKinsey Global Institute (2004) indicates that the foreign direct investment that did find its way to India has had an overwhelmingly positive impact. The introduction of foreign competition in IT, business-process outsourcing, and the automotive industry has prompted Indian companies to revamp their operations and boost productivity, and some have become formidable global competitors. Thousands of new jobs have been created in these industries. Consumers benefit from lower prices, better quality, and a wider selection of products and services, while domestic demand has soared in response to lower prices. MGI's latest research shows that the country must go further in lowering trade and foreign-investment barriers if it is to continue integrating itself into the global economy.

The dynamic growth and competitiveness of India's outsourcing and automotive industries stand in contrast to most of its economy, where continuing restrictions on foreign investment and trade dampen competition and help inefficient companies survive.

India has clearly benefited from closer integration into the global economy. To build on that success, the government must now lower trade and foreign-investment barriers still further.

Getting the full benefit of foreign investment calls for competition within industries, since it forces companies to improve their operations and innovate. Many forms of protection and regulation can stifle competition and thus limit the impact of foreign investment. The consumer electronics industry is a prime example. Still, the entry of multinational players has boosted the local industry's productivity and given Indian consumers more choice and lower prices.

Despite these gains, consumer electronics goods made in India still can't compete internationally, and the country's consumers pay unduly high prices for them. These same problems limit foreign investment and prevent many industries — including banking, heavy industry, and textiles — from reaching their full potential. Ultimately, consumers and workers pay through higher prices and the lower pace of job creation.

India estimates that it needs hundreds of billions of dollars in investment in power, transportation, and telecommunication over the next decade to ensure rapid economic growth to reduce poverty. In India FDI flows are vital for industrial growth as technology and foreign exchange can be accessed through such investment. FDI also helps in raising productivity through better management methods and in creating employment opportunities. It promotes growth by facilitating transfer of technology and help in upgrading skills of the workforce.

In general in India, liberalization of rules governing FDI has contributed to FDI flows. But strong economic policies, strengthening of contract enforcement and implementation of contracts, and reduced risk of nationalization will all have positive effects on FDI flows. A better medium term growth prospectus, greater political stability combined with sound economic policies and continued economic reform process and a heightened tempo of restructuring activities will help India become a desired destination for FDI.

Indian government has cautious policy for FDI also. It has been allowing it in sectors for national priority such as in improving Infrastructure — building of roads, bridges, highways and underground train transportation, and for oil gas exploration and supply. Recent example is of Gas pipe from Iran to India. These practices do boost the industrial pace. FDI flows even keep the Indian stock markets bullish and boosting market activities. Recently in 2005, India is opening more sectors for FDI, such as banking and Real Estate, coal mines and insurance retail sectors; as well allowing higher percentage of FDI such as in telecommunication.

Market forces alone cannot determine economic future. Each country determines and draws a road map for economic reforms that would be based on its own skills, resources, strengths and vulnerabilities. To expect developing countries to continually liberalize, at an extreme pace, even within a rule based regime, may result in opposite of what is desirable.

India's labor laws deter foreign investment in some industries. It is coincidence that software and business-outsourcing companies are exempt from many labor regulations, such as those regarding hours and overtime. Without these exemptions, it would be impossible to perform back-office operations in India. To attract foreign investment in labor-intensive industries, the government should therefore consider making labor laws more flexible. Commenting on the economic survey (2005), FICCI President said, "The Survey has noted that labor laws in competing economies like China and Latin American countries are much more aligned to the requirements of a global industry than Indian laws."

Economic Survey (2005) suggests that India has remained third most attractive investment destination in Asia after China and Hong Kong. Since the FDI norms were liberalized, most of the investments have flown in for data processing, software and consultancy services, followed by pharmaceuticals and automobile industry. Power and services sectors are other big sectors that have attracted foreign investors. However on the flip side it notes that the outlook for industrial sector would be better if infrastructure bottlenecks and shortages, labor market rigidities, entry & exit barriers for firms and land acquisition and multiple stage levels of approvals-clearances are eliminated.

Some Indian policy makers might argue that the reforms proposed here would undermine long-held social objectives, such as creating employment. But the evidence shows that regulations on foreign investment, foreign trade, and labor have actually slowed economic growth and lowered the standard of living. A decade ago, India's per capita income was nearly the same as China's; today China's is almost twice as high.

India's economy has made real progress, but further liberalization will be needed to sustain its growth. The country now has 40 million people looking for work, and an additional 35 million will join the labor force over the next three years. Creating jobs for all these Indians will require more dynamic and competitive industries across the economy.

There is sharing of technology innovative channels since some of these like Internet has wiped out the boundaries. There is indigenous, adaptive and transfer of technology in many areas.

Our second focus is the mass market for the low-end consumers in india (discussed in detail in Chapter 3). These mass markets are of poor, low income and rural markets. Globalization, technology, economic liberalization, economic reforms, foreign direct investment (FDI) have faciliated it. Globalization has shown that there are low-end markets in many of the developing countries and we learnt about the different business practices in which these market needs are met. The other factors have impact, since there is more connectivity due to mobile phones and access to other technology channels and exposure to global products and services and life styles through TV etc. More jobs are created which promote more consumer spend because of economic liberalization, and economic reforms, foreign direct investment (FDI). Therefore, this mass market gets further expanded. Indian businesses must communicate about the business focus to this mass market and also fine tune their business practices as communicated by mass markets demands and expectations and spend.

Our third focus is how these five factors: globalization, technology, economic liberalization, economic reforms, foreign direct investment (FDI) are applied to core competencies, people and processes in business practices.

The competencies of Indian people at all levels, has made India a global player in many businessess and has boosted the business image as well economy of India. As impact of these factors, improved business processes have facilitated production, marketing of products, services and ideas, and technology leading to further economic gains.

Major contribution of the abovementioned factors is in business communication for people (consumer) oriented change through multiple choices to work, to grow, and to consume the products and services; and changing technology and development of people's capabilities through enhanced skill as communication enablers. Technology development whether in telecommunication, transportation, infrastructure such as roads, highways, energy, water, oil etc. communicate about the business practices to deliver these to the people for their benefit. Business technology in the area of ICTs, IT, and manufacturing etc.; whether indigeneous, imported or adapted have contributed to economic gains and communicated feelings of wellbeing and progress to the people.

Secondly, communication about business practices — new or best practices to people is through business schools and other communication skills programs and through exposure to global business practices. Such business communication practices have developed better cadre of business leaders and functionaries who have even global demand. Modern trends are evident in India in new business communication practices based on yesteryears best practices. Changing trends in business education, business culture/s are pushing business enterprises and employees to achieve. Achievement motivation is high.

Thirdly, people in business work place have gained; the work place of today is better than yesterday because of technology innovations. There are improved ways of doing work. Over and above, there is concern and effort for human development as an asset to the business, better employee-mangement relationships and respect for the human potentiality to grow — where it fits the best. People from small towns and rural areas are being given opportunities for new communication skills training to fit in the emerging job markets. There is increased concern for their physical and psychological health. Such an approach has boosted the business productivity and therefore economic gains.

People are always at the core of all economic activity. They gain through employement, enhanced purchasing power, better and multiple consumer choices, new products and services due to global competititon and competitive prices. Due to global competition people learn, develop and upgrade both their local as well global skills. People also call for business social responsibilty at global level whether to combat diseases such as HIV/AIDS, natural disasters like tsunami, or use of computer and Internet for development.

Challenge of globalization for India is to reset its economic priorities to make them people-oriented rather than commodity related. This alone will help country meet the challenges of globalization. The people related economic policies must particularly focus on those who are worst off in society. Though raising economic growth is important, the ultimate objective should be to expand the ability of the most of sections of the society to earn a decent living. This assumes more importance as only by providing for a certain economic security to the poorest of the poor could the country meet the challenges of the globalization. These days there is no way any economy can escape the rapid process of integrating with the world economy. Globalization is a vehicle for progress that we cannot ignore.

Emerging Markets of China

China was not an open society before 80s. It has huge manpower that has the basic capabilities of hard work, diligence, and an innate aptitude for copying and duplicating products to the closest. Its strength is manufacturing goods at low cost because of a large number of cheap labor cost. Earlier the political regime and it philosophies were stifling the economic growth and progress of people in all areas.

In 80s China made a deliberate decision to outshine its neighbors — Japan, Taiwan, and South Korea in economic gains and economic growth and be in competition with them. The thrust was export of manufactured goods. It soon realized it has to open up to the outside market forces and to utilize the basic strengths of its people to the optimum and change its business communication practices.

Since then it has made endeavors to change its bike economy to car and air travel. Expats were/are welcome back in the businesses and growing economy. Earlier, they were stifled and were not ready to come back for fear of stagnation. Factories to manufacture garments to mechanical toys started mushrooming as sweatshops. They needed steel to build factories and oil and electricity to run them. That also needed outside funding.

To compete in international market, they have strengths in manufacturing specially garments, copying and duplicating to the closest details of mechanical hardware processes, low cost, cheap labor, hardworking and diligent people with natural flare for picking communication skills for manufacturing and assembling electronics etc. Its weaknesses have been poor infrastructure both physical such as roads, highways, transport system, telecommunication etc and lack of large amount of funds to improve the infrastructures. A large number of people are educated up to high school and there are less number of people speaking English language that has more or less become international language and an essential requisite for competing in international market successfully. Initially, Western developed markets were shifting their manufacturing hubs because of strengths of China and were attracted by profit margins; and decided to deal with the others in due course. Over and above, Western developed markets were/are baffled by the low transparency in Chinese business communication practices.

Foreign Direct Investments: Sinha Jayant (2005), China soon opened for foreign direct investments and foreign funding aggressively. In 1980s the country positioned itself as a global economic power at lightning speed. GDP growth, driven largely by manufacturing, rose to 9 percent in 2003 after reaching 8 percent in 2002. China used its vast reservoirs of domestic savings to build an impressive infrastructure and sucked in huge amounts of foreign money to build factories and to acquire the expertise it needed. In 2003 it received $53 billion in foreign direct investment and it shows no signs of slowing in 2004, despite the government's attempts to cool off the red-hot economy. Since China first opened its doors to foreign investment, in 1978, multinational companies have sunk more than $400 billion into the country. The beneficiaries of this phenomenal wave vary sharply among industries. In some, such as consumer electronics, foreign money has sharpened the competitiveness of Chinese companies and delivered lower prices to local consumers. In others, such as automotive, the main winners have been multinational companies and their Chinese joint-venture partners, which have only recently begun to share the gains.

Research by the McKinsey Global Institute shows that government policies largely determine these outcomes. Foreign direct investment can spark growth and create national wealth, but competition is needed to diffuse the benefits. Government policies that protect incumbents — such as high tariffs, joint-venture requirements, and local-content restrictions — also shield them from the pressure to improve. Consumers pay the price.

The globalization factor helped China opened to MNCs to communicate with its businesses to set up manufacturing hubs in China and allowing exports to these markets of their finished goods. Following the *glocal model* they put the Chinese skills to manufacture according to MNC export orders specifications. MNC saved in cost and are satisfied with the quality of output and speed. Employment rate in China increased and export businesses expanded. These local events and new business modes are having effects on China emerging as Asian economic power. The global events of MNCs looking for low cost markets has effect on China, when it did open up and change its business practices, to let western markets make China as manufacturing hub. It is thus creating *globalism.* Thus the three factors of globalization, glocalization and globalism have impacted businesses in China and are changing its business communication practices.

China needed funds. It opened up and liberalized its economic policies and welcomed foreign funds, foreign direct investments, and invited foreign companies to set up factories, collaborative businesses and offices speedily without much caution. Since it was confident of handling it in its own way.

The Outsourcing Model for China has been mainly manufacturing of garments and hardware mechanical processes and not knowledge-based industries. China's outsourcing model up to now has been hub-setting model for foreign companies independently and not in Chinese collaboration. Though China is allowing currently, in 2005, Indian knowledge based industries majors to set up their knowledge-base industries. China has extended a red carpet welcome to Indian IT giants like Wipro, Infosys, TCS and Satyam to set up a software development base here that would propel Beijing to become a major global software hub. "We believe co-operation in software industry between China and India is highly complementary and it is a win-win co-operation," deputy director of high-tech industry development at the National Development and Reform Commission, Xu Qin said at the first India-China Software Summit. "We welcome Indian IT heavyweights to set up a base here or build joint ventures with Chinese software companies."

The change occurring in *Chinese Outsourcing Model* is three dimensional: China wants collaborative manufacturing hubs, it wants to build its own brands independently and to export those to foreign markets, it wants to have its own hardware brand in computers and telecommunications, mobile phone etc. China dominates global manufacturing because its labor is cheap. For the moment, most Chinese companies are content being original-equipment manufacturers that build products for Western brands. But some are feeling pressure from the government and competitors to leave behind the anonymous OEM role and become branded players in developed markets. They are focusing on building local capabilites. While many Chinese manufacturers deliver quality that matches that of competitors from other countries, most lack a comparable marketing expertise. Not long ago, Western and Japanese companies were interested in China primarily as a market for their goods. Now retailers and manufacturers are as eager to source their parts and products from China as to sell their own wares to its consumers.

Mass low-end markets: China has low-end and rural mass markets. But so far it has not tapped these consumers or high-end consumers and provided them consumer goods at low prices, which it has been supplying to the world through its exports of manufacturing hubs products. It is a large market with big differences. Rapid economic growth is bringing a wide variety of goods within reach of a growing number of consumers. It is realizing that soon it should focus on its low-end markets that are almost 90% consumers but only if it is of comparative advantage.

Whether China will do it or not for its people; but foreign companies are finding it advantageous and they are focusing on this mass markets to make profits. Foreign companies will continue in the premium segment because the market is still growing and margins are big enough to earn a reasonable return. Most know that to see serious growth they will have to tap into the much larger middle- and lower-income segments, which make up 90 percent (by volume) of China's entire consumer goods market. They will apply new approaches to marketing in these mass low-end markets. They have to stretch premium brands vertically to reach the mass market, for example by tweaking product formulations and packaging while modifying manufacturing practices so that prices can be set at lower levels, a company can make a premium brand appeal to a broader range of consumers.

Until now, few foreign companies have made a serious play for the mass market, partly out of fear of hurting the premium brands they have worked so hard to build. At the same time they do realize; they will not be able to create truly large-scale consumer goods businesses in China without tackling the mass-market segments — or without changing the way they manufacture and market products.

In developed markets, consumer goods companies stretch a brand horizontally by offering, say, additional flavors of a brand of carbonated drinks to attract more of the targeted segment. But in China, where the aim is to appeal to a broad range of consumers at both high- and low-income levels, foreign consumer goods marketers should stretch a brand vertically, could introduce a new brand that offers benefits and features appealing to the middle- or lower-income consumer segments and is priced accordingly.

(India's strategy for mass low-end markets is discussed in comparative section).

Increasing consumer spend is another important point for consideration. History of social and economic dislocation has left an ingrained pattern of thrift in China even as it begins to adopt a consumer culture; its savings rate continues to rise. This parsimony now threatens to slow the country's economic growth. If consumer spending is to keep pace with business investment, China's middle class will need to shed its caution and learn to spend more of its income. China's government can encourage consumer spending by creating tax incentives for home ownership and dispelling worries about the future cost of health care and retirement.

Core competencies: China has developed its core competencies through globalization, economic liberalization and foreign investments. The manufacturing processes are streamlined more and more as businesses expand or new business modes are practiced. They are streamlining their management skills through learning from MNC managements. They have yet to pick marketing expertise (one of their weak point) more so if they want to market their own brands independently. So far they are only supply chain to MNCs. They are still lacking the software applications and development expertise. Observing Chinese determination, they may not be left behind.

So far they have been in nut and bolt assembly for electronics and they do excel in that. But they do want to forge ahead and manufacture their own brands in hardware technology. In 2004, IBM computer was acquired by Chinese business — a step in this direction. They hope expertise in marketing techniques would help them to market the hardware technologies even to the western developed markets.

Through its outsourcing model China has enhanced people's capabilities, communication skills and created more employment for them particularly for their rural population. But it has not developed the consumer spend, consumer choices, human relations for its people.

There is more employment for people but wages are low, so it has not increased the purchasing power. Many members in the family are employed now, so put together, there is more household income for consumer spend. But China has not increased consumer choices for domestic consumers and opened consumer markets for them for the goods that they manufacture.

Young male and females are working in factories in sweatshop conditions. A large number of females are employed (specially in assembly line jobs). They live in cramped dormitories in unhygienic conditions. They have no time for relaxation and leisure time activities, and even for higher education. They are pushed to work like human machines with set targets. Most of these are recruited from villages. They could visit their homes after months, spending lot of time and money, since the transportation of bus is very bad. Only recently, on 2005 Chinese New Year, it has introduced air travel connecting villages with these manufacturing hubs. It is a step to make the workers happy, within 2-3 hrs, and spending the same amount of money, they are able to visit the family and also they do not lose wages for many days spent in traveling.

Even Chinese urbanization model is not people (workers) conducive. They bring people to urbanized factory areas without providing urban facilities of metro cities like Beijing, Shanghai or Guzangdeu. The employees-management relationships are not good. There is low job security and more production target oriented.

Technology factor: In China technology of hardware, ICTs, manufacturing technologies are enabler for promoting businesses. ICTs like computer and mobile telephones are opening up for the people but still there is government censorship for mobile phones communications and on Internet sites.

(how outsourcing offices — call center, BPO and IT hubs in India handle it is discussed in comparative section)

China has achieved economic gains, economic power and capaturing businesses with fast speed and there is credibility about its products, quality, precision and speedy delivery but its business practices communicate some more concerns. It must make its business practices more people oriented. It must encourage and practice better employee-mangement relationships. It must encourage consumerism for its internal markets and handle domestic mass markets itself. It is fast realizing that lack of good, clean and efficient government can severely affect economic programs. Since 2002, Training programs are part of the effort for good, clean and efficient government through bureaucrats exposed to different ways of dealing with Public administration in west. Chinese government objective is to enhance the capability of the government through its trained bureaucrats.

China's impressive economic growth has enhanced its global influence and, some would argue, contributed to a shift in the world's balance of power toward Asia. The country's vast production capacity and appetite for resources are changing the way people around the world live and work. Its rising economic importance makes it a critical component in the strategies of the world's leading companies. China's growth is impressive, but so are the challenges it faces to keep its growth and reforms moving.

Any understanding of business opportunities in China should be grounded in a thorough grasp of the fast-moving changes in its foreign-investment climate, consumer-spending habits, business alliances, and disparities between rural and urban consumers and transparency in business communication practices.

Some of the sectors that are opening up and would provide more opportunites for foreign investment but multinational enterprises are: *China's transportation* and its logistics market remains rudimentary and inefficient, costly and slow. Filling in the industry's gaps could be a promising opportunity for partnerships and joint ventures between Chinese and leading foreign logistics companies. The business of getting goods to market may soon become more competitive in China — with improved services.

Construction boom: China is under construction — the result of rapid economic growth and a government push to upgrade the nation's infrastructure. Foreign contractors have opportunities, though pitfalls can surprise the unwary. Foreign construction companies should choose undertakings that both require their specialized knowledge and project-management skills and offer commensurate rewards. Residential and commercial projects attract low-cost Chinese competitors, but mass-transit and water projects demand high levels of skill and offer an agreeable combination of sustained work and profit potential.

Global chemicals in China: Many of chemical companies 'key' customers have already taken the leap and are moving production there. Meanwhile, Chinese chemical companies, backed by low factor costs, are competing effectively for these customers and are beginning to encroach on global markets. These two trends will have a profound effect on the global value chain for chemicals. They must now also consider the threat posed by its emergence as a major producer.

Shifting to auto parts suppliers in China and India won't be easy for global automakers; and it will not happen overnight. Automakers need to evaluate carefully which items are likely candidates for far-off sourcing and which should be sourced closer to home. Life Insurance and Steel manufacturing are other sectors worth consideration.

Future trading: World futures markets, spurred by the rise of electronic trading and interexchange competition, are now in bloom. Those of developing economies such as China and

India, which have the greatest need for them, are experiencing the fastest growth, but these are also among the countries most likely to hamstring them with shortsighted regulatory policies. Properly functioning futures markets strengthen a country's economy. Excessive capital requirements, restrictions on foreign participation and capital movement, and limits on the types of products traded, all conspire to hamper them.

Comparattive Approaches: China and India

China is more pushing and open for FDI and is utilizing that to build infrastructure, build factories for manufacturing facilities — that is its strength and initial focus. It is focused to provide cheap manufactured goods, good quality and is able to copy, duplicate the process inexpensively. With its vast manpower, it is producing more and more. It is doing well and its economy is booming. The over-fast push has raised few pertinent questions. Is human relations been compromised? Are people treated like machines with no leisure activites? Has it provided the cheap consumer goods to its people and created consumerism at home? Are expats welcome back in businesses with their expertise now?

India is more cautious for FDI, foreign collaborations, and economic reforms. It is opening up slowly and cautiously from one focus to other. There is protectionist attitude to protect domestic companies for steady growth. They do want economic growth and employment for its people but human welfare and human relations development is also of consideration. Expats' expertise has always been utilized well — now, as well earlier. With booming economy, outsourcing models, expats contributing expertise, funding and are in joint ventures.

China should open up more for its people as it is opening up for outsourcing businesses. It's outsourcing manufacturing businesses should be more people conducive and respect human rights.

Compare this with outsourcing offices — call center, BPO and IT hubs in India. Employees are paid fairly high wages. They are provided with local transport, food and gym on the premises and a clean working environment. Recently, BPOs are also providing counseling to mitigate the effect of nightshifts and loss of normal sleep hours. Mostly youngsters join call centers and BPOs after graduating from colleges. Even these outsourcing offices are thinking of providing them free tutions, transport, residence for higher education. So they are not dissatisfied with the demands of jobs and attrition rate gets low, and productivity increases. Going for higher education gives them hope for better future. Even BPO are letting large companies of durables and no-durables open outlets on the premises. So employees can buy on the premises, saving their day-time. It also encourages consumer spend. India's urban model for outsourcing offices is people conducive since most of these offices are around metroes. Many of these employees do come from small towns and villages. These employees enjoy the urban facilites and urban consumer choices. The employees-mangement relationships are good and boost productivity.

India is doing efficiently and cautiously both — opening up businesses for outsourcing, economic liberalization and FDI; and opening the society. These two can develop in parallel. That is how India envisions its problem and development — emerging and surging.

In business practices, India does not strive to match with China. It may have healthy competititon with it. Both differ because their focuses for business development and practices have altogehter different perspectives though they may follow the basic models. But its connotations are different for the two countries. China can learn marketing and management expertise, and business culture adaptation from India. India's business enterprises can learn aggressive business capturing from China. Its workers can learn the value of hardwork and diligence, efficiency and business discipline from within. Both are major contributing factors for any businesss success.

Chinese model of business practices may be good to follow for business success but it cannot overlook the good practices for the development of people in businesses that boost productivity. If employees, people are provided well, given challenging opportunity why would they like to migrate to distant lands, leaving behind the culture, the people they love, and the ties that bond them. They can do more for the country's businesses as expats are doing — providing the expertise in good business practices adapted from other countries. This applies to both India and China.

In India, domestic companies with different marketing strategies are handling its low-end mass markets. The consumer spend in this market is additionally contributing to the domestic capabilities of the companies and creating more revenues for them. China has yet to tap this big and rapid growing market.

In terms of population, China and India are home to the largest number of the poorest people in the world. There are two main ways in which MNEs (multinational enterprises) are helping to alleviate poverty. The first is by investing in the relatively prosperous industrializing areas. In doing so they provide more jobs and raise the income levels of people in these areas. These benefits are now spreading to other parts of these two large countries where, in 10 years or so, abject poverty is most likely to be cut back. The second is by the investment in vital physical infrastructure in the heartland of China and India. This is most often undertaken jointly with indigenous firms and supported by aid agencies and the host governments. It is a necessary preparatory step to further investment by MNEs.

Our above observations are also pointer to the fact that models of globalization, globalism and glocalization; the three factors of economic reforms and liberalization and foreign direct investments and the outsourcing models; when applied to the core competencies, people and processes; have different outcomes for both India and China. Both are emerging markets, focusing on economic gains and being powerful economically. But they are likely to grow in these two directions differently because the characteristics of its people differ, the aspirations as well economic policies, Political leadership and Political Will for its people differ. The market forces will mold the business practices differently for these two countries. As such China and India are taking different paths to economic prosperity as per their business strengths.

In short, Business Communication is important in the above scenarios at various levels. Globalization suggests communication with international businesses through exposure to business styles, practices, products and services of these businesses. Such exposure is through media channels, interpersonal channels and travels and other supporting technologies. Such information and knowledge expand new businesses, innovate others, and create new demands for products and services and promote global partnerships. The two premise of Intercultural Communication: cultural sensitivity, specifically of business culture, and intercultural communication competence is important in these contexts. This is equally important for globalism for having local impact and for glocal model since local talents, local products, public and other business practices would be used.

Public relation as a communicative medium is important to create visibility, credibility, and image building of businesses and their products and services among global partners, foreign countries and their governments, and international media. PR promotes businesses, partnerships and foreign direct investments. We cannot underplay the role of fast growing Information Communication Technologies — both hardware and software that create instant connectivity, global availability and accessibility of business innovations and business solutions.

It is an observation that different emerging markets have their business strengths and weaknesses according to their specific models of business communication practices. Some of these are emerging as booming markets as interplay of abovementioned three factors and other additional models but their markets develop according to models of their predominant business strengths. As such China and India are taking different paths to economic prosperity as per their business strengths.

References

Amadco Lodovico, *India from Emerging to Surging*, McKinsey Quarterly.com, 2001.

Bazerman Max, *Judgment* in Managerial Decision-Making, John Wiley & Sons, 1994.

Boone, Kurt & Block, *Contemporary Business Communication,* 2002.

Bossidy and Ram Charan, *Executive,* Crown Business, New Jersey, 2002.

Bossidy and Ram Charan, *Confronting Reality,* Crown Business, New Jersey, 2004.

Bar Code Information: Skandata.com, Azalea.com, Data ID and other web sites.

The Bar Code Book, by Roger C. Palmer, published by Helmers Publishing, Inc., Peterborough, N.H.

Cappelli and Hamori's *Attributes of Corporate Executives 1980 to 2001,* Research Survey, 2004.

Cappelli Peter, *Interview with Economic Times*, Feb 05.

Colin Mitchell, *Selling the Brand Inside*, Harvard Business Review, 2002.

Carole Macklin, Les Carlson, *Advertising to Children Concepts and Controversies,* Sage Publications, 1999.

Christ Paul, *Internet Tools For Discovering Sales Leads,* KnowThis.com, 2004.

Christ Paul, *Four Technologies to Find More Prospects,* KnowThis.com, 2004.

Christensen Clayton M., *The Innovator's Dilemma,* Harvard Business School Press, 1997.

Marketing With a Dynamic Website, KnowThis.com Dictionary.com.

Corbett Michael, *The 33 Ruthless Rules of Local Advertising,* Pinnacle Books, 1999.

China Today, Special edition McKinsey Quarterly.com, 2004.

China Vital, Special edition McKinsey Quarterly.com, 2004.

Diana Farrell & Adil Zainulbhai, *Richer Future for India,* McKinsey Quarterly.com, 2004.

Diana Farrell *et al.*, *Beyond Cheap Labor in Developing Economies*, McKinsey Quarterly.com 2005.

Drucker Peter, *Management,* Harper and Row, 1974.

Dixon Patrick, *Futurewise: Six Faces of Global Change*, Profile Books, 2003.

Derek H.Chen & Carl.J. Dahlman, *Knowledge and Development: A Cross Section Approach,* World Bank Paper, 2003.

Dunning John H. (Ed), *Regions, Globalization and the Knowledge Based Economy,* Oxford University Press, 2002.

Economic Survey of Apex Economic Associations India, 2005.

Fenwick William C., *New Product Development and Introduction*, 2004.

Ghoshal Sumanta & Bartlett Christopher, *Individualized Corporation,* Harper Perennial, 1999.

Gurcharan Das, *The Elephant Paradigm,* Penguin Books, 2002.

Gurcharan Das, *India Unbound,* Penguin Books, 2002.

Hamel Gary & Prahalad C.K., *Competing for the Future,* Tata McGraw-Hill, 1994.

Hanson J. & Narula Uma, *New Communication Technologies in Developing Countries*, New Jersey, Lawrence Erlbaum Associates, 1990.

Hookway James, *Beyond the Middle Class*, Wall Street Journal, Dec 2004.

Irwin David, *Effective Business Communications,* 2000.

Jagdish Bhagwati, *In Defense of Globalization,* Oxford University Press, 2004.

Jean-Marie Dru, *Disruption,* John Wiley & Sons, Inc., 2000.

John Philip Jones, *Realities and Myths,* Sage Publications, 1999.

John Philip Jones, *Advertising Organizations and Publications: A Resource Guide,* Sage Publications, 2000.

Keefe Joseph F., *Five Trends: The Rise of Corporate Reputation and Corporate Social Responsibility,* NewCircle Communications, 2002.

Kanter, Rosabeth Moss, "*Rising to Rising Expectations*" in WorldLink (Magazine of the World Economic Forum), 2002.

Lydenberg, Steven D., "*The Mainstreaming of Socially Responsible Investing: A Vision for 2006,*" The Journal of Corporate Citizenship, 2003.

Liberthal Kenneth & Prahalad C.K., *The End of Corporate Imperialism,* Harvard Business Review, Aug 2003, Vol. 81, 109-17.

London Ted, *Interview with Development Gateway,* World Bank, 2005.

McKinsey Quarterly.com 2003, *How to Make After-Sales Services Pay Off.*

Morgan Michael, *Making Innovations Happen*, Kogan Page, 2002.

Narula Uma, *Diffusion of Cell Phone in India and Social Change* (forthcoming, research publication), 2005b.

Narula Uma, *Handbook of Communication Perspectives, Models, Communication Strategies,* Atlantic Publishers & Distributors, New Delhi, 2005a.

Narula Uma, *Communication Perspectives: Cultural Diffusion, Dynamics and Challenges,* HarAnand Publications, New Delhi, 2000.

Narula Uma, *Media Communication Technologies : New Perspectives,* HarAnand Publications, New Delhi, 2001.

Narula Uma, *The Cultural Challenge of Communication Technology*, American Behavioural Scientist, Vol. 32,

No. 2, Nov-Dec 1988, 94-207, Sage Publications, Newburyport, USA.

Norderstreng Kaarle and Schiller Herbert, *National Sovereignty and International Communication,* Ablex, New Jersey, 1979.

Prahalad C.K. & Venkat Ramaswamy (a), *The Future of Competition: Co-creating Unique Values with Customers,* Harvard Business School Press, 2004.

Prahalad C.K. & Stuart Hart (b), *The Fortunes at the Bottom of the Pyramid,* 2004.

Prahalad C.K. (c), *Interview with Hindustan Times,* New Delhi, Aug 18, 2004.

Prahalad C.K. (d), *The Invisible Market,* Across the Board Sept/Oct, 2004.

Prahalad C.K. & Al Hammond, *Serving the World's Poor, Profitably,* Harvard Business Review, 2004.

RFID Technology: Intermec.com/rfid, Videojet.com/accusort.com, paxar.com/rfid, siemens.com/rfid, Zebra.com/rfid, aanza autorid.net, Wikipedia, rifd.org, rfid-tagging.net,

Richard Cross & Janet Smith, *Pathways to Customer Loyalty,* NTC Business Books, 1995.

Robbin Lee Zeff, & Bradley Aronson, *Advertising on the Internet,* Wiley John & Sons, 1999.

Rouse Michel J. and Sandra Rouse, *Business Communications: A Cultural and Strategic Approach,* 2000.

Ryan M.J., *Attitudes and Gratitude,* 2000.

Schwartz Barry, *The Paradox of Choices: Why More is Less,* Ecco., 2004.

Sinha Jayant, Diana Farrell, Tarun Khanna and Jonathan R. Woetzel, *China Today,* The McKinsey Quarterly, 2004 Special Edition.

Seth Godin, *Permission Marketing,* 2004.

Soni Vivek, *Three Approaches to Creating New Businesses,* Business Workshop Presentation, Feb 4.

Strunk & White, *The Elements of Style,* Crown Books, 2000.

Surowwiecki James, *The Wisdom of Crowds,* Doubleday, 2004.

Seely, Brown and Hagel, *Innvoation blowback: Disruptive Management Practices in* McKinsey quarterly, Jan 2005.

Seely, Brown and Hagel, *Brand Building in Emerging Markets,* McKinsey quarterly.com *2003.*

Thomson (Ed), *Handbook of Business Strategies*, Crown Books, 2002.

Thurow Lester, *Building Wealth,* Harper Collins Publishers, 1999.

Twitchell James, B., *Twenty Ads That Shook the World,* Crown Publishing Group, 2000.

Winston Fletcher, *Advertising,* Advertising Profile Books Ltd, 1999.

Appendix

APPENDIX 1 : SYMBOLOGIES

Standards: Many bar code applications must share common bar codes between different vendors. The UPC symbology has a standards committee that assigns manufacturer and product codes for well over one million products. That is the reason that a product manufacturer can put a bar code on a package without fear of duplication. If you are in a situation where some type of industry committee has set up standards, it is frequently in your best interest to conform to that standard, even if it imposes other limitations.

Density: Each symbology can encode a different number of characters in a given space with all other factors being the same. Numeric-only bar codes such as Interleaved 2 of 5 can encode many more numbers in a given space than a more flexible symbology such as Code 128. In many cases this is critical. Even if one symbology is capable of making a bar code of the required size, you may get a better first read rate using a different symbology. Note that some scanners, particularly wands, are built for a particular density. Make sure that your input device matches the density of the bar code you will use.

Readability: Some bar codes are inherently more readable than others. For example, tests show that Code 128 (which is one of the most flexible symbologies) is easily and successfully read by most readers. This is a case where the symbology is better in nearly every way than the competition. In other cases, you may sacrifice readability for some other requirement. Always use the most readable symbology you can, and test it using the actual equipment you plan to use.

Durability: Some symbologies are more durable than others. As a rule, those with better readability are more durable than others. You should always test your bar codes by subjecting them to some abuse and making sure your equipment will still read them.

Setup: Many bar code readers have certain symbologies disabled in their default configuration. If at all possible, it is best to use a symbology that the reader will read "out of the box." This will cut down on your setup time and reduce user confusion when a reader is added or replaced. If a new reader requires configuration, be sure to leave detailed instructions and materials at the site. (Keep a copy for yourself for when users lose the ones you gave them).

Acceptance: Your bar codes may need to be compatible with those of companies you do business with. As far as possible, use symbologies that are already in place.

Conflicts: Your bar codes should avoid conflicts. For example, if you disable symbologies that you're not using, you can keep an employee's candy bar out of your inventory.

To *summarize*: For general-purpose use, Code 128 is usually the best choice. It provides use of the full (128-character) ASCII set as well as the best readability and reliability available. If you are making a general-purpose system that needs to read only numbers and uppercase letters, you can use Code 39. If you need numbers only, you should use Interleaved 2 of 5 or Code 128. In any case, avoid symbologies that require reconfiguration of the reader.

Checksums: These are additional characters appended to bar codes to guarantee good reads. Checksums are necessary on some bar codes that are prone to errors. For example, Interleaved 2 of 5 is a very dense, numeric-only bar code, but it is prone to substitution errors. You should always use a checksum on this code. Other codes, such as Code 128 and Code 39, are self-checking and seldom require a checksum. Most bar code readers can be configured to use.

Code 128 symbology is a very compact bar code for all alphanumeric applications. The full (128-character) ASCII character set can be encoded in this symbology without the double characters found in extended Code 39. If the bar code has four or more consecutive numbers (0‹9), the numbers are encoded in double-density mode (where two characters are encoded into one character position). Code 128 also has five special, nondata function characters. These are generally used to set reader parameters or return parameters. Code 128 actually has three different character-code subsets. It has two forms of error checking, making it a very stable bar code. Checksums are not required. If you have your choice, Code 128 is generally the best all-around choice you can use.

Code 39 (or Code 3 of 9) is the most common bar code in use for custom applications. It is popular because it can support both text and numbers (A‹Z, 0‹9, +,-, ., and), it can be read by almost any bar code reader in its default configuration, and it is one of the oldest of the modern bar codes. Code 39 is a variable-width bar code, and it can support any number of characters that the reader can scan. Code 39 is specified in many military and government specifications. Code 39 bar codes are self-checking and are not prone to substitution errors. They generally do not require checksums.

Interleaved 2 of 5

Also known as 2 of 5, this is a numeric-only bar code that prints out a little larger than the UPC-A bar code when 10 digits are encoded. This symbology has the flexibility to encode any even number of digits. If you have an odd number, a leading zero is added. This bar code is an excellent candidate for numeric-only applications, and it is the best symbology to use for fixed-mount readers. Because Interleaved 2 of 5 is prone to substitution errors, you should always use a checksum.

UPC (Universal Product Code) is the standard bar code for items for sale to the public. It is the code seen on items at the local supermarket. UPC-A is a fixed-length, numeric-only bar code. It contains 1 digit for a system number,

5 digits for the manufacturer number, 5 digits for the product number, and one checksum digit. The position and value of the digits is standardized by a grocery industry committee. UPC-A and UPC-E also allow two- or five-digit supplemental numbers. UPC-A and UPC-E codes have an automatic checksum. UPC-E is ideal for small packages, because it is the smallest bar code available. This symbology contains the same information as UPC-A, except that at least four zeros are suppressed. Only tags with the system character of 0 can be encoded with this symbology. UPC-A and UPC-E codes have an automatic checksum. Interleaved 2 of 5 is almost as dense and does not have the format considerations.

Extended Code 39 is a derivative of Code 39. This symbology uses combinations of two standard Code 39 characters for every character in the ASCII character set (0—127). This symbology allows lowercase letters and control characters, at the expense of size. This makes the code very big if you have very many lowercase or special characters. Most bar code readers in their default configuration will not read Extended Code 39. If you want to use this symbology, you will probably need to configure the reader. If you need to read both uppercase and lowercase, you should use Code 128.

Code 93 and Extended Code 93 are compressed versions of Code 39 and Extended Code 39. This symbology supports the same characters as Code 39, but in a smaller character width. This is a more difficult symbology to read, and many readers do not support it. Both Code 93 and Extended Code 93 have automatic checksums.

UCC 128. This bar code is a 19-digit, fixed-length bar code that uses Code 128 C to generate the bar code. This bar code is specifically used on shipping containers by those who ship items with UPC codes. UCC 128 has automatic checksums.

Codabar bar codes can include numeric characters, six punctuation characters (-$:/.+), and spaces. There are also four special start/stop characters, which are A, B, C, and D. Codabar is useful for encoding dollar figures and mathematical figures. These bar codes are slightly larger than Interleaved 2 of 5 bar codes. Codabar requires start and stop characters. The Codabar symbology is self-checking, but you can use a mod 16 or mod 10 checksum.

The EAN/JAN-13 code is used for overseas applications where a country code is required. The UPC-A symbology is actually a subset of the EAN/JAN-13 symbology. This bar code is composed of 2 numbers for the country code, 10 numbers for the data characters, and a checksum. The checksum is generated automatically. The EAN/JAN-8 code is also used for overseas applications where a country code is required. This is similar to the EAN/JAN-13 except that only 5 numbers are used.

The MSI bar code is used most often in the grocery industry for shelf labels. This is a numeric-only code that stands up well to wear and tear. This code is not self checking, and so a checksum is highly recommended. It supports three types of checksums.

Zip+4 and DPBC POSTNET. This bar code is the special code that is placed on the lower right portion of an envelope. This bar code is used to speed mail through the postal service (by automated sorting) and get reduced rates.

2D (Two-Dimensional) Bar Code Symbologies

A 2D bar code symbology allows vast amounts of data on a single bar code by storing data in 2 dimensions. A common demonstration of the technology is a single bar code no larger than a standard UPC bar code that contains the entire Gettysburg Address. Some common 2D bar code symbologies include PDF 417, DataMatrix Code, and MaxiCode.

Subject Index